CONSCIENCE

Conscience

A Biography

Martin van Creveld

REAKTION BOOKS

For Benda, a true friend in need

Published by Reaktion Books Ltd
33 Great Sutton Street
London EC1V 0DX, UK
www.reaktionbooks.co.uk

First published 2015
Copyright © Martin van Creveld 2015

Printed and bound in Great Britain
by TJ International, Padstow, Cornwall

A catalogue record for this book is available from the British Library

ISBN 978 1 78023 454 0

Contents

Introduction

As a Jew, an Israeli and the son of Holocaust survivors, several of whose relatives were killed during the German occupation of the Netherlands in 1940–45, I have long been interested in the following question: did the Nazis, especially those who ordered and perpetrated mass murder, have a conscience? Was there anything they did simply because they considered it good? Was there anything so evil that it made them shrink? Is there any indication that, either during or after the event, they were tormented by remorse? If not, and given that many of us see conscience as the factor that separates man from the beasts, does this mean that they were somehow other than human? Is it possible that, coming out of God knows where, there suddenly appeared a group of people so essentially different from what we believe ourselves to be as to almost form a different species? If so, how did such a thing happen? Since it happened once, could it happen again?

Conscience should not be confused with morality: that is, the ability to distinguish between good and evil. Rather, it is that part of the human soul, built-in or acquired, that makes us behave and act on the basis of that distinction. It is also that which, if we have already committed an act we judge as evil and not good, makes us experience guilt, remorse and regret. It keeps us awake at night, gnaws at us and gives us no rest. Unless the act has been repented and/or atoned for, it can result in severe psychological problems. As Shakespeare put it in *Richard III* (1:iv):

> it makes a man a coward. A man cannot steal but it accuseth him; a man cannot swear but it checks him; a man cannot lie

7

with his neighbour's wife but it detects him. 'Tis a blushing shame-faced spirit that mutinies in a man's bosom. It fills a man full of obstacles; it made me once restore a purse of gold that by chance I found. It beggars any man that keeps it; it is turned out of towns and cities a dangerous thing; and every man that means to live well endeavours to trust to himself, and live without it.

Reader note, these are the words of a professional 'murderer' – a hitman, as we would say – employed by the king to get rid of his enemies. For him, 'it' is what urges those who have it to respect social norms, as he occasionally did. However, there is another face to the matter. Given the right circumstances 'it' can, and sometimes does, make some of us act *against* those norms, even to the point of trying to demolish them and blow them right into the stratosphere.

Negative or positive, conscience does all this, or at any rate is supposed to do all this, regardless of whether the act in question was known to ourselves alone or to others too; of whether it succeeded or ended in failure; and of any reward or punishment that did, or did not, follow. It does so, in other words, regardless of the cost its owner may incur. Strictly speaking, a conscience that takes cost into consideration is not a conscience at all. A conscience that meets these conditions may be rarer than diamonds. However, it does exist. To paraphrase the great eighteenth-century British philosopher David Hume (1711–1776),[1] conscience is the bridge between the world that is and the world that, on the basis of what is normally known as the contrast between good and evil, we feel should have been or should be.

At first I thought I would limit my enquiries to the Third Reich. Later I changed my mind and decided to delve into the subject as a whole. But I still wanted to devote a special chapter to the Nazis. This was because their crimes, by almost universal consent, were perhaps the worst of all, so their consciences, if they had such a thing, could be used as a kind of measuring stick for the rest. But where to start? Is conscience an invention? If so, who invented it, when, where, how and to what purpose? What social need did its invention meet, and how did it interact with other elements of human culture such as religion, philosophy, state power and psychology? Is it limited to 'civilized' peoples belonging to the 'higher' races, as many Western people believed, at least until 1945? Or is it something all human beings, by virtue of being human, have or at least are capable of having? What are we to make of the many peoples – including, as we shall see, Jews until the end of the nineteenth century – whose language does not have a word for it? Do non-Western civilizations share our ideas of it? How to account for those, such as the above-mentioned Nazis, who have shown few signs of having it? Taking 1945 as the starting point of the 'modern' world, what has happened to conscience since then? Given current advances in robotics on the one hand and in neuroscience on the other, does conscience have a future and, if so, of what kind?

To make things more complicated still, some modern ethologists have suggested that certain animals also show signs of having something like a conscience. The tone was set by Charles Darwin. In *The Descent of Man* (1871), Darwin raised the following question. Suppose life is indeed a struggle for existence in which the fittest come out on top: how then did the faculties that restrain that struggle, such as empathy, altruism and morality, evolve and maintain themselves? In response, he wrote:

> The following proposition seems to me in a high degree probable – namely, that any animal whatever, endowed with well-marked social instincts, the parental and filial affections being here included, would inevitably acquire a moral sense or conscience, as soon as its intellectual powers had become as well, or nearly as well developed, as in man . . .
>
> I do not wish to maintain that any strictly social animal . . . would acquire exactly the same moral sense as ours. [Yet an] inward monitor would tell the animal that it would have been better to have followed the one impulse rather than the other. The one course ought to have been followed, and the other ought not; the one would have been right and the other wrong . . .
>
> It has often been assumed that animals were in the first place rendered social, and that they feel as a consequence uncomfortable when separated from each other . . . but it is a

more probable view that these sensations were first developed, in order that those animals which would profit by living in society, should be induced to live together, in the same manner as the sense of hunger and the pleasure of eating were, no doubt, first acquired in order to induce animals to eat.[2]

Such a conscience is essential for any kind of animal that, first, raises its young and, second, lives in the company of others of its kind. Many other biologists, evolutionists and ethologists have addressed the issue, with no very great success. On the contrary: the deeper we penetrate into the microscopic mechanisms that govern the heredity and evolution of all living creatures, the more baffling the problem.

For example, a famous book by a well-known present-day biologist describes the way in which heredity and evolution is dominated by 'selfish' genes. Genes are packets of DNA, a material that carries the heredity of a living organism whose one 'wish' in its 'life' is to replicate itself. The volume in question does not mention conscience even in the index.[3] Can a gene have a conscience? Certainly not in anything like the ordinary sense of the term. To return to Hume's definition of conscience, it seems to presuppose four things. The first is an understanding of the self as a separate entity – what is commonly known as consciousness. The second is knowledge of the world in which that self exists and operates; the third, an understanding of the difference between good and evil; the fourth, freedom to use conscience as the basis for connecting the two. All these are things bits of matter cannot have. Or can they?

Many animals, especially birds and mammals, display solicitous behaviour towards their offspring. Does that mean the animals in question have a moral choice? The question preoccupied Frans de Waal, an American professor of zoology and a leading expert on chimpanzees and their smaller cousins, bonobos. He believes that they are capable of refraining from certain actions, even those that are beneficial to themselves, if they perceive that these actions are harmful to others of their species. Citing some experiments, he says that ape A will refrain from pressing a lever that makes ape B receive an electric shock and scream in pain, even if, by pressing it, A will be able to obtain food.[4]

As de Waal says, the ability, and willingness, to refrain from certain actions perceived as harmful to others even if they are beneficial to oneself seem to indicate a capacity for empathy. But is empathy the same as conscience? Even more intriguing are the following questions. Suppose A had in fact pressed the lever and watched B suffering. In that case, would he have experienced guilt and remorse? Would he have reproached himself for what he did? Would he have been unable to sleep at night? Having finally fallen asleep, would he have nightmares? Would he want to confess his 'sin' to somebody so as to feel relief and, perhaps, gain atonement? And finally: is the reluctance to press the lever inborn or is it acquired as part of that animal's socialization?

De Waal on his part takes the behaviour he and others have witnessed as proof that conscience, rather than originating in religion – as Christians in particular have long maintained – has its roots in our biology. He believes his chimpanzees are capable of showing contrition as well as the need to make amends for an injury they inflicted on others.[5] But what does the animal in question actually *feel*? Does it have some understanding of good and evil, however rudimentary? Scientists may go on forever inserting electrodes into the animal's brains and tracing the electrochemical changes that are taking place inside them. Without language as a means of communication, it means very little. Attempts by philosophers to answer the question seem to have fared no better.

Such being the case, I intend to skip the question and proceed straight to humans. The difference between humans and all the rest is that they can use language to share their thoughts, feelings and beliefs. Even so, formidable methodological difficulties persist. Supposedly conscience is that inner voice all of us have that always knows whether what we are about to do, or what we have done, is right or wrong, morally speaking. The problem is that, being inner, it is only accessible to others through the spoken or written word. Palaeontologists tell us that *Homo sapiens* took on his present patterns of behaviour, language included, about 50,000 years ago.[6] By contrast, the earliest forms of writing were only invented around 5,000 years ago. Even so, a great many societies remained illiterate. From antiquity on, a few of those were visited by people from literate ones who were interested in the question at hand and wrote down their impressions. The rest are beyond our reach and will forever remain so.

Two other important problems must be noted. First, the language on which we depend for our enquiries is capable of being used equally well to express thought and to conceal it. What people say or write either about themselves or about others by no means always reflects what they really feel, believe and think, least of all in matters of conscience. Second, even if we did succeed in establishing the truth in respect to what few individual cases can be accommodated on the pages of a single volume, there still would be no way to know how widespread the effects of conscience have been within any given society.

The outline of the volume is as follows. Chapter I deals with the Old Testament and traditional Judaism, both of which had precious little use for conscience. It also covers the classical Greeks who invented it and the Greek and Roman Stoics who adopted and developed it for their own purposes. Chapter II examines the ways in which Christianity and conscience interacted from the time of Paul the Apostle onwards. Passing through the Reformation, it ends by taking a look at the peculiar Protestant trio of religion, secular government and conscience that ruled much of Northern Europe for centuries on end and to a considerable extent continues to do so today.

Chapter III returns to the Renaissance. It traces the way in which conscience became separated first from politics and then from religion, finally focusing on 'the state' and 'duty' instead. This chapter also presents what was probably the most important, and certainly the most eloquent, challenge to conscience ever: the one presented by Friedrich Nietzsche. Chapter IV takes us into the twentieth century. Here the key figure is Sigmund Freud, who was especially interested in the link between conscience and neurosis. His influence on twentieth-century thought was and remains unsurpassed. It is not his fault that, after his death, his therapeutic methods have so often been distorted and even turned into the opposite of what he intended them to be. The chapter also takes a brief look at two other systems of thought that developed alternatives to conscience: Japanese Shintoism and Chinese Confucianism.

Chapter v brings us back to the original starting point, namely the role conscience played, or did not play, in the Third Reich. Here I distinguish between those who commanded, those who executed and those, a relative handful, who resisted. Chapter vi deals with recent attempts to anchor conscience in three new idols: to wit, universal human rights, health and the environment. Finally, Chapter vii takes a look at those who have long claimed that the very idea of conscience is nonsense. In other words, that man is merely a machine, the behaviour of which is governed not by some internal voice with freedom to choose but by stimuli, positive or negative, coming from outside. Given rapid advances in robotics and brain science, this is probably the most important problem of all.

To end this introduction, a word about sources. As always, I hoped to obtain a reasonably good understanding of what I thought were the most important issues at hand. As so often, I was surprised to find that a comprehensive study of the subject does not exist. To be sure, works about conscience in this or that society, this or that context, this or that thinker, abound. An attempt to use them all would have resulted in an encyclopaedia capable of killing an ox, if an ox could read it. I was forced to put aside, not to say ignore, countless beautiful flowers, old and especially new, that no doubt deserved better. In presenting the product, I can only hope for readers' indulgence at not having done more.

I
At the Beginning

Early Stirrings

Hermann Rauschning (1887–1980) was a Nazi activist who ended up fleeing Germany and writing several anti-Nazi books. In 1932–4 he had many conversations with Adolf Hitler who, he says, once described conscience, *Gewissen* in German, as a 'Jewish invention'. His own mission was to rid the world of it.[1] The claim was anything but original. It can be traced back at least as far as Friedrich Nietzsche's *The Genealogy of Morals* of 1887. Be that as it may, many would say that in making the claim, Hitler and Nietzsche were paying Judaism the greatest compliment ever. For isn't conscience the most basic quality of all, that which distinguishes human beings from beasts?

Alas both for Hitler and for those who have sought to show how wonderful Judaism, and hence Christianity, is, the truth is that the Old Testament does not even have a word for conscience. According to the book of Genesis (3:1–21), Adam and Eve lived together innocently in the Garden of Eden. They were accosted by a serpent which suggested that they eat of the forbidden fruit of the tree of knowledge. It told them that, as a result, they would be 'as gods, knowing good and bad'. Having eaten, their eyes were opened. 'They knew that they were naked', made themselves belts out of fig leaves, and were expelled from the Garden, never to return.

Some would no doubt argue that nudity is merely a question of custom and/or convenience. As such it has little, if anything, to do with right and wrong. After all, people of many ethnic groups have walked around naked in the past and some do still. Others would answer that the real question is sexual morality. For monotheists of all persuasions, the latter is inextricably linked with sin. Heaven forbid that consenting adults should do what they like, with whom they like, whenever they like, in any way they like! In any case the ability to distinguish right from wrong is merely the prerequisite for conscience, not conscience itself.

Following Abel's murder by Cain, the Lord tells the latter that 'the voice of thy brother's blood crieth unto me from the ground.' Cain's problem was that he was unable to conceal his crime sufficiently well, not that his conscience troubled him. Later too it was his punishment, not remorse, which he says was 'greater than [he] can bear' (Genesis 4:13). Several other passages in the Old Testament mention people's inner organs, especially the heart, as the place where their sins are recorded even against their will. 'The sin of Judah is written with a pen of iron and with the point of a diamond; it is graven upon the table of their heart, and upon the horns of your altars' (Jeremiah 17:1). 'The Lord examines hearts and kidneys' (Psalms 26:2); 'O Lord of hosts, that judgest righteously, that triest the reins [kidneys] and the heart' (Jeremiah 11:20). In none of these cases is there any question of a feeling of guilt or remorse. All the text says is that the Lord can look right into the human soul and will know what sinners have done regardless of how hard they work at concealing their thoughts.

Exodus 21–3 has a long list of laws concerning the relationship between people. It opens with the Fifth Commandment ('Honour thy father and thy mother') and proceeds through the remaining ones. Next it addresses other questions, such as the rules applicable to slavery, kidnapping, murder, assault, inflicting injury through negligence, illicit sex, rape, sorcery, bestiality, usury, the way strangers, widows and orphans should be treated, and more. Later, as Moses was approaching the end of his life, he repeated the injunctions in the book of Deuteronomy. Anxious that the People of Israel should not abandon his legacy, he made them solemnly swear to maintain them (27:15–26). Whoever breaks the oath he has taken and does any of these things shall be *arur*, a term whose full power is not conveyed by the usual English translation, 'laid under a curse'.

Three other terms often used in connection with transgression and crime are *avon*, *hattat* and *asham*. All are associated with guilt in the legal sense of the word: that is, culpability. All demand expiation in the form of restitution, ritual sacrifice or punishment. One modern student has tried to show that, since those who carry *asham* are required to confess, the term can also mean the *feeling* of guilt. However, a close reading of the relevant passages in Leviticus and Numbers does not support that idea. Indeed the student in question admits that his translation of the terms differs 'from all extant ones'.[2] Thus *asham* does not correspond to conscience, which is the innermost voice of all. That is why David, as the putative author of Psalms, famously begs the Lord to 'create in me a clean heart . . . and renew a right spirit in my inward parts' (Psalms 51:10).

One sentence in the Old Testament (Psalms 73:21) says that 'I was pricked in my reins.' Another (Psalms 1:7) speaks of the 'torment of the kidneys' at night. In Modern Hebrew both expressions signify acute remorse. However, in all the books of the Old Testament, only a few figures seem to have had a conscience as we have defined it. The first was Joseph. When Potiphar's wife asked him to sleep with her, he said that he could not bring himself to do this 'great wickedness' or sin against God (Genesis 39:7–10). The second was King Saul. At one point he found out that the young outlaw David, whom he was persecuting with might and main, had been in a position to kill him but refrained from doing so. 'Then said Saul, I have sinned; return, my son David; for I will no more do thee harm, because my soul was precious in thine eyes this day; behold, I have played the fool, and have erred exceedingly' (1 Samuel 26:21). The outcome was peace between the two men, though it did not last for long.

The third was David himself. On one occasion he was addressed by a courageous woman, Abigail. Prostrating herself at his feet, she pleaded with him not to kill her husband, Nabal the Carmelite, in retaliation for the latter's refusal to pay protection money. In her own words, she wanted to make sure 'that this [the eventual murder] shall be no grief unto thee, nor offence of heart unto my lord . . . that thou has shed blood causeless' (1 Samuel 25:31). He saw her point and did as she said. Somewhat later, after her husband had died of more or less natural causes, he married her. Briefly, David understood that unjust action now would lead to remorse at a later stage: he had a conscience.

These cases seem clear-cut: a clear choice had to be made, and was made, between good and evil. However, three others in which David was involved are much less so. First,

> it came to pass . . . that David's heart smote him because he had cut off Saul's skirt. And he said unto his men, the Lord forbid that I should do this thing unto my master, the Lord's anointed, to stretch forth mine hand against him, seeing that he is the anointed of the Lord. (1 Samuel 24:5)

The problem here is the likelihood that the Lord might grow angry if he, David, lifted a hand against His anointed. So he refrained from doing so.

Second, having slept with the woman Bathsheba and sent her husband, Uriah, to his death, David does indeed admit that 'I have sinned against the Lord', but only after the prophet Nathan had told him in no uncertain terms that the Lord was furious and that, by way of punishment, He would 'take away thy wives before thine eyes, and give them unto thy neighbor, and he shall lie with thy wives in the sight of this sun' (2 Samuel 12:11). Whereupon, according to tradition, David composed Psalm 51, in which he mentions his 'broken and contrite heart' (1) and asks that the Lord 'have mercy upon [him]' (27).

The third case involving David took place after he had already ruled Israel for many years. 'And again the anger of the Lord was kindled against Israel, and He moved David against them to say, "go, number Israel and Judah".' David did so, learning that his kingdom, which at that time covered parts of what are today Syria and Jordan, comprised 1,300,000 people, women and children not included. 'And David's heart smote him after that he had numbered the people. And David said unto the Lord, I have sinned greatly in that I have done; and now I beseech thee, O Lord, take away the iniquity of thy servant; for I have done very foolishly' (2 Samuel 24:10–11). As with Bathsheba, his remorse was not spontaneous. Earlier that day another prophet, Gad, had told David that he had sinned and angered the Lord. Thus the king behaved just as my dogs do. First he violated what he knew was the express command of the Lord (Exodus 30:11–15). Next, he begged for forgiveness; then, in the belief it had been granted, he wagged his tail. As to the Lord's behaviour, first using David as his tool against His people and then punishing them for what the king had done to them, it can only be called psychopathic.

However many transformations Judaism may have undergone, it still continues to exercise considerable influence both in its own right and by way of its links to Christianity and Islam. The fact that the Hebrew language is still in use, albeit in a much-modified form, also permits some extraordinary insights into the nature and evolution of the concept that interests us. Both in the Old Testament and in subsequent Jewish literature the organs in which thought originates are said to be the kidneys and the heart. To be sure, there are occasional references to matzpun, which is Modern Hebrew for 'conscience'. However, in the Bible the term means 'something hidden'. So, for example, in Obadiah 1:6: 'How are the things of Esau searched out! How are his hidden things sought up!' The 'things' in question also differed from the modern idea of conscience in that they could lead the person who had them not only towards good deeds but to bad ones too.[3]

In the entire Septuagint, the Greek version of the Old Testament that was created somewhere between 300 and 200 BC, what is commonly understood as the Greek word for 'conscience' only occurs once (Ecclesiastes 10:20). But even in this case the translation does not fit the original Hebrew text. As the context makes quite clear, the term meant not conscience but 'hiding' or 'privacy'. The reason why Judaism was unable to develop conscience was because it centres on 'a consuming fire, even a jealous God' (Deuteronomy 4:24). Whatever He has commanded is good. Whatever He has prohibited is bad. Advocates will say that the approach is not moral but legalistic; critics, that it is based simply on caprice.

Instead, Judaism has come up with two other ideas. The first is that 'from youth on, man's heart is driven towards evil' (Genesis 8:21; the translation is mine). The second, whose existence is made necessary by the first, is repentance. Those who have done wrong, either in their relationship with God or with their fellow men, are always given the opportunity to repent of their deeds. Indeed a well-known Talmudic saying, often repeated and commented upon, has it that 'those who repent [literally, 'turn around'] are more worthy than those who have never sinned.' The reason, we are told, is because changing one's ways is harder than never deviating from the old ones.

The Old Testament has quite some stories of individuals and groups who, after a shorter or longer period during which they did 'that which is evil in the eyes of the Lord', decided to change their conduct. Here and there they acted on their own initiative; for the most part, though, they did so at the Lord's express command, transmitted by one prophet or another. Those prophets, both major and minor, regularly accompanied their demands that the people repent and return to the ways of the Lord with the most bloodcurdling descriptions as to what would happen to them if they failed to do so. 'Behold, the day of the Lord cometh, and the spoil shall be divided in the midst of thee. For I will gather all nations against Jerusalem to battle; and the city shall be taken, and the houses rifled, and the women ravished', said Zechariah (14:1–2).

Granted, the Old Testament also incorporates two important texts, Proverbs and Ecclesiastes, where leading what we would call a moral life is equated not so much with obedience as with wisdom. However, doing so is presented as a once-for-all decision, not a prolonged struggle against ever-present temptation. Even so, a clear threat is not lacking: 'The wicked shall be cut off from the earth, and the transgressors shall be rooted out of it' (Proverbs 2:22).[4] In any case, in the eyes of most orthodox Jews none of the books in question is nearly as important as the Pentateuch. It is the Pentateuch, and not the Old Testament as a whole, part of which is publicly read in synagogue one Shabbat after another. It is the commandments of the Pentateuch, too, which 'thou shalt bind . . . for a sign upon thine hand, and they shall be as frontlets between thine eyes' (Exodus 13:9 and 13:16; Deuteronomy 6:8).

Presumably it was precisely because people could not be relied upon to repent of their own free will that the Book of Leviticus established the annual Day of Atonement:

> And this shall be a statue unto you; that in the seventh month, on the tenth day of the month, ye shall afflict your souls, and do no work at all, whether it be one of your own country, or a stranger that sojourneth among you; for on that day shall

the priest make an atonement for you, to cleanse you, that
ye may be clean from all your sins before the Lord . . . And
this shall be an everlasting statue unto you, to make an
atonement for the children of Israel for all their sins once a
year. (Leviticus 16:29–34)

According to later interpretations, possibly such as were influenced
by Christianity, the underlying assumption is that none of us, being
human, is without sin. Offences committed against fellow humans
may be expiated by ordinary means such as restitution, compensation
and asking for pardon. Not so those against the Lord, who sees everything and overlooks nothing. How does one make the Lord forgive
a sinful act? One fasts, prays and begs for forgiveness. Thus repentance
was institutionalized. But does repentance carried out by fiat once a
year really deserve to be called conscience?

To cap it all, many of the things the Lord did and demanded of
those who believed in Him were irrational, even contradictory.[5] So
much so, in fact, that an entire book, that of Job, was needed to try
and reconcile people with them. Yet questioning His commands was
prohibited. Such a framework is known as theonomy, from the Greek
theos, god, and *nomos*, law. The objective of the commandments that
formed the framework was precisely to prevent the evil drives in
man's heart from gaining the upper hand. They represented, and
still represent, a sort of dam: always threatened by the flood, it must
be maintained at all cost. All this left very little room for individuals
to develop an autonomous conscience. Some would argue that it did
not even leave much room for morality. The obvious case in point is
the book of Joshua. Here the Lord not only sanctioned but expressly
commanded the Israelites to carry out the most immoral acts, such
as exterminating the populations of captured cities to the last man,
woman, child and even head of cattle. Surely anyone with a conscience
should have refused to carry them out?

The demand for unconditional obedience explains why the hundreds upon hundreds of commandments that make up Jewish practice
are as detailed as they are. Just those governing female hygiene during
and after menstruation take up a book over 200 pages long. Starting
in the second and third centuries AD, trying to ascertain the precise

meaning of the numerous, often complex and esoteric injunctions was the task of the rabbis. Some injunctions are trivial, such as whether a woman may put on make-up on the Sabbath (it depends: she is allowed to use powder, but ointment is prohibited). Others are deadly serious: under what conditions should a Jew allow himself to be executed rather than violate the Lord's commands? Over the centuries hundreds of thousands of similar questions were referred to rabbis all over the Jewish world, who in turn would consult the Old Testament, the Talmud and the opinions of other rabbis before giving their answer. That process is ongoing: new so-called Q&A tomes keep being published. Recently the entire voluminous literature has been put on the Net for easy access. All this left plenty of room for scholarship and casuistry, but relatively little for the individual's inner voice, or conscience.

Some subsequent Jewish traditions allowed more room for 'the Lord God, merciful and gracious, long-suffering and abundant in goodness and truth, keeping mercy for thousands, forgiving iniquity and sin'. But make no mistake: 'That will by no means clear the guilty; visiting the iniquity of the fathers upon the children, and upon the children's children, unto the third and to the fourth generation' (Exodus 34:6–7). The basic assumption remained always the same: namely that, compared with the clarity of revealed truth and the punishments by which it is accompanied, the promptings of the heart, or kidneys as the case may be, are but fragile. Men will always find a thousand ways to justify their behaviour. That is why Maimonides (1135–1204), one of the greatest Jewish sages of all times, says: 'Any person who accepts the . . . commandments and is meticulous in observing them is thereby one of the righteous . . . [But] *this is only the case if he accepts them because God commanded them* in the Torah [my emphasis].'[6] Jews, in other words, should *practise* their religion. Compared with day-to-day observance, what they believe – some would say even *whether* they believe – is secondary: obeying the commandments arguably makes a conscience superfluous.

The German philosopher Arthur Schopenhauer once said that many people confuse conscience with the commandments of the religion to which they belong.[7] Some recent studies, noting that religious people are more likely than non-believers to base any altruistic behaviour they may engage in on God's commands, seem to back him up.[8] Religion, in other words, is not the parent of conscience but an alternative to it. To this day, anyone who can read the *pashquills*, or placards, pasted to the walls of Jerusalem's orthodox neighbourhoods will see that many of them list sins the community has allegedly committed. They call for *teshuva*, repentance; but *matzpun* is never mentioned.

Still staying with Judaism, change only got under way early in the twentieth century. It was driven partly by the ongoing process of secularization and partly by the nascent Zionist Movement. The two, of course, were linked. Secularization meant that, except among the orthodox who still claimed to adhere to it and to obey it as they always had, the divine commandment was no longer obeyed and a suitable substitute had to be found. Zionism for its part led to attempts to revive the Hebrew language so as to meet the needs of a modern society and state.

Joining the effort, linguists started considering how to render such concepts as conscience, *conscience*, *conscienza*, *Gewissen* and their equivalents in other European languages. In the end, a writer by the name of Joseph Brenner (1881–1921) hit on *matzpun*, thus giving the term a new meaning very different from the original one. Later still Modern Hebrew added expressions such as 'the sufferings of conscience', 'pangs of conscience' and 'a clean conscience'. All were adapted from various European languages. All reflect Gentile European patterns of thought more than they do traditional Jewish ones. As *matzpun* was assigned a new meaning, *asham*, but not its close relatives *avon* and *hattat*, underwent a parallel development. To its original meaning, legal culpability, Modern Hebrew added the *feeling* of guilt; in other words, conscience.

To sum up, the Führer got it wrong – would that doing so were his only crime! Contrary to what he said or is alleged to have said, modern Jews took the idea of conscience from Christianity, or rather the Christian peoples among whom they lived after finally leaving the ghetto during the nineteenth century, not the other way around. Not so in traditional Judaism: until the very last decades of the nineteenth century people who were about to commit, or who had already committed, an evil deed worried mainly about the divine commandment. That commandment made itself heard either by way of a written text that was the source of all moral understanding or through the mouths of prophets, priests and, later, rabbis who were responsible for studying and interpreting it.

Like conscience, the divine commandment could, and sometimes did, lead to repentance. However, conscience either does not imply any punishment or else, as Shakespeare's 'murderer' says, is one in its own right. Not so the divine commandment, which operates in a different way entirely. When the Lord is pleased the outcome is prosperity in the form of flocks, herds, fields and a large number of children. Nowadays a nice house, an expensive car, a good stock portfolio and exclusive holidays in favourable spots around the world would no doubt be added. When not, and unless forgiveness is asked for and granted, His terrible swift sword will inflict punishment either in the present world or in the next one. This being the case, purists would say that listening to the commandment, and doing as it says, is not a question of conscience at all.

From Homer to Aristotle

Contrary to the common view, Judaism in either its biblical or subsequent forms cannot account for our modern Western idea of conscience. The more so because, during much of its history, those subsequent forms were vehemently rejected by the Gentile world. So where did the idea originate? The answer may come as a surprise to some readers. Its foundations are found not in any monotheist religion but in the pagan cultures of Greece and Rome. Considering how close the Nazis always felt to the Greeks, the warlike Spartans in particular, this is ironic indeed.

That is not to say that it was there right from the beginning or that its meaning was identical with the common modern one. From Friedrich Nietzsche down, many commentators have noted that the Homeric poems – which, along with the Bible, have acted as the real fountainhead of all subsequent Western culture for thousands of years – have nothing to say about the subject.[9] The poems do indeed distinguish between good, *agathos*, and bad, *kakos*. But those terms had nothing to do with protecting the weak against the depredations of the strong. The reality, says Nietzsche, was just the opposite. 'Good' were the qualities that the ruling warrior-aristocrats claimed for themselves; anything that made them healthier, stronger, more fear-inspiring and more powerful. 'Bad' was what the same men associated with the lowly and the servile; and, ultimately, with those who were pitiable because they were disgusting, and disgusting because pitiable. The same goes for *kalos*, beautiful, and *aischros*, ugly or deformed. Indeed so closely linked were 'beautiful' and 'good' in Greek life and thought, especially early Greek life and thought, that they were fused into a single word.[10]

Nor were good and evil laid down once and for all by God as in Judaism and, later, Christianity. Humanity did not need to have its eyes opened either by eating the apple or by receiving some heaven-mandated commands that would tell it how to keep the two apart. Instead, the aristocrats *created* those concepts for themselves. In so doing they did not only express their humanity – it *was* their humanity, the striving to find out their potential and live up to it as much as they could. In this scheme of things good was equivalent to the kind of excellence, including courage, the desire to rule and physical prowess, that enabled one to become stronger, conquer and rule over others. 'Bad' was cowardice and the kind of despicable behaviour that made a person give way to the 'good' and, even more important, turned him into less than what he should be. To Nietzsche, whom I am following here, all this was a sign of healthy minds that had not yet been corrupted by 'slave morality' and conscience.

What is true in relationships among men also applies to the relationship between them and the gods. For example, in the first part of the *Iliad* Apollo is angry with the Greeks and causes a plague to rage among them. However, he only does so because King Agamemnon has taken the daughter of Charises, Apollo's priest, as his concubine. A god, like any man, must defend his own. In this entire long story not a word is wasted about either sin or conscience.[11] If Zeus' wife, Hera, his brother, Poseidon, and his daughter, Athena, hate Troy and are bent on bringing about the city's destruction, then this has nothing to do with any virtues or vices its unfortunate citizens may have. If the same Athena dislikes Hector and actively helps Achilles to kill him, this is not because Hector is a bad person but in spite of the fact that he is a very good one indeed.

Not a word of condemnation is heard about Achilles' abuse of Hector's body, let alone over the fact that he and his fellow warriors attacked countless inoffensive cities, laid them waste, killed the men and carried off the women and enslaved them. Such attacks were a normal part of life. Men could and did deplore them – yet what fate had ordained, not even the gods could change. This is not to say that Homeric people were incapable of kindness. Patroclus consoles the girl Briseis for the death of her family. Achilles himself is kind to King Priam, who has come to beg for the body of his fallen son. The Phaeacian princess Nausicaa overcomes her fears and helps the ship-wrecked Odysseus. So, later, does her father King Alcinous.[12] None of the four expects any reward for his or her deeds. The last two are simply following the rules of hospitality which, Nausicaa says, were ordained by Zeus.

To use Nietzsche's famous phrase, what we see here is a world beyond, others would no doubt say beneath, good and evil. It is one into which conscience has not yet been introduced. What we do find is *aidos*, a hard-to-translate concept. Applied to women, it can mean either purity or modesty. It is that which will prevent them from engaging in sexual misconduct and, in general, aggressive or pro-vocative behaviour considered inappropriate for their sex. In art, its presence is indicated by women dressing in mantles that cover their bodies, bowing their heads and lowering their gaze. In Euripides' *Phaedra* it is *aidos* that prevents the heroine from committing adultery. In the same author's *Ion* the heroine, Creusa, feels *aidos* not because she has done wrong but because she has been raped or, to put a less brutal interpretation on it, seduced – then as today, it was not always easy to say which was which – by Apollo. The idea long survived the passing both of the archaic age and of the classical one. Many other passages carry the same message. Briefly, feminine *aidos* always had a powerful erotic element. The same applies to its Latin equivalent, *pudicitia*.[13]

With men the situation is more complicated. As with women, *aidos* can mean shame, especially in a sexual context. Indeed the Greek word for the genitals of people of both sexes is *aida*, 'shameful parts'. A good example of this kind of *aidos* in action is provided by Odysseus trying to hide his nakedness from the Phaeacian princess

Nausicaa and her maids.[14] Most of us today share that feeling and do our best to keep our private parts out of public view. Where we differ is that we rarely think of conscience in this context: if I were to go about naked, then presumably this is not because I am bad but because I have no 'inhibitions'. However, the Greek male *aidos* also has another role. It is the kind of embarrassment that makes men act in ways they and the societies in which they live consider honourable and prevents them from doing the opposite.[15]

Thus, in respect to *aidos*, men bear a double burden. Some men are simply shameless. Penelope's suitors disregard honour and do whatever they think will gain them the hand, and the wealth, of the lady. Much later, the Roman emperor Caligula actually boasted that he did not know shame.[16] Ordinarily, though, *aidos* is something most men do feel. What is at issue is not the clash between good and bad. It is the one between honour and advantage; as a result, *aidos* can be an obstacle to effective action. At one point in the *Iliad* the hero Diomedes is about to go on a dangerous reconnaissance mission. King Agamemnon, with whom he consults, advises him not to let *aidos* disturb him. He, Diomedes, should select as his companion the man best suited for the job, not one who is his social equal.[17] More often *aidos* is what makes men overcome their fears and face danger, such as when the Achaeans are 'ashamed' not to accept Hector's challenge to a duel.[18] Towards the end of the *Iliad* Hector's *aidos* makes him order the Trojan army to stand and fight Achilles rather than withdraw behind the walls. The outcome is a disaster, culminating in Hector's own death.[19]

None of these male choices have much to do with morality, hence with conscience as we understand the term. In the first case a surfeit of *aidos* may lead to failure. In the last three, to the contrary, insufficient *aidos* will result in disgrace.[20] How can the Achaean heroes avoid an encounter with the magnificent Hector and still look others, and themselves, in the face? How can Hector avoid meeting Achilles in battle, even though he knows full well that doing so will result in his own death? After all, it was only a short while ago that he himself had told his wife Andromache that war was a man's business and his first of all.[21] Many of us might consider disgrace a small price to pay for survival – a living dog, it is said, is better than a dead lion.

The Homeric poems, the Iliad in particular, see things differently. Their central message is that, against the background of an inexorable fate none of us is able to avoid, aidos is what distinguishes heroes from the common herd and makes for a life worthy of being lived.

Throughout the thousand years of classical antiquity the Iliad and the Odyssey enjoyed canonical status. Complete or fragmentary, the surviving texts outnumber those of all other literary productions of the period combined. Plato quoted them and Aristotle taught them to his student Alexander the Great. Every educated person was supposed to study them and model himself on their heroes. All this proves how powerful the frame of reference they created was. The poet Hesiod, who wrote somewhat later than Homer, also saw aidos in terms of the clash between honour and utility. Unlike Homer, though, he provides some indications that aidos was not entirely a question of listening, or not listening, to one's 'gut feeling'. Instead it was linked with the rules of justice, or dike, as laid down by Zeus with respect, for example, to the treatment of guests and of supplicants. Transgressors might expect punishment at the hands of the goddess Nemesis, best described as the personification of vengeance. The difference is that Hesiod wrote for, and about, the lowly and the weak, not the noble and the powerful. He saw aidos as something a poor man could ill afford if he were to achieve his goals in life.[22] He exhorts his brother Perses to forget his aidos, roll up his sleeves and work for a living.

Plutarch says that the future reformer Solon (c. 638–558 BC), while still a young man, was left without means by his spendthrift father. His friends were prepared to help, but he felt 'ashamed' to ask them. Instead he engaged in commerce, travelled widely, gained experience and thus prepared for his future role as a reformer.[23] Much later, he wrote a poem that illustrates the vast gap between Greek ideas and our own. Having carried out his brief and given Athens a new set of laws, Solon left the city and went abroad to allow them to take hold. This caused some people to blame him for not using the exceptional powers he had been granted to elevate himself to become the city's ruler. Solon, in other words, was a coward who had opted out of the fierce, unending competition that was the essence of Greek (male) life. In response he wrote that he had no reason to 'be ashamed'.

He had done the honourable thing, even if it meant going against public opinion.[24] According to one modern student, this is the first time in Greek literature that we encounter *aidos* in the sense of a clash between 'what others say' and one's own inner voice.[25]

As the fifth century BC unfolded the Greek city-states, with Athens at their head, gradually became more democratic. The fact that commoners were now able to participate in government and even rise to the highest positions may have caused the close link between aristocratic, beautiful and good on the one hand and low-class, ugly and bad on the other to lose some of its force. In Aeschylus' tragedy *Persians*, which dates to 472 BC, *aidos* is closely linked to the 'dread' that makes ordinary people reluctant to look the ghost of King Darius in the face. One is reminded of the passage in the Old Testament Book of Esther, which says that anybody who spoke to the Persian king without receiving permission first put his life in jeopardy.[26] *Aidos*, in other words, has embarked on a process, parallel to the political one, whereby it liberated itself from its early association with high social status.

The list of Greek texts, archaic ones in particular, which use *aidos* or any of its several derivatives in ways that do not correspond, or only partly correspond, to the later idea of 'conscience' could be extended forever. Probably the first literary figure who may be credited with having possessed something of the kind is Sophocles' King Oedipus. Yet even here some doubts persist. As the plot goes, an oracle tells Oedipus' father Laius that he is destined to die at the hands of his own son. Thereupon he exposes Oedipus, but, as so often happens in ancient myth, the infant is found and raised in the royal court of Corinth. Later Oedipus himself is told, this time by the famous Oracle at Delphi, that he is destined to kill his father and marry his mother. Horrified, he leaves Corinth, where he has grown up, in an effort to avoid his fate. However, he is involved in a quarrel and ends up killing a stranger. Later still he marries the stranger's widow. When the truth emerges and the real identity of all three is revealed, even the sun, the all-seeing god, is affronted by the sight of the offender.

The word *aidos* is not used. However, Oedipus certainly experiences the most intense guilt and remorse. Unable either to be looked at or to look the world in the face, he stabs out his own eyes. What is at work here is the ancient conflict between a man, the world's opinion of him and his own inability to look that opinion in the face. But why should he feel that way? There is no question that he did not consciously prefer wrong over right. He did not deliberately set out to commit first parricide and then incest. On the contrary, having heard the oracle, he did whatever he could to avoid what by any standards are among the most evil deeds of all. His failure was preordained by fate. Why should a man be blamed for what he cannot escape? Is a crime unwittingly committed really a crime? Or is Aeschylus telling us that, at some level which Freud would have called the unconscious, Oedipus had been perfectly aware of what was happening? That the real message of the play is that, when everything is said and done, he *always* should have known or should know or did know?

In Sophocles' play, Oedipus' daughter Antigone took the opposite route. Like so many tragic figures, Antigone, whose name means 'unbending', is caught in a conflict. On the one hand is her wish to bury her brother Polynices, who was killed while leading an uprising against Creon, king of Thebes. On the other is Creon's command that Polynices' body should be left for the birds and the animals to devour. Since denial of the customary rites meant that the soul of the deceased would never come to rest, this was a terrible punishment indeed. In giving the order Creon relies on the need to maintain authority – without it, any society would quickly fall to pieces. He also calls on public opinion: 'Don't you feel', he asks her, '*aidos* in differing from these men [the assembled members of the chorus, who represent the latter]?'

'It is no unseemly deed', Antigone proudly declares, 'to honour one's kin.'[27] Her answer must have hit the mid-fifth-century Athenian audience like a bombshell. All the more so because she does not lose a word on gods, or justice, or reward, or punishment; and all the more so because the speaker is not a man (the Greek term for 'courage' is 'manliness') but a woman. A member, in other words, of the sex which Sophocles himself, through the mouth of Antigone's sister Ismene, characterizes as 'timid'. The text leaves no doubt that she is putting her own judgement first.[28] The old world in which what is and is not disgraceful is decided by convention clashes with Antigone's new one. Knowing her life will be forfeit, she follows an inner voice. It alone tells her what is right and what is wrong; conscience has been born.

This was by no means the end of the matter. In the plays of Sophocles' slightly younger colleague Euripides (480–406 BC), the old and the new meanings of *aidos* often appear side by side. As in Homer, the term is still often used to describe both the quality that prevents men from fleeing from the battlefield and that which women feel, or are supposed to feel, in the face of anything overtly sexual. In *Electra* the heroine is a king's daughter. At one point she was considered fit to marry a god, Castor. Later she came down in the world until she was forced to wed a simple peasant. Yet the husband in turn is reluctant to consummate the marriage. As he sees it, for her to sleep with him would be a shameful act; for him, a manifestation of hubris.[29] His is a form of reluctance born out of a combination of bashfulness and deference not too different from the kind of thing Creon vainly expects Antigone to show.

In *Orestes*, Euripides takes another step. Here the eponymous hero kills his mother, Clytemnestra, in order to avenge his dead father, Agamemnon. Later, meeting his uncle Menelaus, Orestes says that he is 'in agony . . . knowing with himself that he had done terrible things'.[30] The verb he uses to describe his feeling is *suneidenai*, 'to share knowledge', or 'to be aware'. As a result he comes under attack by the monstrous Erinyes, or Furies, who 'look like night'. They give him no rest, haunt him as he tries to flee and all but drive him mad. The question is, does he see them as real? In that case his sufferings have more to do with divine retribution of the kind so often described in the Old Testament than with true remorse. Or are the Erinyes merely the personification of his own persecutory hallucinations? In that case one may say that he was suffering pangs of conscience. Neither this text nor any other provides a direct, unambiguous answer.

From yet another one of Euripides' plays, *The Suppliants*, we learn that people wished to avoid *aischune*, literally 'the sense of shame', for fear of becoming *kakoi*, bad.[31] The way Euripides and his contemporaries increasingly saw it, this wish, or feeling, was not innate. Instead, we are told, it was something children of both sexes could acquire. They did so by following their elders' example in the same will lead to *metanoia*, remorse. Conversely, 'not having knowledge of oneself of having committed any injustice is a cause for great satisfaction.'[42] In view of the persistent Greek tendency to personify various qualities and give them the names of gods, whether the jurors whom Antiphon addresses are supposed to act out of fear of divine retribution or in the name of 'pure' conscience is hard to say. The same Antiphon also warns jurors that *hamartia*, error, is itself a source of harm. As one modern scholar has pointed out, seldom is it possible to say whether the harm arises from fear of the consequences or from the individual's own self-reproach; whether what the texts refer to is crime, sin or a subjective feeling of guilt. Greeks during the classical period did not think in such terms.[43]

Socrates' speech was delivered in front of hundreds of citizen-jurors. He must have taken it for granted that his arguments, though they would probably not be accepted (they were not), would at least be understood by the majority. A third instance was Isocrates (436–338 BC). Like Antiphon, Isocrates wrote speeches for defendants at court. Such was his reputation that he could charge as much as twenty talents – more than half a ton – of silver for each speech. 'Never hope', he once wrote, 'to conceal any shameful thing which you have done. For even if you do conceal it from others, you will still know with yourself.' And again: 'Do not emulate those with the most possessions, but those who do not know of anything bad with themselves. For it is with such a psyche that one can lead the happiest life.'[44]

In Athens, the theatre played a much greater role in public life than in any other society at any other time and place.[45] It was used to imbue the people with the city's values; at one point spectators even started to be paid for attending. The audience were not supposed to be passive consumers of culture. Considerable numbers of young men were expected to participate in the chorus, thus interacting with the actors and, indirectly, the playwrights too. Doing so was an essential part of their education. Citizens also regularly voted for the best plays of the year and awarded prizes to the authors. Did they do so without understanding the issues the plays raised? Surely for most of them that was not the case. Following the abortive expedition against Syracuse in 415–13 BC, some Athenian prisoners of war were able to draw attention to themselves by reciting lines from Euripides.[46]

way as they learnt to speak without any need for formal tuition. Obeying the commands of *aidos* and *aischune* will result in a good reputation.[32] Conversely, the absence of *aischune* in a mid-fifth-century BC adult, whether an aristocrat or commoner, is considered a certain sign of a deficient education. With both the desire to avoid evil and remorse present, the self-regulating human experience we call conscience is complete.

The next critical name is that of the philosopher Democritus (c. 460–370 BC), best known to the modern world for his invention of atomic theory (about which more later). Democritus, only brief fragments of whose work have survived, resembled Euripides in that he put great emphasis on the role of education as the fount of virtue. That specifically includes the virtue we know as conscience. The key point he raises is that positive law alone is unlikely to guarantee proper behaviour by the individual. What is needed is a good understanding of the reasons that might lead to such behaviour. As he says, 'do not abstain from wrongdoing because of fear, but because of what must be done.'[33] Other fragments elaborate on the message and reinforce it. Thus fragment 264b reads as follows:

> One should not feel embarrassment before other people to any greater extent than one does before oneself, nor should one do wrong if no one is going to know any more than if everyone is. One should be ashamed in front of oneself above all. And let this be established as a law in one's own soul, so as to do nothing inappropriate.

To which fragments 84 and 244 add:

> The one whose does unseemly things should be ashamed in front of himself first of all . . . Even if you are alone, do not say or do anything base. Learn to be shameful in front of yourself much more than in front of other people.

Speaking of a juror who for reasons of pleasure or profit has knowingly acquitted a guilty man, Democritus says that such a juror will have to carry his deed in his heart.[34] Yet he is also a realist: knowing men, he has some doubts as to whether everybody will be persuaded by this. That is why, like Hesiod two centuries earlier, he adds the link to justice and, with it, fear of punishment.[35] Still, the difference between embarrassment in front of others on the one hand and self-reproach on the other has been clearly stated.

According to Plato, Socrates (469–399 BC) in his final speech before the court told the jurors that, from his youth on, he had heard 'a voice which comes to me and always forbids me to do something which I am going to do'. He did not keep what he heard to himself. At the price of neglecting his own affairs and remaining poor, he chose to be 'that gadfly God has given the state and all day long and in all places and always fastening upon you, arousing and persuading and reproaching you'.[36] In modern terms what he is saying is that he is their conscience. That is precisely why they decided to execute him. Different versions of the same speech have him saying that he was 'aware with himself' that he was innocent: that is, that his conscience was clear. Once he had been condemned to death, he did not choose to flee and 'disgrace' himself.

When Plato refers to aidos, as he often does, normally what he means is the quality which tells people (men, really; on the whole, Plato is not very interested in women) to adopt certain forms of behaviour and avoid others. Nevertheless, from time to time we get a hint that embarrassment may be directed not merely towards others but towards oneself too. The best-known case is the Seventh Letter, which he wrote in 366 BC, when he was already an old man. In it he explains how the tyrant of Syracuse, Dionysius II, accepted the advice of his uncle Dion and invited him, Plato, to come over and act as an adviser. One reason that induced him to accept was his long-standing friendship with and respect for Dion; the other was 'a feeling of shame with regard to myself [my emphasis], lest I might some day appear to myself wholly and solely a mere man of words, one who would never of his own will lay his hand to any act'.[37] Another indication of the way in which Plato understands aidos is the fact that he locates it in the part of the soul that seeks timē, honour.[38] It is that which makes a person feel embarrassed, angry even, for falling short of his, and rarely her, ideal self-image.[39] This still is not quite what we mean by conscience, but it does come pretty close.

The first author who explicitly classifies aidos as an emotion, pathos, much like others such as fear, pity, confidence, joy, liking and hating, is Aristotle.[40] Like other emotions, he says, it is associated with physiological changes that take place in the body. For example, 'being angry is a boiling of the blood and hot stuff around the heart.' Today we would speak of an accelerated heart rate, enhanced electrical activity in certain parts of the brain and increased secretions of certain hormones. Proceeding in his systematic way, Aristotle defines aidos and its synonym, aischune, as 'a kind of pain or disturbance concerning those evils (ills, misfortunes) which seem to lead to ill-repute, whether they be present, past or future'.[41] Like so many other Greeks, he uses the Homeric heroes' fear of disgrace to illustrate his case. Conversely, shamelessness entails 'a kind of contempt or indifference with regard to the same things'.

Dependent as we are on written texts, so far our discussion has been limited to high culture – some of the greatest culture ever, to be sure, but high culture nevertheless. To what extent did the idea of conscience or, to use an exact translation of the Greek expression, 'knowledge with one self' enter the popular mind and affect everyday behaviour? One clue is provided by the speeches of 'sophists', literally 'cunning' or 'wise' men. They were written on behalf of clients who were supposed to deliver them in court; that was because the use of lawyers was not allowed and defendants had to represent themselves. Repeatedly during the last decades of the fifth century BC we find appeals to the juries in murder trials to ensure that their verdicts would be in accordance with aidos as well as eusebeia, piety. To prevent bribery, Athenian courts regularly consisted of hundreds of jurors. Some exceptionally sensitive cases were even tried by popular assembly as a whole, though we do not know how well attended the meetings were. This fact indicates that such ideas were understood by, and relevant to, the mental processes not merely of a small group of literati discussing philosophical ideas but of a much larger number of ordinary citizens.

For example, Antiphon of Rhamnus (480–411 BC) was a professional writer of court speeches. In one speech designed for the benefit of a person who was standing trial for murder, the accused is made to call upon the jury to acquit him. Failing to do so, he warns them,

The fact that countless vases were painted with scenes from the very myths the tragedians used to introduce their audiences to the idea of conscience, among others, points in the same direction.

In summary, the framework Homer created and others maintained for a millennium or so had more to say about the clash between honour and advantage than about the one between good and bad; more about disgrace in front of others than about self-reproach. Yet starting around the middle of the fifth century BC, here and there we find flashes of what can only be called conscience proper. The best sources are Sophocles, Euripides, Democritus and, to some extent, Plato. Unlike the Homeric heroes, Sophocles' Antigone does what she considers right and proper without any regard to the consequences – that is, her own death. Doing so, she has earned the right to be called the inventor of conscience. Euripides' Orestes 'knows with himself' that he has done terrible things. He suffers torments on that account, though whether they were self-inflicted, as the use of the term conscience would demand, or the handiwork of the vengeful Erinyes is not entirely clear. The most explicit classical Greek author of all was the philosopher Democritus. Not only did he speak of 'shame in front of oneself', but he raised the question of whether people would act conscientiously even in the absence of either other people or laws to govern their conduct. Plato, by mostly sticking to the conventional framework, did not go quite so far. However, as the Seventh Letter shows, he too knew self-reproach and acted on it.

The first to define *aidos* as a feeling was Aristotle. Like Homer four centuries or so earlier, he saw it mainly as a wish to avoid ill repute. Judging by the surviving fragments of Antiphon, Socrates' apology and the speeches of Isocrates, rhetoricians often used such arguments in courts of law. In addition, large numbers of adult citizens (and perhaps their wives and daughters as well) were exposed to them by way of the theatre. Many of the plays in which they occur were actually awarded prizes. These facts seem to show that the emerging ideas surrounding conscience were not simply limited to a handful of literati. Instead they were understood, and perhaps to some extent even acted upon, by a considerable section of the population at large.

Enter the Stoics

Throughout the archaic and classical periods Greek ideas of conscience never quite liberated themselves from their early association with honour, justice and law – both human and divine – as well as reward and punishment. A choice between good and evil seldom entered into them. However, shortly after the year 300 BC this began to change. The shift had everything to do with the emergence of Stoic philosophy.

Stoicism in turn was linked to two broader developments, one religious and the other political. The first was that people ceased to believe in the existence of personal, anthropomorphic, gods. No longer did Zeus, Poseidon, Hera, Athene, Apollo and the rest keep a close watch on the world and actively intervene in events. Their place in creating the world was taken by the Uncreated, the Eternal and the Cause of All,[47] whereas day-to-day happenings were the province of fortune. Hope for, and fear of, divine rewards and retribution started waning. So did the perceived usefulness of religious ceremonial, prayer, sacrifice, vows and the like. To keep men and women on the straight and narrow, other methods were needed.[48] The second development was the demise of the independent city-state and the rise of powerful monarchies governed by despots ('masters', in Greek). Claiming divine or semi-divine status, often arbitrary and capricious, these rulers had it in their power to do literally *anything* – and were often not shy of boasting of the fact.

It was in response to these conditions that the Stoic movement, as well as some others that concern us here, developed. Some Stoics, notably Cicero and Cato the Younger, lived during periods of transition from democracy/republic to despotic government and did their best to resist it. Most, however, took absolute government for granted. They advised people to reconcile themselves with it, and in general opposed any attempt to dispute it or change it.[49] As we shall see, for this and other reasons they won the admiration of Immanuel Kant (1724–1804), the German philosopher who probably did more to develop the modern idea of conscience than anybody else. All depended on the emperor's 'indulgence' for their very survival.[50] Yet this helplessness, the fact that they were to a considerable extent unable to control their own fates, made them put a strong emphasis on individual autonomy and self-motivation.

Judaism bet its hand on divine commands, and Homer trusted in pride and fear of disgrace. By contrast, the Stoics emphasized reason. All men, they argued, are by nature inclined to put their own survival first. They have the *potential* for exercising reason; in other words, the ability to distinguish between virtue and it opposite or, to use the Stoics' own language, between that which was according to nature and that which was not.[51] It was each man's duty to himself to exercise virtue and avoid vice as much as possible. Not for the sake of others, but for their own; why be less than that which your nature enables you to be? Should the worst come to pass, with fortune raining down its blows and circumstances making a virtuous life impossible, there was always suicide, which offered a way out while at the same time forming the supreme manifestation of one's independence, even one's humanity.

The founders of Stoicism were Zeno (c. 334–262 BC) and his students Cleanthes (c. 330–c. 230 BC) and Chrysippus (c. 279–c. 206 BC). All three were prolific writers, but only isolated fragments of their works have survived. All three are known to have argued that morality consisted of acting in accordance with the laws of nature, though whether doing so meant knowing the natural sequence of causation and 'flowing' with it, or performing one's duties, or enjoying those things that were in accordance with nature, was never made entirely clear. Curiously enough, the first extant writer to provide us with relatively plentiful information on the way in which the Stoics understood 'conscience' was a Jew, Philo of Alexandria (c. 20 BC–AD 50). Philo was the scion of a wealthy and aristocratic family who studied Greek philosophy and understood its worth. He also had extensive ties both in the Jewish and the Roman world.

Between them, Philo's voluminous writings contain more references to 'knowledge with oneself' (*syneidēsis*, the closest Greek comes to the modern conscience) than those of any other Stoic author. In *The Unchangeableness of God* he calls it 'a pure ray of light' that drives away the 'sicknesses' in the soul that led us to 'guilty and blameworthy actions'.[52] In *The Confusion of the Tongues* he says that it 'convicts and pricks' even those who lead a 'godless' life.[53] In *On the Decalogue* he says that every soul has for its birth-fellow and house-mate a monitor . . . whose way is to admit nothing that calls for censure, whose nature is ever to hate evil and love virtue, who is its accuser and its judge in one . . . As accuser, he censures, accuses and puts the soul to shame; and again as judge, he instructs, admonishes and instructs its ways. And if he has the strength to persuade it, he rejoices and makes peace. But if he cannot, he makes war to the bitter end, never leaving it alone by day or night, but playing it with stabs and deadly wounds until he breaks the thread of its miserable and ill-starred life.[54]

No mention here of the 'jealous' God, 'visiting the iniquity of the fathers upon the children unto the third and fourth generations of them that hate me; and showing mercy unto the thousands of them that love me, and keep my commandments' (Exodus 20:5–6). To the contrary, in his frequent use of the term *syneidēsis* Philo overrode the Septuagint. To repeat, the latter only employs it once and then in an entirely different way.[55] His purpose was to convince his Gentile contemporaries that Judaism was not the exclusivist, separatist and frankly outrageous creed many of them thought it was.[56] Rather, correctly understood, it agreed with the most advanced philosophy of the age.

Another key figure was Epictetus (c. AD 55–135). In a fragment attributed to him (perhaps falsely), he refers to conscience as a facet of the mature mind.

When we are children our parents deliver us to a pedagogue to take care on all occasions that we suffer no harm. But when we are become men, God delivers us to our *syneidēsis* to take care of us. This guardianship we must in no way despise, for we shall displease God and be enemies of our own civilization.[57]

Keep in mind that, for Epictetus as for the Stoics in general, God, nature and the universal law that rules it amount to the same thing.[58] Wisdom and virtue consist of following that law; discovering the law is the task (by no means an easy one, given man's subjectivity and proneness to error) of philosophy. In all this there can be no question of divine reward and punishment. Another one of Epictetus' fragmentary texts runs as follows:

> To the kings and tyrants of this world, their bodyguards and their arms used to afford the privilege of censuring certain persons, and the power also to punish those who do wrong, no matter how guilty they themselves were; to the Stoic it is his conscience [*syneidēsis*, 'knowledge with oneself', 'awareness'] which affords him this power . . . When he sees that he has watched over men, and toiled on their behalf; and that he has slept in purity . . . and that every thought which he thinks is that of a friend and servant to the gods.[59]

Many other writers make similar use of the term.[60] The most important ones among them are Diodorus' fellow historians Dionysius of Halicarnassus (c. 60–7 BC), Josephus (like Philo, a Jew who wrote in Greek, AD 37–c. 100) and Plutarch (AD 46–120).

On occasion 'conscience' is still confused with fear or shame, reminding us of the way people thought about it before the Stoics started polishing it, so to speak, and made it stand on its own. Normally the term is used in the context of deeds that have already been committed. However, here and there it is referred to as a judge of a deed that is merely being contemplated. As such it can prevent action, provoke it or open the road to certain courses of conduct. In one of his treatises Philo retells the above-mentioned tale of Potiphar's wife trying to seduce the good-looking Joseph while her husband, Joseph's master, was absent. Instead of sticking to the text of the Septuagint, though, he embroiders it: 'What would be my inward feelings if I agreed to this unholy act?' he makes Joseph ask.

> What my looks when I face him, iron-hearted though I be?
> No, conscience will take hold of me and not suffer me to look him straight in the face even if I can escape detection. And that cannot be, for . . . even if no other knows of it or reports the knowledge, which he shares with me, all the same

I shall turn informer against myself through my colour, my looks, my voice, convicted, as I just said, by my conscience.[61]

A Stoic, says Epictetus, should try to achieve the good things in life, money, position and family included. However, he should only do so for as long as he can preserve his self-respect, his trustworthiness and his magnanimity, since these are the most important goods of all.[62]

The Latin term for conscience is *conscientia*. Like its Greek equivalent, its literal meaning is 'knowledge with' oneself. It is often used by the lawyer and politician Cicero (106–43 BC) and, above all, the philosopher Seneca (4 BC–AD 65), in whose works it appears some 50 times. Both Cicero and Seneca had studied Greek philosophy under teachers with Stoic leanings. To both of them *conscientia* is a sort of guide or judge of personal conduct. Either it accuses a person as a result of what he has done, or it enables him to manage his affairs in such a way as to make it unnecessary to feel remorse.[63] *Conscientia*, Seneca says, 'places a janitor at the entrance of the interior man'. Unlike knowledge that is shared with others, it is hidden within the individual man with regard to his own wrong deed. Free of divine commandments, men must live in accordance with 'nature'. Such a life, he adds, should be composed above all. Nothing that rushes headlong can ever be well-ordered.[64]

As far as the available evidence goes, the first to combine the term 'conscience' with some adjective was Cicero, who speaks of *praeclara conscientia* (clear, or beautiful, conscience) and of *recta conscientia*. Other expressions found in his work include *conscientia maleficiorum* – consciousness of an evil deed committed; *conscientiae labes* – a wounded conscience; and the need to refer everything to conscience (*ad conscientiam referre omnia*).

The most famous Stoic to combine 'conscience' with 'good' was Emperor Marcus Aurelius. The scion of an aristocratic family, highly educated by some of the best contemporary minds, during his youth he seems to have considered taking up the philosopher's abstemious way of life.[65] Rather than realizing that dream, in AD 161 he found himself the absolute ruler of perhaps 80 million people and the most powerful person in the 'known world'. Between 170 and 180 he spent much time on the German frontier, where he had gone, as he himself put it, 'to hunt Sarmatians'. Apparently he wrote his *Meditations* during his moments of leisure with no intent of publication. The relevant passage runs as follows:

Keep thyself then simple, good, pure, serious, free from affectation, a friend of justice, a worshipper of the gods, kind, affectionate, strenuous in all proper acts. Strive to continue to be such as philosophy wished to make thee. Reverence the gods, and help men. Short is life. There is only one fruit of this serene life, a pious disposition and social acts. Do everything as a disciple of Antoninus [Aurelius' imperial predecessor, Antoninus Pius]. Remember his constancy in every act which was conformable to reason, and his evenness in all things, and his piety, and the serenity of his countenance, and his sweetness, and his disregard of empty fame, and his efforts to understand things; and how he would never let anything pass without having first most carefully examined it and clearly understood it; and how he bore with those who blamed him unjustly without blaming them in return; how he did nothing in a hurry; and how he listened not to calumnies, and how exact an examiner of manners and actions he was; and not given to reproach people, nor timid, nor suspicious, nor a sophist; and with how little he was satisfied, such as lodging, bed, dress, food, servants; and how laborious and patient; and how he was able on account of his sparing diet to hold out to the evening, not even requiring to relieve himself by any evacuations except at the usual hour; and his firmness and uniformity in his friendships; and how he tolerated freedom of speech in those who opposed his opinions; and the pleasure that he had when any man showed him anything better; and how religious he was without superstition. Imitate all this that thou mayest have as good a conscience [*eusyneidēsis*, good knowledge with yourself], when thy last hour comes, as he had.[66]

In marked contrast to the modern view, the emphasis is not on the act (good or bad), nor on its consequences (good or bad), but on the agent who commits it. The objective is to attain long-term equilibrium, self-mastery and, above all, autonomy. Whereas the motto of the kings of Scotland was 'nobody who hurts me will escape unpunished', the Stoic one might be 'nothing can hurt me.' These qualities in turn will be achieved by, and express themselves in the form of, justice, steadiness, affability, the avoidance of excess and moderate living. Such a way of life will enable a person to work on behalf of human society, of which he is necessarily a member and which he must seek to serve as much as he can.[67] Above all, it will endow him with an austere kind of peace and enable him to face anything, death included. No mention is made of the need to make a moral choice between good and bad.

Seen from a modern point of view, Aurelius' conscience left something to be desired. It neither prevented him from having Sarmatian prisoners of war beheaded nor from watching 'obstinate' Christians being thrown to the beasts in the Colosseum. Seneca on his part says at one point that, as part of his attempts to prepare for possible blows of fortune, he travelled in a modest cart instead of the luxurious one which, as a rich man, he could well afford. Hardly a question of conscience, one would think – and not a very Stoic thing to do either, since Seneca admits his embarrassment in the face of the ridicule others might cover him with if they saw him. Yet he does not lose a word about his real sins, including making a fortune by flattering members of the imperial family and also committing adultery with an imperial princess.[68]

Once again, one may well ask: was the idea of conscience as understood by the Stoics during the Hellenistic and Roman periods limited to a small elite? Or did it make its impact felt in broader circles as well? Some attempt has been made to show that the latter was the case and, by so doing, prove the existence of links between it and Christianity, most of whose early adherents were lower-class people. But the evidence is far from impressive. In Greece, so widely taught were the Homeric epics that, throughout antiquity, even moderately literate men could hardly escape their influence. The Athenian plays were watched, and perhaps even participated in, by large segments of the population, and citizens often acted as jurors as part of their day-to-day duties.

way as they learnt to speak without any need for formal tuition. Obeying the commands of *aidos* and *aischune* will result in a good reputation.[32] Conversely, the absence of *aischune* in a mid-fifth-century BC adult, whether an aristocrat or commoner, is considered a certain sign of a deficient education. With both the desire to avoid evil and remorse present, the self-regulating human experience we call conscience is complete.

The next critical name is that of the philosopher Democritus (c. 460–370 BC), best known to the modern world for his invention of atomic theory (about which more later). Democritus, only brief fragments of whose work have survived, resembled Euripides in that he put great emphasis on the role of education as the fount of virtue. That specifically includes the virtue we know as conscience. The key point he raises is that positive law alone is unlikely to guarantee proper behaviour by the individual. What is needed is a good understanding of the reasons that might lead to such behaviour. As he says, 'do not abstain from wrongdoing because of fear, but because of what must be done.'[33] Other fragments elaborate on the message and reinforce it. Thus fragment 264b reads as follows:

> One should not feel embarrassment before other people to any greater extent than one does before oneself, nor should one do wrong if no one is going to know any more than if everyone is. One should be ashamed in front of oneself above all. And let this be established as a law in one's own soul, so as to do nothing inappropriate.

To which fragments 84 and 244 add:

> The one whose does unseemly things should be ashamed in front of himself first of all . . . Even if you are alone, do not say or do anything base. Learn to be shameful in front of yourself much more than in front of other people.

Speaking of a juror who for reasons of pleasure or profit has knowingly acquitted a guilty man, Democritus says that such a juror will have to carry his deed in his heart.[34] Yet he is also a realist: knowing men, he has some doubts as to whether everybody will be persuaded by this. That is why, like Hesiod two centuries earlier, he adds the link to justice and, with it, fear of punishment.[35] Still, the difference between embarrassment in front of others on the one hand and self-reproach on the other has been clearly stated.

According to Plato, Socrates (469–399 BC) in his final speech before the court told the jurors that, from his youth on, he had heard 'a voice which comes to me and always forbids me to do something which I am going to do'. He did not keep what he heard to himself. At the price of neglecting his own affairs and remaining poor, he chose to be 'that gadfly God has given the state and all day long and in all places and always fastening upon you, arousing and persuading and reproaching you'.[36] In modern terms what he is saying is that he is their conscience. That is precisely why they decided to execute him. Different versions of the same speech have him saying that he was 'aware with himself' that he was innocent: that is, that his conscience was clear. Once he had been condemned to death, he did not choose to flee and 'disgrace' himself.

When Plato refers to *aidos*, as he often does, normally what he means is the quality which tells people (men, really; on the whole, Plato is not very interested in women) to adopt certain forms of behaviour and avoid others. Nevertheless, from time to time we get a hint that embarrassment may be directed not merely towards others but towards oneself too. The best-known case is the Seventh Letter, which he wrote in 366 BC, when he was already an old man. In it he explains how the tyrant of Syracuse, Dionysius II, accepted the advice of his uncle Dion and invited him, Plato, to come over and act as an adviser. One reason that induced him to accept was his long-standing friendship with and respect for Dion; the other was 'a feeling of shame *with regard to myself* [my emphasis], lest I might some day appear to myself wholly and solely a mere man of words, one who would never of his own will lay his hand to any act'.[37] Another indication of the way in which Plato understands *aidos* is the fact that he locates it in the part of the soul that seeks timē, honour.[38] It is that which makes a person feel embarrassed, angry even, for falling short of his, and rarely her, ideal self-image.[39] This still is not quite what we mean by conscience, but it does come pretty close.

The first author who explicitly classifies *aidos* as an emotion, or *pathos*, much like others such as fear, pity, confidence, joy, liking and hating, is Aristotle.[40] Like other emotions, he says, it is associated with physiological changes that take place in the body. For example, 'being angry is a boiling of the blood and hot stuff around the heart.' Today we would speak of an accelerated heart rate, enhanced electrical activity in certain parts of the brain and increased secretions of certain hormones. Proceeding in his systematic way, Aristotle defines *aidos* and its synonym, *aischune*, as 'a kind of pain or disturbance concerning those evils (ills, misfortunes) which seem to lead to ill-repute, whether they be present, past or future'.[41] Like so many other Greeks, he uses the Homeric heroes' fear of disgrace to illustrate his case. Conversely, shamelessness entails 'a kind of contempt or indifference with regard to the same things'.

Dependent as we are on written texts, so far our discussion has been limited to high culture – some of the greatest culture ever, to be sure, but high culture nevertheless. To what extent did the idea of conscience or, to use an exact translation of the Greek expression, 'knowledge with one self' enter the popular mind and affect everyday behaviour? One clue is provided by the speeches of 'sophists', literally 'cunning' or 'wise' men. They were written on behalf of clients who were supposed to deliver them in court; that was because the use of lawyers was not allowed and defendants had to represent themselves. Repeatedly during the last decades of the fifth century BC we find appeals to the juries in murder trials to ensure that their verdicts would be in accordance with *aidos* as well as *eusebeia*, piety. To prevent bribery, Athenian courts regularly consisted of hundreds of jurors. Some exceptionally sensitive cases were even tried by popular assembly as a whole, though we do not know how well attended the meetings were. This fact indicates that such ideas were understood by, and relevant to, the mental processes not merely of a small group of literati discussing philosophical ideas but of a much larger number of ordinary citizens.

For example, Antiphon of Rhamnus (480–411 BC) was a professional writer of court speeches. In one speech designed for the benefit of a person who was standing trial for murder, the accused is made to call upon the jury to acquit him. Failing to do so, he warns them, will lead to *metanoia*, remorse. Conversely, 'not having knowledge of oneself of having committed any injustice is a cause for great satisfaction.'[42] In view of the persistent Greek tendency to personify various qualities and give them the names of gods, whether the jurors whom Antiphon addresses are supposed to act out of fear of divine retribution or in the name of 'pure' conscience is hard to say. The same Antiphon also warns jurors that *hamartia*, error, is itself a source of harm. As one modern scholar has pointed out, seldom is it possible to say whether the harm arises from fear of the consequences or from the individual's own self-reproach; whether what the texts refer to is crime, sin or a subjective feeling of guilt. Greeks during the classical period did not think in such terms.[43]

Socrates' speech was delivered in front of hundreds of citizen-jurors. He must have taken it for granted that his arguments, though they would probably not be accepted (they were not), would at least be understood by the majority. A third instance was Isocrates (436–338 BC). Like Antiphon, Isocrates wrote speeches for defendants at court. Such was his reputation that he could charge as much as twenty talents – more than half a ton – of silver for each speech. 'Never hope', he once wrote, 'to conceal any shameful thing which you have done. For even if you do conceal it from others, you will still know with yourself.' And again: 'Do not emulate those with the most possessions, but those who do not know of anything bad with themselves. For it is with such a psyche that one can lead the happiest life.'[44]

In Athens, the theatre played a much greater role in public life than in any other society at any other time and place.[45] It was used to imbue the people with the city's values; at one point spectators even started to be paid for attending. The audience were not supposed to be passive consumers of culture. Considerable numbers of young men were expected to participate in the chorus, thus interacting with the actors and, indirectly, the playwrights too. Doing so was an essential part of their education. Citizens also regularly voted for the best plays of the year and awarded prizes to the authors. Did they do so without understanding the issues the plays raised? Surely for most of them that was not the case. Following the abortive expedition against Syracuse in 415–13 BC, some Athenian prisoners of war were able to draw attention to themselves by reciting lines from Euripides.[46]

The fact that countless vases were painted with scenes from the very myths the tragedians used to introduce their audiences to the idea of conscience, among others, points in the same direction.

In summary, the framework Homer created and others maintained for a millennium or so had more to say about the clash between honour and advantage than about the one between good and bad; more about disgrace in front of others than about self-reproach. Yet starting around the middle of the fifth century BC, here and there we find flashes of what can only be called conscience proper. The best sources are Sophocles, Euripides, Democritus and, to some extent, Plato. Unlike the Homeric heroes, Sophocles' Antigone does what she considers right and proper without any regard to the consequences – that is, her own death. Doing so, she has earned the right to be called the inventor of conscience. Euripides' Orestes 'knows with himself' that he has done terrible things. He suffers torments on that account, though whether they were self-inflicted, as the use of the term conscience would demand, or the handiwork of the vengeful Erinyes is not entirely clear. The most explicit classical Greek author of all was the philosopher Democritus. Not only did he speak of 'shame in front of oneself', but he raised the question of whether people would act conscientiously even in the absence of either other people or laws to govern their conduct. Plato, by mostly sticking to the conventional framework, did not go quite so far. However, as the Seventh Letter shows, he too knew self-reproach and acted on it.

The first to define *aidos* as a feeling was Aristotle. Like Homer four centuries or so earlier, he saw it mainly as a wish to avoid ill repute. Judging by the surviving fragments of Antiphon, Socrates' apology and the speeches of Isocrates, rhetoricians often used such arguments in courts of law. In addition, large numbers of adult citizens (and perhaps their wives and daughters as well) were exposed to them by way of the theatre. Many of the plays in which they occur were actually awarded prizes. These facts seem to show that the emerging ideas surrounding conscience were not simply limited to a handful of literati. Instead they were understood, and perhaps to some extent even acted upon, by a considerable section of the population at large.

Enter the Stoics

Throughout the archaic and classical periods Greek ideas of conscience never quite liberated themselves from their early association with honour, justice and law – both human and divine – as well as reward and punishment. A choice between good and evil seldom entered into them. However, shortly after the year 300 BC this began to change. The shift had everything to do with the emergence of Stoic philosophy.

Stoicism in turn was linked to two broader developments, one religious and the other political. The first was that people ceased to believe in the existence of personal, anthropomorphic, gods. No longer did Zeus, Poseidon, Hera, Athene, Apollo and the rest keep a close watch on the world and actively intervene in events. Their place in creating the world was taken by the Uncreated, the Eternal and the Cause of All,[47] whereas day-to-day happenings were the province of fortune. Hope for, and fear of, divine rewards and retribution started waning. So did the perceived usefulness of religious ceremonial, prayer, sacrifice, vows and the like. To keep men and women on the straight and narrow, other methods were needed.[48] The second development was the demise of the independent city-state and the rise of powerful monarchies governed by despots ('masters', in Greek). Claiming divine or semi-divine status, often arbitrary and capricious, these rulers had it in their power to do literally *anything* – and were often not shy of boasting of the fact.

It was in response to these conditions that the Stoic movement, as well as some others that concern us here, developed. Some Stoics, notably Cicero and Cato the Younger, lived during periods of transition from democracy/republic to despotic government and did their best to resist it. Most, however, took absolute government for granted. They advised people to reconcile themselves with it, and in general opposed any attempt to dispute it or change it.[49] As we shall see, for this and other reasons they won the admiration of Immanuel Kant (1724–1804), the German philosopher who probably did more to develop the modern idea of conscience than anybody else. All depended on the emperor's 'indulgence' for their very survival.[50] Yet this helplessness, the fact that they were to a considerable extent unable to

control their own fates, made them put a strong emphasis on individual autonomy and self-motivation.

Judaism bet its hand on divine commands, and Homer trusted in pride and fear of disgrace. By contrast, the Stoics emphasized reason. All men, they argued, are by nature inclined to put their own survival first. They have the *potential* for exercising reason; in other words, the ability to distinguish between virtue and it opposite or, to use the Stoics' own language, between that which was according to nature and that which was not.[51] It was each man's duty to himself to exercise virtue and avoid vice as much as possible. Not for the sake of others, but for their own; why be less than that which your nature enables you to be? Should the worst come to pass, with fortune raining down its blows and circumstances making a virtuous life impossible, there was always suicide, which offered a way out while at the same time forming the supreme manifestation of one's independence, even one's humanity.

The founders of Stoicism were Zeno (*c.* 334–262 BC) and his students Cleanthes (*c.* 330–*c.* 230 BC) and Chrysippus (*c.* 279–*c.* 206 BC). All three were prolific writers, but only isolated fragments of their works have survived. All three are known to have argued that morality consisted of acting in accordance with the laws of nature, though whether doing so meant knowing the natural sequence of causation and 'flowing' with it, or performing one's duties, or enjoying those things that were in accordance with nature, was never made entirely clear. Curiously enough, the first extant writer to provide us with relatively plentiful information on the way in which the Stoics understood 'conscience' was a Jew, Philo of Alexandria (*c.* 20 BC– AD 50). Philo was the scion of a wealthy and aristocratic family who studied Greek philosophy and understood its worth. He also had extensive ties both in the Jewish and the Roman world.

Between them, Philo's voluminous writings contain more references to 'knowledge with oneself' (*syneidēsis*, the closest Greek comes to the modern conscience) than those of any other Stoic author. In *The Unchangeableness of God* he calls it 'a pure ray of light' that drives away the 'sicknesses' in the soul that led us to 'guilty and blameworthy actions'.[52] In *The Confusion of the Tongues* he says that it 'convicts and pricks' even those who lead a 'godless' life.[53] In *On the Decalogue* he says that

every soul has for its birth-fellow and house-mate a monitor
. . . whose way is to admit nothing that calls for censure,
whose nature is ever to hate evil and love virtue, who is its
accuser and its judge in one . . . As accuser, he censures,
accuses and puts the soul to shame; and again as judge, he
instructs, admonishes and instructs its ways. And if he has
the strength to persuade it, he rejoices and makes peace. But
if he cannot, he makes war to the bitter end, never leaving it
alone by day or night, but playing it with stabs and deadly
wounds until he breaks the thread of its miserable and
ill-starred life.[54]

No mention here of the 'jealous' God, 'visiting the iniquity of
the fathers upon the children unto the third and fourth generations
of them that hate me; and showing mercy unto the thousands of
them that love me, and keep my commandments' (Exodus 20:5–6).
To the contrary, in his frequent use of the term *syneidēsis* Philo overrode
the Septuagint. To repeat, the latter only employs it once and then
in an entirely different way.[55] His purpose was to convince his Gentile
contemporaries that Judaism was not the exclusivist, separatist and
frankly outrageous creed many of them thought it was.[56] Rather,
correctly understood, it agreed with the most advanced philosophy
of the age.

Another key figure was Epictetus (c. AD 55–135). In a fragment
attributed to him (perhaps falsely), he refers to conscience as a facet
of the mature mind.

When we are children our parents deliver us to a pedagogue
to take care on all occasions that we suffer no harm. But
when we are become men, God delivers us to our *syneidēsis*
to take care of us. This guardianship we must in no way
despise, for we shall displease God and be enemies of our
own civilization.[57]

Keep in mind that, for Epictetus as for the Stoics in general, God,
nature and the universal law that rules it amount to the same thing.[58]
Wisdom and virtue consist of following that law; discovering the law

is the task (by no means an easy one, given man's subjectivity and proneness to error) of philosophy. In all this there can be no question of divine reward and punishment. Another one of Epictetus' fragmentary texts runs as follows:

> To the kings and tyrants of this world, their bodyguards and their arms used to afford the privilege of censuring certain persons, and the power also to punish those who do wrong, no matter how guilty they themselves were; to the Stoic it is his conscience [*syneidēsis*, 'knowledge with oneself', 'awareness'] which affords him this power . . . When he sees that he has watched over men, and toiled on their behalf; and that he has slept in purity . . . and that every thought which he thinks is that of a friend and servant to the gods.[59]

Many other writers make similar use of the term.[60] The most important ones among them are Diodorus' fellow historians Dionysius of Halicarnassus (c. 60–7 BC), Josephus (like Philo, a Jew who wrote in Greek, AD 37–c. 100) and Plutarch (AD 46–120).

On occasion 'conscience' is still confused with fear or shame, reminding us of the way people thought about it before the Stoics started polishing it, so to speak, and made it stand on its own. Normally the term is used in the context of deeds that have already been committed. However, here and there it is referred to as a judge of a deed that is merely being contemplated. As such it can prevent action, provoke it or open the road to certain courses of conduct. In one of his treatises Philo retells the above-mentioned tale of Potiphar's wife trying to seduce the good-looking Joseph while her husband, Joseph's master, was absent. Instead of sticking to the text of the Septuagint, though, he embroiders it: 'What would be my inward feelings if I agreed to this unholy act?' he makes Joseph ask.

> What my looks when I face him, iron-hearted though I be? No, conscience will take hold of me and not suffer me to look him straight in the face even if I can escape detection. And that cannot be, for . . . even if no other knows of it or reports the knowledge, which he shares with me, all the same

I shall turn informer against myself through my colour, my looks, my voice, convicted, as I just said, by my conscience.[61]

A Stoic, says Epictetus, should try to achieve the good things in life, money, position and family included. However, he should only do so for as long as he can preserve his self-respect, his trustworthiness and his magnanimity, since these are the most important goods of all.[62]

The Latin term for conscience is *conscientia*. Like its Greek equivalent, its literal meaning is 'knowledge with' oneself. It is often used by the lawyer and politician Cicero (106–43 BC) and, above all, the philosopher Seneca (4 BC–AD 65), in whose works it appears some 50 times. Both Cicero and Seneca had studied Greek philosophy under teachers with Stoic leanings. To both of them *conscientia* is a sort of guide or judge of personal conduct. Either it accuses a person as a result of what he has done, or it enables him to manage his affairs in such a way as to make it unnecessary to feel remorse.[63] *Conscientia*, Seneca says, 'places a janitor at the entrance of the interior man'. Unlike knowledge that is shared with others, it is hidden within the individual man with regard to his own wrong deed. Free of divine commandments, men must live in accordance with 'nature'. Such a life, he adds, should be composed above all. Nothing that rushes headlong can ever be well-ordered.[64]

As far as the available evidence goes, the first to combine the term 'conscience' with some adjective was Cicero, who speaks of *praeclara conscientia* (clear, or beautiful, conscience) and of *recta conscientia*. Other expressions found in his work include *conscientia maleficiorum* – consciousness of an evil deed committed; *conscientiae labes* – a wounded conscience; and the need to refer everything to conscience (*ad conscientiam referre omnia*).

The most famous Stoic to combine 'conscience' with 'good' was Emperor Marcus Aurelius. The scion of an aristocratic family, highly educated by some of the best contemporary minds, during his youth he seems to have considered taking up the philosopher's abstemious way of life.[65] Rather than realizing that dream, in AD 161 he found himself the absolute ruler of perhaps 80 million people and the most powerful person in the 'known world'. Between 170 and 180 he spent

much time on the German frontier, where he had gone, as he himself put it, 'to hunt Sarmatians'. Apparently he wrote his *Meditations* during his moments of leisure with no intent of publication. The relevant passage runs as follows:

> Keep thyself then simple, good, pure, serious, free from affectation, a friend of justice, a worshipper of the gods, kind, affectionate, strenuous in all proper acts. Strive to continue to be such as philosophy wished to make thee. Reverence the gods, and help men. Short is life. There is only one fruit of this serene life, a pious disposition and social acts. Do everything as a disciple of Antoninus [Aurelius' imperial predecessor, Antoninus Pius]. Remember his constancy in every act which was conformable to reason, and his evenness in all things, and his piety, and the serenity of his countenance, and his sweetness, and his disregard of empty fame, and his efforts to understand things; and how he would never let anything pass without having first most carefully examined it and clearly understood it; and how he bore with those who blamed him unjustly without blaming them in return; how he did nothing in a hurry; and how he listened not to calumnies, and how exact an examiner of manners and actions he was; and not given to reproach people, nor timid, nor suspicious, nor a sophist; and with how little he was satisfied, such as lodging, bed, dress, food, servants; and how laborious and patient; and how he was able on account of his sparing diet to hold out to the evening, not even requiring to relieve himself by any evacuations except at the usual hour; and his firmness and uniformity in his friendships; and how he tolerated freedom of speech in those who opposed his opinions; and the pleasure that he had when any man showed him anything better; and how religious he was without superstition. Imitate all this that thou mayest have as good a conscience [*eusyneidēsis*, good knowledge with yourself], when thy last hour comes, as he had.[66]

In marked contrast to the modern view, the emphasis is not on the act (good or bad), nor on its consequences (good or bad), but on the

agent who commits it. The objective is to attain long-term equilibrium, self-mastery and, above all, autonomy. Whereas the motto of the kings of Scotland was 'nobody who hurts me will escape unpunished', the Stoic one might be 'nothing can hurt me.' These qualities in turn will be achieved by, and express themselves in the form of, justice, steadiness, affability, the avoidance of excess and moderate living. Such a way of life will enable a person to work on behalf of human society, of which he is necessarily a member and which he must seek to serve as much as he can.[67] Above all, it will endow him with an austere kind of peace and enable him to face anything, death included. No mention is made of the need to make a moral choice between good and bad.

Seen from a modern point of view, Aurelius' conscience left something to be desired. It neither prevented him from having Sarmatian prisoners of war beheaded nor from watching 'obstinate' Christians being thrown to the beasts in the Colosseum. Seneca on his part says at one point that, as part of his attempts to prepare for possible blows of fortune, he travelled in a modest cart instead of the luxurious one which, as a rich man, he could well afford. Hardly a question of conscience, one would think – and not a very Stoic thing to do either, since Seneca admits his embarrassment in the face of the ridicule others might cover him with if they saw him. Yet he does not lose a word about his real sins, including making a fortune by flattering members of the imperial family and also committing adultery with an imperial princess.[68]

Once again, one may well ask: was the idea of conscience as understood by the Stoics during the Hellenistic and Roman periods limited to a small elite? Or did it make its impact felt in broader circles as well? Some attempt has been made to show that the latter was the case and, by so doing, prove the existence of links between it and Christianity, most of whose early adherents were lower-class people. But the evidence is far from impressive. In Greece, so widely taught were the Homeric epics that, throughout antiquity, even moderately literate men could hardly escape their influence. The Athenian plays were watched, and perhaps even participated in, by large segments of the population, and citizens often acted as jurors as part of their day-to-day duties.

The diffusion of Stoic thought was entirely different. Becoming a Stoic meant undergoing a thorough, prolonged and in some ways painful education of the kind that could only be obtained at the schools some teachers set up in various cities. It also implied a considerable amount of leisure. For the vast majority who did not have that leisure and that education, the only way to familiarize themselves with the ideas in question was by listening to itinerant preachers in the marketplace.[69] They may have made an occasional half-informed reference to *syneidēsis* and *conscientia*, but hardly more.

Further narrowing its influence, Stoicism explicitly aimed at the wise alone. True, there was no correlation between wisdom and ancestry, social status or anything else. Yet from Zeno on Stoics tended to see most of mankind as made up of hopeless fools, slaves to those very fears and passions from which their own doctrine set out to liberate them. Real Stoics, Seneca wrote, were as rare as the phoenix.[70] Philo himself complained that he could not make his fellow Jews abandon the literal interpretation of the Old Testament and its jealous God in favour of a more liberal, allegorical view of things.[71] His lifelong attempts to interest members of the secularly minded Graeco-Roman elites in the marvels of the Jewish tradition did not carry very far either.[72] Epictetus in his *Handbook*, one of the principal surviving Stoic documents, adds that those who engage in philosophy are apt to be ridiculed by the mob, which, his contemporary Juvenal claimed, cared only for bread and circuses.[73]

No doubt there were some, such as the famous orator Quintilian (AD 35–c. 100), who held that mere mastery of the métier was not enough and that a speaker's effectiveness depended on his moral character above all. To some extent even Cicero shared that view. Certainly he used the term *conscientia* quite often not only in his letters but in his speeches as well. On the other hand, as Quintilian himself comments, there must have been more than one lawyer who put *victoria* ahead of *bona conscientia*.[74] Seneca in his tragedies, including one about Agamemnon and one about Oedipus, sought to provide examples of Stoic doctrine in action. However, in Rome the theatre never became nearly as important a tool for educating the masses as it had been in classical Athens, where thousands watched each performance. In fact it is not at all certain whether Seneca's plays were

even performed. They may have been intended for recitation in the various clubs that were a common feature of many ancient cities from classical through Hellenistic and all the way into Roman times.

As the frequent use of the dialogue form of literature shows, the basic assumption was that ideas originate neither in solitary study nor in 'brainstorming' but in relaxed conversation among friends.[75] Some clubs are known to have had, as their purpose, engagement in serious intellectual pursuits. Still, the number of people who had the leisure and the inclination to deliberate about reason, conscience and morality in general must have been somewhat limited. Many clubs probably spent their time debating gladiators, horse-racing, athletics or food – then as now the usual subjects of conversation.[76] Others became centres where various mystery cults, most of them imported into the empire from the East, were practised. Led by Christianity, such cults had the advantage that they appealed to people's emotions, not their intellects.

In summary, Stoicism emerged against the background of far-reaching social and political changes. As the Hellenistic age opened, the position of the individual in relation to society became stronger because the community to which he belonged lost its sovereignty and, with it, some of the power it had previously exercised over each citizen separately. However, it also became weaker owing to the rise of despotic government in which he had no say whatsoever. The combination of individualism and helplessness explains the emphasis first on *syneidēsis* and later on *conscientia*. The Stoics turned these concepts into mainstays of their philosophy. In so doing they explicitly separated them both from their early religious connotations and from the desire, as expressed by Hector and others, to avoid disgrace in anybody's eyes except their own.

Nevertheless, Stoic ideas only partly overlap with the modern, secular concept of conscience. Both start from the assumption that there is no personal God who rewards or punishes either in this world or the next one. Both emphasize the inner voice as opposed to external commandments, whether divine or human. But here the similarities stop. As Aurelius makes perfectly clear, *eusyneidēsis* means the pre-eminence of reason over emotion – never the opposite, as is so often the case with us. It also stands for avoidance of excess,

benevolence and tolerance. Finally it demands iron control of one's feelings in the face of both gain and loss – that of power, money, social position, health, even wife and children, specifically included. Nothing, says Epictetus, should be valued so highly as to make a person grovel, upset somebody else or be upset by him, or resort to flattery in order to obtain it.[77]

In principle any wise adult, regardless of race, creed and social condition, can adopt the Stoic philosophy and live accordingly. The same applies to gender, though in practice the role women played in the movement seems to have been minor. If any important female Stoic thinkers existed, they have left no trace. The Stoics postulate that by following the path, one will be able to cope with life as it comes, be spared the need to look backward with regret and depart with 'good knowledge with oneself'. Is such a life really possible? Both Zeno and Cleanthes enjoyed a high reputation for consistency and integrity. So, centuries later, did Cato the Younger, who ended by killing himself rather than living by the grace of his enemy Caesar, as well as Epictetus and Marcus Aurelius. Cicero was more controversial. At the age of 60 he married a young girl, Publilia, who had been his ward, primarily for her money. Many saw Seneca as a hypocritical scoundrel who came to the bad end he deserved.

Moreover, already in antiquity some doubted whether such self-control, assuming it was possible, was in fact admirable. The true Stoic, they argued, was not a man but a monster devoid of love, remorse or pity. He, rarely she, trained himself to be unaffected by anything except the desire to maintain his or her own peace of mind. Yet even this particular interest, to the extent that it did not automatically 'flow' from the soul but required an active effort, constituted a paradox. However that may be, certainly it is not covered by what we mean by conscience.[78]

II

The Christian Centuries

From Paul to Augustine

The word *syneidēsis*, the closest the ancient Greeks ever came to the idea of conscience as a moral compass, only appears in the Septuagint once. In the New Testament it figures no fewer than 32 times.[1] Usage is not spread evenly among the various books, epistles and so on. Since *syneidēsis* does not appear in the Gospels we may safely assume that Jesus did not use it. Like the Hebrew prophet who preceded him, he was simply giving voice to what God had told him; so why should he?

Practically all the occurrences originate in Paul the Apostle. Paul was a Jew from Tarsus, a large and important city in what is now south-eastern Turkey. It was the capital of the Roman province of Cilicia and had a population made up many different ethnic groups. Some modern scholars have tried to show that, as in the case of Jesus Himself, everything in Paul's opus is deeply rooted in contemporary Judaism. Others argue that Paul's Jewish learning went no further than whatever was available in his native city, presumably not very much. The question is unlikely to be resolved. In any case, since conscience does not figure in the Old Testament, clearly Paul could not have derived the idea from the mainstream Jewish tradition of his time. The various Dead Sea Scrolls and the Talmud are not very helpful either.

Are we, then, to conclude that Paul took his ideas on conscience from the Gentile world, the Stoics in particular? Many Fathers of the Church thought so. Superficially there is much to support this view. Defending himself in front of the Sanhedrin, the 71-member high court that judged the Jewish community in Palestine during the

Hellenistic and Roman periods, Paul says that 'I have lived in good conscience before God' (Acts 23:1). While the God he has in mind is very different from the Stoic one, the expression could have been used, and in one way or another was used, by numerous Stoic thinkers. Elsewhere Paul says that he has served God 'with a pure conscience'. Deacons, he adds, should be 'grave, not double tongued, not given to much wine, not greedy of filthy lucre; holding the mystery of the faith in a pure conscience' (2 Timothy 1:1; 1 Timothy 3:8).

Nevertheless, in everything pertaining to conscience the apostle's links with Stoicism are no less problematic than his relationship with his Jewish roots.[2] Following a visit to Jerusalem during which he was almost killed, Paul decided to give up on his fellow Jews. Henceforward his main audience consisted of Gentiles outside Palestine. His works betray a familiarity with many important aspects of Gentile life such as the Isthmian Games, gladiatorial combat and the theatre (1 Corinthians 4:8–13). Yet it has been argued that, unlike Philo with whom he is sometimes compared, Paul was not well versed in the higher aspects of Greek philosophy.[3] In fact he went out of his way to pour scorn on that philosophy, informing the Corinthians that he did not wish to resort to highfalutin philosophical language. Instead, he explained, he relied on a far more effective method which, thanks to God's power, yielded better results (1 Corinthians 1:2–16; Galatians 3:5).

Furthermore, the principal Pauline tenets were that metaphysics and the afterlife mattered; that a personal God did exist and had revealed Himself in words and deeds; that the God in question, having created the world, always remained closely involved in governing it on a day-to-day basis, rewarding the righteous and punishing evildoers both in this life and the next one; and that man, following the Fall, was fundamentally evil and in need of redemption. Man, in other words, was guilty from the moment of conception on. This guilt could be expiated, and redemption found, not in seeking excellence by following nature and reason but solely through the Lord, Jesus Christ.

When Paul, immediately after saying that people should have their hearts 'sprinkled from an evil conscience', suggested that they do so by adopting a way of life centring on the sacrifice Jesus made on their behalf, he left Stoicism far behind (Hebrews 10:22). Justice, not the feeling of guilt on the one hand and mercy on the other, had always been the Stoic motto. No self-respecting Stoic would have regarded Paul's ideas as anything but nonsense, let alone anticipated many subsequent Christian practices such as pretending to eat God's body, begging Him to forgive one's sins and engaging in such outlandish behaviour as tearfully confessing in front of each other (the original title of Aurelius' *Meditations* was 'To Myself'), repentance, self-mortification and withdrawal from the world. Stoics were supposed to lead a useful life. They were to serve mankind as a whole, regardless of social position, nationality or creed, to the best of their ability.

The differences between the two creeds being as large as they are, one is not surprised to find other instances where Paul uses *syneidēsis* in entirely new ways. The most outstanding ones are Romans 9:1 and 2 Corinthians 1:12. In the former Paul calls on Christ, the Holy Ghost and 'my conscience' as witnesses that he is not lying but speaking the truth. In the latter, 'our conscience' – meaning his own and that of Timothy, his 'brother unto the church' – serves a similar function. Its synonyms are 'simplicity and godly sincerity . . . [and] the grace of God'; its opposite is 'fleshly wisdom'. Both dicta form part of Paul's lifelong efforts to establish his own credentials as a genuine apostle, indeed the most impotent apostle of all.[4] The same applies to 1 Corinthians 4:4, where he says that he 'know[s] nothing by [him]self', and also to 2 Corinthians 4:2 and 5:11. Twice he suggests that the members of the congregation consult their *syneidēsis* as to whether he, Paul, was or was not a genuine messenger of the Lord.

In Romans 13:1–7 Paul says that secular rulers are 'ministers of God'. Their mission is to terrorize the bad while leaving the good alone; thus obeying them is not just a question of 'wrath' but of 'conscience'. We are getting closer to the most revolutionary use of the term *syneidēsis*, which is found in yet another passage of the same letter. Not by accident, that letter is by far the longest and most important of the apostle's writings. In many ways it is the granite foundation of what was soon to develop into an entirely new religion. Once again, the background is formed by the fact that around the time of Christ Judaism had long solidified into a ritualistic religion. As such, its essence consisted not of belief but of obedience to the Law. Turning his main efforts towards the Gentiles, Paul was forced to dispense with most of that Law. Especially important were the commandments concerning circumcision and eating kosher food.[5]

'The Law', he went on, 'is not made for a righteous man, but for the ungodly and for sinners, for unholy and profane, for murderers of fathers and murderers of mothers, for manslayers, for whoremongers, for them that defile themselves with mankind, for manstealers, for liars, for perjured persons' (1 Timothy 1:9–10). By contrast, 'when the Gentiles, which have not the law, do by nature the things contained in the Law, these, having not the Law, are a law unto themselves; which shew the work of the Law written in their hearts, their conscience also bearing witness' (Romans 2:15). In other words, 'knowledge with oneself' was made to take the place of formal Jewish Law. It was what made the Gentiles, or at least those among them who followed where Paul pointed, righteous in the eyes of the Lord, even though they did not practise the Law, or know anything about it.

Clearly there is a paradox here. Retaining the Jewish framework in which he had been raised, Paul asked his Gentile followers to forsake their pagan deities and/or philosophies and take up unconditional belief in a single creator who, keeping a close watch over the world, would reward the good and punish the bad. On the other hand, having emptied *syneidēsis* of its Stoic-inspired links with 'nature' and 'reason', he substituted it for the biblical commandments. As he did so he combined it with faith, an apparent contradiction since conscience, certainly conscience as the Stoics had understood it, presupposes freedom of choice. The latter cannot be reconciled with the existence of an all-knowing, all powerful God in constant touch with the minutest affairs of the world.

From this point on Christianity and conscience, and perhaps even more so elaborate discussions of the precise meaning of conscience and its implications, have been marching hand in hand. There is hardly a single Christian 'great' who did not have something to say about it. Among the earliest participants in the debate was St Origen (AD 184–254). Commenting on the above-mentioned passage in Romans, he says:

> [It] appears necessary to discuss what the Apostle is referring
> to by 'conscience', whether it is something substantially

different from the heart or the soul. For it is said elsewhere of the conscience that it condemns and is not condemned, and that it judges man but is itself not judged . . . As John says, 'If our conscience does not condemn us, we have confidence before God' [1 John 3:21; however, the term John uses is *kardia*, heart, not *syneidēsis*]. And again Paul himself says in another passage, 'this is our boast, the testimony of our conscience' [2 Corinthians 1:12]. And so I perceive here such great freedom that indeed it is constantly rejoicing and exulting in good works but is never convicted of evil deeds. Instead it rebukes and convicts the soul to which it cleaves. In my opinion the conscience is identical with the spirit, which the Apostle says is with the soul as we have taught above. The conscience functions like a pedagogue to the soul, a guide and companion, as it were, so that it might admonish it concerning better things or correct and convict it of faults.[6]

Origen's rough contemporary, the Christian apologist Marcus Minucius Felix, hit the nail on the head when he wrote that 'you are afraid that somebody may know what you are doing; we are afraid of conscience alone.'[7] Around AD 135 the Athenian orator Aristides, seeking to fend off persecution of the Christians, explained what this meant, or was supposed to mean:

[They] are the ones, beyond all the [other] nations [sic] who have found the truth. For they know the God who is creator and maker of everything, and they worship no other God but him . . . They do not commit adultery, they do not engage in illicit sex, they do not give false testimony, they do not covet other people's goods, they honour father and mother, and love their neighbours, they give just decisions. Whatever they do not want to happen to them they do not do to another. They appeal to those who treat them unjustly and try to make them their friends; they do good to their enemies . . . If they have male or female slaves or children, they urge them to become Christians so that they can hold them in affection,

and when they do become such, they call them brothers without distinction . . . They are humble and gentle and modest
and honest, and they love one another. They do not overlook
widows, and they save orphans; a Christian with possessions
shares generously with anyone without. If they see a stranger,
they bring him into their own home and greet him like a real
brother – for they call one another 'brothers' not by physical
connection but by the soul.[8]

In this text there is no mention of any laws; only knowledge of 'the
God' and 'the soul'.

As the Christian belief in an omnipotent God spread, the Stoic
one in fortune declined. Indeed Lactantius (AD c. 250–c. 325), an
adviser to the first Christian emperor, Constantine I, opined that, in
referring to it, Seneca had written 'delirious nonsense'. We Christians,
he added, 'know that there is a depraved and deceitful spirit who is
hostile to the good and an enemy of justice, who does the opposite
of good'.[9] Next in line was St Jerome (AD 347–420). Jerome, whose
original name was Eusebius Sophronius, was a Gentile, a native of
Stridon in the borderlands between today's Croatia and Slovenia. He
was a much-travelled man of immense learning; in his prime he was
the darling and reputed lover of leading aristocratic ladies in Rome.
Much of his fame is due to the fact that he spent the last decades of
his life in a hermit's cell near Bethlehem busily translating the Bible
into Latin. It was in this context that he called on 'my conscience,
and those who lived with me' as witnesses of his heroic and apparently
not altogether successful efforts to learn Hebrew.

More pertinently, he spoke of 'that spark of conscience, scintilla
conscientia, which had not been quenched even in the heart of Cain
when he was driven from paradise'.[10] Not only did Jerome turn conscientia
into the accepted translation of syneidēsis, but he sometimes introduced
the term even where neither the Hebrew nor Greek texts, both of
which he used, say nothing of the sort. A good example is his gloss
to Ezekiel 1:10, the famous passage in which the prophet explains the
vision God had sent him. He had seen, Ezekiel says, four 'living
creatures'. Each had four faces. One was like that of a man; one like
that of a lion; one like that of an ox; and one like that of an eagle.

Earlier on, Origen had suggested that the story should be understood allegorically and that each of the beasts represented a facet of the human soul. However, there was a problem. Plato, whose work greatly influenced both Origen and Jerome, had suggested that the soul was made up of three parts (the appetitive, the spirited and the rational), not four. It was to overcome this difficulty that Jerome added another part, *syntērēsis*, a variation of *syneidēsis* whose literal meaning is 'careful watching'. It was, he said, represented by the eagle.[11] The irony is that Plato, though he was well aware that some people were governed by internal sanctions and, though he did write about *aidos*, never used the term *syneidēsis*. Had he read Jerome, very likely he would have considered the introduction into the soul of a fourth, self-accusatory part as a sign of morbidity.

The most important Father of the Church to busy himself with *conscientia*, as with everything else, was St Augustine (AD 354–430). Augustine was educated at Carthage, long since rebuilt after its destruction in 146 BC, a major city of the empire and a centre of Christian learning. As a student he led or, by some accounts, pretended to lead the life of a libertine so as to be appreciated as a man among men. Hence his famous prayer, 'Grant me chastity and continence, but not yet.'[12] At the age of 32, as he converted to belief in the One and True God, he left this phase behind.

Perhaps more than any previous Fathers of the Church, Augustine was obsessed with the idea of original sin. It was, he explained, not so much a question of nudity as of sexual desire; the drive which, while indispensable for generation, also threatened to make men and women forsake both God and reason and make them indistinguishable from animals.[13] Whether this obsession originated in the felt need to defend himself against his enemies, or was rooted in some kind of psycho-pathological background, cannot be examined here.[14] Certainly it was not made easier by the fact that, as a non-Jew, he could not resort to the rigid framework Judaism had erected for dealing with that very problem. How to avoid sin and the punishment it brought in its wake, both in this world and the next, became the central concern of his life.

The question made him 'stand bare in his own sight'.[15] His attempts to answer it resulted in the *Confessions*, which he wrote while aged 45 or so. The book both reflected the spirit of contemporary Christianity and laid down the essence of that spirit for future generations. It became the forerunner of an entirely new literary genre, one about which Luther would also have a lot to say.[16] Stoic self-discipline was supposed to make people more and more serene. By contrast, for Augustine the road to redemption led through great mental turmoil. The trouble was that man was born by way, and out, of sin. He could never escape this condition by his own efforts, remaining forever in debt to the God who had sacrificed Himself on man's behalf. This left only one answer to the problem: complete and unconditional faith in, and imitation of, God. As one modern historian put it, Augustine's world was 'measured by the cross'.[17] Those who do not have the faith, even including infants who die before they are baptized, will inevitably go to hell.

Like Jerome before him, Augustine was an admirer of Cicero, the man who had done more than anybody else to bring Stoic thought, including the idea of *conscientia*, to Rome. He even went so far as to claim that he had converted to Christianity after reading the *Hortensius*, a work of Cicero that is now lost. It is said that anyone who claims to have read Augustine in his entirety is lying. The exception appears to be a German scholar, Johan Stelzenberger. In the late 1950s he carried out the monumental task of collecting and studying all 900-plus of the saint's references to the term.[18] As with Cicero and Seneca before him, its literal meaning is 'knowledge with oneself'. For example: 'there is no knowledge of letters more innate than the writing of conscience – against doing unto another what one would not have done to himself.'[19] However, Augustine differs from Seneca, Cicero and the remaining Stoics in that he uses the word exclusively in reference to questions pertaining to good and evil. He leaves out the rest, including the kind of qualities needed to cope with the ups and downs of fortune, thus taking us straight into the heart of the Christian way of seeing things.

Trying to explain what it is all about, Augustine provides various definitions of conscience. Following Seneca, he calls it the key to the inner man. Perhaps echoing Felix, he says that it is the only relevant witness: to wit, the one who is always present regardless of external circumstances. It is the one mechanism that can prevent men from committing such sins as rash judgement, slander and vain suspicions; sins, in other words, of a kind for which there is normally no legal punishment. The struggle against sin was not a one-time act ending with a decisive victory. Instead it was continuous, lasting through most, if not all, of life.

> Desire revolts, but you do not consent. The wife of your neighbour delights you, but you do not assent. You turn away your mind, you turn in to the secret chamber of your mind. Outside you see the roaring of desire and you publish a verdict against it, thus purifying your conscience.[20]

Most important of all, he calls conscience 'God's seat [in man]'.[21] To the Stoics, who lived in a world ruled not by personal gods but by impersonal fortune, *conscientia* was ultimately the product of reason. By contrast Augustine, more than any of his pagan or Christian predecessors, emphasized the link between it and religious faith. For him conscience is the voice of God, capable of being received by every human soul. By operating inside that soul, it enables the latter to distinguish good from evil and, of course, act accordingly, as nothing else can. The decisive innovation is that he saw the believer's conscience and God's voice as identical. To use his own words, it is that which 'sets those shameful errors of mine before my face, that I might see and hate them'.[22]

Asked how the Christian life differed from the pagan one, Augustine answered that where day-to-day behaviour such as eating, drinking, taking wives and having children was concerned, there was no difference. However, the frame of reference in which everything was rooted was different indeed. 'We refer [all these things] to the legitimate and divine precept, which is love that comes from a pure heart, *a good conscience* [my emphasis], and faith unfeigned.'[23] In stressing that, for him and his fellow Christians, the role of conscience was to act as a substitute for the Law, he liked to quote and interpret the above-mentioned passage from Romans.[24] Conversely, it is only conscience, along with charity, a pure heart and, most important of all, 'faith unfeigned' that can turn obedience to the Law from a purely mechanical act into a moral one leading to redemption.[25]

In this way the break between Christianity and both its parents, the Jewish one from which it had sprung and the Stoic one it had adopted and tried to adapt to its own needs, was complete. In the creation and early development of a new religion the concept of conscience, which Augustine used in his own unique way, played a critical role.

Conscience in the Age of Faith

In Western history, probably no other period was as thoroughly imbued with, not to say dominated by, religion as the Middle Ages. This is not necessarily to say that people were more religious, let alone more scrupulous, than either before or after. But it does mean that religion played a central role in the culture. That role was amply reflected in art as well as the political, economic and social power of the organized Church. With God omnipresent and close at hand, people were often hard pressed to express themselves in any terms except religious ones. It was also an age when most scholars, following Paul and Augustine, thought of conscience as inseparably bound up with their own Christian faith. That is why the eleventh-century *Chanson de Roland* and the thirteenth-century *Book of Huon*, for example, speak of 'false paynims'.[26] It also explains why, in the view of many theologians, agreements with non-Christian rulers did not have to be kept and non-Christian prisoners of war could be enslaved.

One of those who turned his attention to the problem was St Dorotheus of Gaza (505–565). Like so many others he took his cue from St Jerome. A spark of *syneidēsis*, Dorotheus believed, was present in every human being. Along with Augustine, he insisted that it could only come into its own when it was combined with, indeed made part of, faith in Jesus Christ. 'When God created man, He breathed into him something divine, as it were a hot and bright spark added to reason, which lit up the mind and showed him the difference between right and wrong.' While the Patriarchs did not know Jesus Christ, they were still able to please the Lord by exercising it. However, Dorotheus argued, time had caused conscience to be all but buried. Only divine revelation by way of the Law and the prophets kept it alive. Finally, with the appearance of Jesus Christ, 'our power either to bury it again or when we obey it, to allow it to shine out and illuminate us' was restored. For Dorotheus, conscience included such things as keeping one's needs modest and one's shirt clean. 'A man who hangs his tunic or blanket in the sun and through negligence leaves it there to spoil – this is all against the conscience.' With Dorotheus the position of the Orthodox Church in respect to conscience was essentially complete.[27]

In the West the debate concerning conscience was only reopened during the twelfth century as part of a general revival of learning. Much the most important views in the field were those of Peter Abelard (1079–1142). To his contemporaries he appeared larger than life, an adolescent prodigy celebrated as a theologian and teacher. His students, who came from all over Europe, were said to number in the thousands. Like other twelfth-century scholars Abelard was interested in questions such as the origins of good behaviour and bad; the way responsibility for it was shared, or not shared, by an omnipotent God on the one hand and man on the other; and how to tell them apart in such a way as would accord with the tenets of religion. 'There was', a modern scholar says, 'a general feeling for the importance of conscience as providing a subjective norm of morality and for intention as a source of morality, itself influencing the degree of merit accorded to man by God'.[28]

The concrete question, evidently the most extreme case he can think of, he poses as follows. Were those who persecuted the martyrs and Christ, torturing and executing them in all kinds of gruesome ways, sinners?[29] On the face of it the answer was positive; or else Christ would not have said 'Forgive them, Father, for they know not what they do.'[30] However, since it is the intention that counts, and since sin was 'contempt of God or consenting to what one believes should not be consented to', 'we cannot say that they [that is, the persecutors] have sinned in this.' Furthermore, 'those who do not know Christ and therefore reject the Christian faith because they believe it to be contrary to [the God they have been taught to believe in], what contempt of God have they in what they do for God's sake and therefore think they do well?' Hence the title of the relevant chapter: 'That there is no sin unless it is against conscience'. 'Those who persecuted Christ or his disciples', he concludes, 'who they thought should be persecuted, sinned in deed, yet they would have sinned more gravely in fault if they had spared them against their own conscience.'

Thus Abelard distinguishes between two kinds of sin, the less grave and the more so. The former need not detain us; as to the latter, whoever acted in good conscience, even on the basis of error, had not committed it. Real sin only applied to those who went 'against their conscience'.[31] Thus conscience was turned into the ultimate arbitrator between good and bad. Abelard even compared those who followed it, or at any rate did not go against it, to those who accidentally killed a person during a hunt.[32] This did not quite amount to saying that all religions were equally true (or false). However, it did absolve non-Christians, provided they had acted according to their conscience, from some of the worst sins of all. Indeed Abelard went so far as to call the idea that children who had died before being baptized were sinners and thus unable to achieve salvation 'absurd'.[33]

Abelard's chief opponent was St Bernard of Clairvaux (1090–1153). In him the principle of fervent and unhesitating faith was incarnated. Both men were formidable personalities, causing the struggle between them to assume almost epic dimensions. In Bernard's own words, 'A new Gospel is being forged for peoples and communities, a new faith is being propounded, a foundation that is different from what has been established.'[34] The most intense clashes took place at the Council of Sens in 1140 or 1141. Abelard lost and paid the price. His works were provided with a warning note advising readers to treat him with caution. Tried for heresy and condemned, he was forced to burn one of his books, locked up in a monastery, released and tried again. The persecution never relented until his death.

Yet his method of enquiry, alternately adducing arguments of pro and con before using reason to reach a firm conclusion, was to become almost standard. One of the most perfect examples of this may be found in the work of Philip the Chancellor (c. 1160–1236). Like Abelard, Philip was associated with Notre Dame in Paris. What set him apart was the fact that, unlike so many others, he referred not merely to Latin authors but to Greek ones, primarily Plato and Aristotle, whose works had become available in translation.

This enabled him to comment on *synteresis*, a corrupt form of *syneidēsis* often used during the Middle Ages. He even drew comparisons between it and *conscientia*. The difference between the two was that *conscientia*, being based on human reason, could be mistaken. Not so *synteresis*, whose origin was divine; following Jerome, Philip defined it as the fourth part of the soul. It was the element which 'murmured' in answer to the will to sin, or else in response to a sin already committed. The essential point was that, though both the will and its counterpart, *synteresis*, were rooted in the soul, neither was inevitable in the sense of robbing those who experienced them of their free will to choose between good and bad. The relationship between them was that of symmetrical opposites. Just as sin could be eliminated by means of grace, so *synteresis* might be extinguished, at least in some people, by a 'pile of wickedness'.[35]

What St Augustine had been to early Christianity – that is, the great synthesizer – St Thomas Aquinas (1225–1274) was to the Christian Middle Ages. Italian born, Aquinas was destined by his aristocratic family to become a Benedictine monk. However, early on he came under the influence of a Dominican teacher in Naples and decided to join the Dominicans instead. This led to a long conflict with his mother and brothers who at one point kidnapped him and for two years held him under house arrest. Legend has it that they sent him a prostitute in the hope of seducing him, without success, since he drove her away with a burning stick and vowed to remain celibate. These events formed the background for a life of study during which he familiarized himself with every field of medieval knowledge. In addition to philosophy and theology he studied arithmetic, geometry, astronomy and music, not to mention his contributions to psychology, the law of war and economics.

This impressive polymath was known as the 'Angelic Doctor'. The nickname seems to have been intended partly as a compliment and partly, perhaps, as an ironic comment on his tendency to bring in angels as part of his argument. His thoughts about conscience are concentrated in two works, *Disputed Questions Concerning the Truth* and *To Santa Sabina*.[36] Like Philip, Aquinas held that *synteresis* could not be wrong. Unlike Philip, he thought that this inability was due to the fact that it was rooted in higher reason. The latter, in other words, was reunited with the voice of God as heard by, indeed incorporated into, the human soul. To return to the case of those who killed the apostles in the belief that doing so would please God, they are guilty because they based their action on false *higher* reason. If they were ignorant, then this was because they had not sought truth hard enough. On the question as to whether *synteresis* can be extinguished, in other words whether some people do not have it (in which case, presumably, they cannot be guilty of anything), Aquinas took a position in between those of his predecessors. It cannot be extinguished, he says, but it can certainly be impeded.

Methodologically speaking, a striking feature of all this is the use made, or not made, of the sources. There are hardly any references to the Old Testament, which at that time was only available in Latin and in a relatively small number of copies. Given this fact, and given also the small role conscience plays in Judaism, that is not surprising. Nor was an attempt made to systematically explore the meaning of *synteresis* (*syneidēsis*) as found in the new one. Perhaps the explanation is that the basic question – that is, the relationship between God's omnipotence on the one hand and freedom of will, including the will to sin and to repent, on the other – never changed. It had been there since the time Lactantius criticized Seneca over the latter's belief in Fortune.

Trying to square the circle, various scholars were forced to make finer and finer distinctions. Thus Philip drew a line between the infallible *synteresis* and the fallible *conscientia*, one that many of his successors found useful. Less useful was his statement that, since it was not clear whether it was a potentiality or a disposition, it was best described as a dispositional potentiality. Abelard separated grave sins from lesser ones, whereas Aquinas distinguished between simple and higher reason, extinguishing conscience and impeding it. Numerous others racked their brains to invent their own twists and turns. For example, the great William of Ockham (1289–1349) distinguished between invincible and culpable error.[37] Following one's conscience in respect to the latter was a sin; one ought to have known better. However, doing the same in respect to the former was to do good. This was because God wanted man to follow what he believes to be right reason, whereas acting against it was sinful. The more numerous and more complex the distinctions, the less useful they became in separating the true from the false, the good from the bad. This hair-splitting, so typical of late scholasticism in particular, gave it a bad name that has lasted to the present day.

This in turn raises the question as to the extent to which these unending debates affected the 'real' world outside the walls of such great centres of ecclesiastical learning as Rome, Naples, Cologne and Paris. Or was it merely a question of a relative handful of scholars, many of whom led an itinerant life and moved from one city to another in order to teach, going round and round like dogs trying to catch each other's tails? Here it is important to note that, much like certain arguments among rabbis over obscure passages in the Talmud (and, some would say, among many modern academics as well), some of the medieval disputations may not have been meant seriously. Instead they were elaborate games that learned preachers played among themselves. The objective was to trump one's fellows, gain recognition and entertain both participants and bystanders. As Abelard found out to his cost, occasionally a game might get out of hand and turn serious. Both parties gathered allies, ecclesiastical and lay. Politics would intervene, threatening disastrous consequences for the contestants and possibly others as well. Originally, though, many debates were mere games. As if to emphasize the point, some were even put into verse.[38]

Surely not every member of ancient civilization was literate, let alone a philosopher. On the other hand there is little doubt that there were numerous towns and that many, perhaps most, of their citizens could read and write. Such knowledge was essential for administration, trade and, not least, the exercise of organized religion.[39] In Greece at any rate the theatre also played an important role in educating the masses. As we saw, it was precisely in the theatre that something like conscience first made its appearance. The contrast with medieval civilization, which was essentially rural, was striking. For several centuries from the fall of Rome until the so-called Twelfth-century Renaissance almost the only literate persons were priests.[40] The vast majority who lived in the countryside rarely if ever saw any kind of written document and could not even sign their names. Whatever little the people in question knew about theological debates could only have reached them at nth hand from preachers who themselves were often ignorant, sometimes all but illiterate. How much attention they paid to what they were told is impossible to say. Not to mention the fact that in many outlying areas, pre-Christian, heathen ideas lingered for centuries.[41]

At the time Paul wrote, around the middle of the first century AD, and for quite some time afterwards, Christian communities were small, isolated and, as Aristides' description of them makes clear, concerned above all with preserving their sanctity. That explains how he could expect conscience to play the enormous role he had assigned to it. It also explains why so much early Christian literature is hortatory by nature: there simply were no leaders with the authority needed to do more. However, no large group of people, let alone entire societies, can be set apart from others and governed by such methods, especially not over long periods of time. As Christianity matured and spread it changed its character from a rebellion against established society into one of the tools, indeed the most important tool, for holding it together and policing it.

To do this, the old methods had to be replaced by different ones. Some were ritualistic, others legal or semi-legal. Several (but not, as we saw, the idea of conscience itself) may have been borrowed from the various Dead Sea Sects. Famously the oldest Christian ritual was baptism, a sort of cleansing, even rebirth, already mentioned in the Gospels themselves.[42] The Lord's Supper, or Eucharist, is first mentioned in 1 Corinthians 11. Interpretations of its significance may have differed. They may have started as expressions of group solidarity; others increasingly saw them as miraculous occasions during which the Lord was present and His body was literally consumed. By the second century AD it too had become firmly established. Lesser rituals included prayer, the singing of hymns and fasting (1 Corinthians 7:5). By the time of Augustine at the latest, a lively debate as to what was and was not part of religious practice had developed.

The most important rituals were the sacraments. Church dogma traced their efficacy in securing salvation back to St Peter. It was to him that Jesus had given the keys to heaven as well as the power to loosen and bind sinners, both in the present life and in the next one. Later in the New Testament He extended that power to all His disciples, or so the Church, in its interpretation of the text, claimed (Matthew

16:13–20 and 18:15–20). Some sacraments, such as anointment and marriage, were voluntary. Some, such as baptism, confirmation and the last rites, were once in a lifetime events. Others, such as the Eucharist and confession (penance), had to be repeated on a regular basis. In 1215 the Fourth Lateran Council obliged all Christians to confess at least once a year. Some sacraments were supposed to be practised by the entire community. One and a half – that is, anointment and drinking wine during the Eucharist – were strictly limited to the clergy alone. To the sacraments were added various lesser rituals, such as sprinkling holy water, lighting candles, wearing amulets with texts from the New Testament on them and going on pilgrimages. On the negative side were penance, various forms of abstinence and, on occasion, various forms of tormenting and even torturing the self.

The more time passed, the more numerous the rituals and the greater their role in shaping day-to-day life. Side by side with the rituals there grew up long lists of things Christians were and were not supposed to do. During the Middle Ages by far the most important lists were those of virtues and sins. Enormous intellectual capital was expended in defining them, interpreting them, applying them to any number of concrete cases by means of examples and devising all kinds of penalties for them.[43] Presumably in an attempt to make them more popular and easier to memorize, from time to time the lists were even put into verse. Often they were accompanied by detailed drawings of the delights awaiting the virtuous and the punishment meted out to sinners. As early as AD 600 the *Penitential of Columban*, apparently put together by some otherwise unknown Irish priest, had the following to say about adultery: 'A man shall do penance for three years, abstaining from juicy food and from his own wife, and giving to the husband the price of the violated honor of his wife, and so shall his guilt be wiped off by the priest.'[44] Not a word here about conscience, incidentally. Not only were the lists long and detailed, but they varied according to the calendar. Some sins were much worse if committed at certain seasons or on certain days. Thus, gradually, the earthly framework of Christianity, so to speak, was put in place.

Two other elements of that framework have to be mentioned here. The first is good works in the form of charity. During part of the Christian centuries, the Crusades in particular, such works also included fighting in the name of religion, whether against the infidels or against heretics that had risen within the Christian community itself and were pointed out by the Pope. Especially during the century from 1535 to 1648, when Christians regularly fought each other in the name of God, it was standard practice for priests to absolve the troops, each on their own side, before the slaughter started. Good works enabled those who performed them to gain absolution from sin and cancellation or commutation of the punishment that normally went with it. Regular lists were prepared, explaining how many merit points each kind of good work was worth.

The second element is formed by various methods meant to cleanse the sinner from his sin, such as sprinkling holy water, wearing amulets and the like. Originally these were supposed to be the outward symbols of internal change. Soon, however, they started taking the place of such change. Most famous, or infamous, of all were the indulgences that enabled absolution to be had in return for payment.[45] When they first appeared during the eleventh century these payments were linked to the sacraments and were meant as a concrete expression of contrition. At the same time, since the proceeds were supposed to be devoted to charity, they themselves represented a certain kind of good work. Like the rest, though, very quickly they cast off from their moorings and became independent, so to speak. In the process the uninitiated increasingly saw them as an instrument by which pardon was bought not merely here on earth, as the Church's official doctrine never ceased to maintain, but in the afterlife as well.

That view, in turn, was useful towards raising revenue; hence it was by no means as strongly discouraged by the clergy as, strictly speaking, it should have been. Briefly, indulgences were understood as part of a comprehensive strategy whose purpose was to enable sinners to escape hell and reach paradise. The practice climaxed during the second half of the fifteenth century. One is reminded of the five-year-old child whose grandmother taught him to say 'please' when he asked for something. On one occasion, when she refused a request, he said: 'But granny, I did say "please"!'

All this justifies the term 'practising Catholics', meaning those who regularly observe the standard Catholic routines such as attending Church, undergoing confirmation, participating in Mass, confessing sins, repenting and so on. To be sure, some of the requirements were relatively trivial. The list never grew nearly as detailed or as strict as the Jewish one. Some of the most important commandments, including circumcision and the injunction to abstain from eating un-kosher food, were not included. Not even the austere Calvin, whose insistence that Christians obey the Second Commandment ('thou shalt not make unto thee any graven image, or any likeness of any thing') led to riots and the destruction of countless works of art, demanded that they should be (Exodus 20:4–6). This was no accident. After all, one reason for establishing the list was precisely to institute forms of behaviour that would separate Christians from Jews, enabling the new religion to expand far beyond its tribal limits. As Aquinas and many others emphasized, for Christians faith in Jesus, and the grace by which it had been granted, always retained their central role.[46]

Still the danger that actions, rituals, ceremonies and indulgences originally devised as *signs* of grace would be understood as procedures for *conferring* it persisted. Along with the rewards and punishments for compliance and non-compliance, they formed an elaborate points system. One worthy citizen of Nuremberg calculated that by visiting a certain church, of which he himself happened to be the master, and participating in its rituals, his fellow citizens could receive an annual total of 367,759 days of remission from penance. Since there are only 365 days in the year this was much the best possible investment, yielding a return of just over 100,000 per cent![47] This book-keeping mentality, as it has been called, threatened to bury conscience under its weight. Other things being equal, the less learned any person or group the greater the temptation, and the greater also the danger that they might succumb to it.

As one would expect, attitudes were anything but uniform. Some priests resisted the growing emphasis on ritual, insisting that external forms of devotion were insufficient and that they should be accompanied by internal contrition and repentance. The outcome, in Luther's words, was to 'pervert' the promise of penance 'into a most violent tyranny, and into the establishment of a dominion that is more than temporal'.[48] Many others, notably the well-known preacher and author John of Paltz (d. 1511), simply gave up.[49] In writing his books, Paltz's intention was to provide his fellow priests with some guidance towards solving the day-to-day problems they encountered. One of his principal suggestions was that they stop probing too deeply into their flock's 'conscience'. Many people did not understand the meaning of the term. Nor were they able to bring convincing proof that it did in fact make them feel contrite.

Priests would be performing their duty if they did their level best to help people achieve absolution principally on the basis of deeds. In this way a whole series of practices, originally understood as means towards ends, were turned into ends, *became* ends. Human, all too human, Nietzsche would have said.

Luther and After

In much of Central Europe, the second half of the fifteenth century witnessed a paradox. On the one hand there was a growing sense of devotion. This 'churchliness', as it has been called, may have been a reaction to the great plague that had struck in the previous century. It expressed itself in church attendance, a much increased number of festivals, processions and pilgrimages and the founding of any number of new monasteries and fraternities.[50] It was also the heyday of the school known as the *devotio moderna*. Originating in the Netherlands, the school's central purpose was precisely to do away with many of those trappings. Instead it focused on the individual's inner faith and on leading a life based, as far as possible, on that of Jesus; as the title of its most important text, Thomas à Kempis's (1380–1471) *The Imitiation of Christ*, so clearly suggests.

The leading representative of this approach was Desiderius Erasmus (1467–1536). Born in Rotterdam, Erasmus was the illegitimate son of a priest. He received the best available education and spent some time as a monk before gaining a dispensation from the Pope. Thereupon he rejoined the secular world as a secretary and itinerant scholar. Like many others discussed in this volume, he never married or raised a family. He owed his fame as 'the prince of humanists' primarily to his expertise in ancient Greek. This provided him with unrivalled access not only to the New Testament but to the ancient sources, many of which were just then being brought to the West by refugees from Ottoman-ruled Constantinople.

Erasmus was a splendid writer – at one point he presented his readers with a sample of 50 different prefaces meant to flatter those to whom they might dedicate their work. He also had a keen sense of humour, using it to lampoon all sorts of superstitious practices. All this turned him into the leading intellectual of his age. His weakness, like that of so many of his fellow humanists, was that he was an unrelenting, sometimes insufferable highbrow. He never found within himself either what it takes to reach the masses or the sheer courage to break with the Church whose abuses he was always pointing out. Thus the task of saving the Christian conscience from the semi-oblivion for which it seemed destined devolved on his somewhat younger contemporary Martin Luther (1483–1546).

Of Luther, Johann Wolfgang von Goethe (1749–1832) once wrote that 'between ourselves, the only interesting thing about the entire matter is [his] own character. And it is this character, too, which makes any real impression on the masses; everything else is confused rubbish.'[51] As we shall soon see Goethe was right, but not in the sense he intended to be. Like Augustine, the only saint whose works he considered worth reading, the young Luther became obsessed with sin and remained so for the rest of his life. He always doubted whether he was sufficiently contrite to be saved.[52] Nor was his state of mind improved by the fear that what comfort he did find might in reality have been occasioned by the Devil to mislead and ensnare him. His friend and collaborator of 25 years, Philipp Melanchthon (1497–1560), says that he was seized by such 'violent terrors' that he had to take to his bed and almost died.[53] From time to time he made attempts to gain reprieve by orgies of fasting (as much as two or three days at a stretch), vigils and prayer. They did not help.

Paradoxically Luther was also energetic, physically robust and rather coarse. For many years, the image he presented – that of a man who ate, drank and enjoyed having sex with his wife – was the exact opposite to that of the ascetic saint the Church had cultivated for so long. He was also courageous and determined. Another major strength was his incomparable mastery of German. In the whole of history, arguably only Heine and Nietzsche rivalled him in this respect. He used this mastery to write any number of letters and theological tracts, many of them dripping with vitriol. While not without a sense of humour, his real speciality consisted in hurling invective in every direction; in this respect he had no peer.[54] Both in public and in private he routinely called his enemies, and those whom he chose to regard as such, 'asses', 'blockheads', 'mad dogs', 'whoremistresses' and 'devil's s–t'. His devastating reply to one of Erasmus' polite homilies left the sage gasping for breath. At one point even his wife, a former nun named Catherine von Bora, suggested that he tone down his violent phrases.[55]

All this has given rise to any number of studies designed to unravel Luther's psychological make-up.[56] To return to Goethe, the really important point is a different one: namely Luther's determination to throw out the 'confused rubbish' which, in his view, had been covering the truth of religion for centuries past. The rubbish consisted of all kinds of irrelevant false beliefs, rituals and practices. Especially important in this respect were the indulgences. Having attacked them in his famous Ninety-five Theses of 1517, Luther's opposition to them became the clue to everything that followed. Other practices, such as the worship of saints and the collection of relics, also came under fire. As his thought developed, he came to see all these as resting on false interpretations of Scripture as God's own word. They had been imposed by the authority of the Church and were kept alive by its refusal to have the Bible translated into the vernacular. What concerns us here is the point at which he finally arrived. He explicitly turned his own conscience, which as in all of us was rooted in his character, into the ultimate guarantor of his interpretation of Scripture. It was this fact, rather than any more or less weird traits he may have displayed, that made his character 'interesting'.

By Luther's time the German word *Gewissen*, conscience, already had a considerable history behind it.[57] Like *synteresis*, a term to which he often referred, and *conscientia*, its literal meaning is 'knowledge with oneself'. Like them, though, it could also be used in the sense of 'consciousness' or 'firm knowledge'. Thus its significance went far beyond the moral one which is our topic in this study. The young Luther in his lectures and sermons often referred to it. Like his scholastic predecessors, he focused on such questions as its origins, whether it was part of reason or the will, whether it could be found in the soul of everybody and so on. At one point he echoed Jerome in claiming that 'we are not so totally inclined towards evil that there is not a remainder of us which is affected toward good, as is evident in the *synteresis*.'[58] Yet in the Ninety-five Theses, much the best-known piece he ever wrote, it is not mentioned. As the attacks on him multiplied during the following years the role it played in his thought started to increase again. At the same time he narrowed down its meaning until it referred almost exclusively to a person's duty to obey Scripture and little else.

The most important occasion was the Council of Worms in April 1521. This was two and a half years after he had proclaimed that, since there was no mention of the papacy in either the Old Testament or the New, it did not form a rightful part of the Church and had no authority over believers. The importance of the occasion was indicated by the fact that Emperor Charles v, as the highest Christian secular authority of all, was present in person. The meeting took place in the town hall, one of the largest in all of Germany. In front of the assembled dignitaries the Pope's representative, Johann Eck, assistant to the archbishop of Trier, presented Luther with copies of his writings, asking him whether they were his and whether he stood by their contents. Thus challenged, Luther appeared to hesitate; whether, as some claim, that was because he had expected much worse and was taken by surprise, or because, like most great leaders, he possessed a keen sense of drama, is moot. He answered the first question in the positive but asked for time to think about the second. Having been granted 24 hours in which to do so, he spent them praying and talking to friends.

When the Council reassembled on the next day it found the accused transformed. Taking the bit between his teeth, Luther explained that the

> Papists . . . by their most evil teachings and examples have laid waste all Christendom, body and soul. Nobody can deny or dissemble this: the experience and the complaint of all men bear witness that by the laws of the Pope and man-made doctrines, the consciences of the faithful have been most wretchedly ensnared, tormented, tortured.

A little later, following some disputation, like a bullet delivered straight to the head, he uttered the most famous words of his entire career:

> Unless I am convinced by the testimony of the Scriptures or by clear reason (for I do not trust either in the Pope or in councils alone, since it is well known that they have often erred and contradicted themselves), I am bound by the Scriptures I have quoted and my conscience is captive to the Word of God. I cannot and will not recant anything, since it is neither safe nor right to go against conscience. May God help me. Amen.[59]

Some sources, trying to make the occasion even more dramatic, claim that he added, 'Here I stand, I cannot otherwise.' Nice words, except that he never uttered them. Even so, the critical role of conscience in Protestantism had been established once and for all. Examined in private later on, Luther repeatedly made the same point. In matters of religion, conscience – which he identified with the word of God – bound him to pay heed to Scripture and Scripture alone.[60]

By that time Luther had already become the most admired reformer Europe had ever seen. Wherever he was announced, thousands of people flocked to see him. Many factors made his meteoric rise possible. One was the use of print. Thanks to his enormous literary output, amounting to no fewer than 111 volumes, he was ideally suited to exploit it and benefit from it. But that was only part of the story. All over Europe, resentment against the Church was widespread. Particularly hated were its corruption and its venality, recently put on show as it tried to secure funds for the construction of St Peter's Cathedral in Rome. Furthermore, as Luther himself had observed when visiting the Eternal City in 1510, it appropriated all the luxuries of secular lords: palaces, sumptuous banquets, expensive carriages, hordes of retainers and stables full of mistresses included. The Church was envied for its enormous riches – in Germany, it owned some 20 per cent of all land. Inside Italy it was often seen as an organization more interested in safeguarding its own power than in promoting anybody's spiritual welfare. Outside Italy it was seen as a foreign institution with few native roots.

Thus all that was missing was somebody who would set the tinderbox alight. When that somebody appeared he very quickly swept away centuries of hoary ecclesiastical beliefs, injunctions, prohibitions, practices and rituals. Indeed not the least surprising fact about the Reformation was the speed with which it spread from its centre in Saxony. Legions of self-appointed reformers suddenly sprang forward. They affected – or infected – not just Germany but Switzerland, large parts of France, the Low Countries, Scandinavia, England, Scotland, Poland, Bohemia and Hungary.

Eleven centuries earlier Luther's favourite, St Augustine, had understood conscience as the voice of God, implanted in the soul of man by means of grace and faith. Luther explicitly shared that view; 'It is only the blood of Christ', he wrote, 'poured out [for the remission of sin] which cleanses the conscience through faith in the word of Christ.'[61] Better suffer from a serious illness than from pangs of conscience.[62] What was really revolutionary was his insistence that his followers do away with priests as intermediaries and holders of the keys. From now on everybody was conscience-bound to read the Bible on his (or her, though Luther does not explicitly say so) own in an effort to understand what it really said, and act accordingly. It was to enable them to do so that he produced his great literary masterpiece, the *Lutherbibel*.

Certainly Luther made far more people busy themselves with, if not always pay heed to, 'conscience' than ever before.[63] This emphasis enabled him to do away with the sacraments as necessary – and, in the eyes of many Catholics, sufficient – instruments of salvation. He specifically attacked the Fourth Lateran Council, claiming that it had been 'the greatest plague on earth'. It had bewildered the consciences of all the world, brought many souls to despair and degraded all mankind's faith in Christ. The principle of confession, which served as 'proof' that a person did in fact have a conscience, was retained. However, it was transformed from a formal duty into a right the individual might or might not choose to exercise. The requirement that the confessant submit to a rigorous examination or confess all his or her sins was also dropped. As Luther saw it, confessing every trivial detail was foolish; confessing everything, beyond human capabilities. To think that doing so was possible was a sign of hubris. A person should confess as much as he saw fit and was able to. The rest he should leave to God and God's grace.[64]

As mounting attacks on the Inquisition showed, the gift of freedom Luther brought was highly appreciated. To be sure, there was much debate about the extent of that freedom. But neither at that time nor later was there a question of a complete rollback. Yet the coin also had another face. Even as he made confession less onerous, Luther turned Protestantism into the religion of conscience – not, needless to say, 'a conscience seared and deformed by human traditions, but a conscience which is expert in the commandments of God' – par excellence.[65] The first of his Ninety-five Theses said it all: 'Our Lord and Master Jesus Christ, when He said *Poenitentiam agite* [do penance, Matthew 4:17], willed that the whole life of believers should be repentance.' Repentance, that is, for a sin they had committed not by any voluntary word or deed but simply by entering the world as humans rather than, say, elephants or bees.

There were two reasons why he was able to do this. First, Protestants, having reformed and taken on their consciences as their guides, now considered themselves as having direct access to the truth such as no other religion had ever possessed or, in their own view, could possess. Second, the sixteenth- and early seventeenth-century Protestant God was much stricter and more interventionist than His Catholic colleague. Nothing and nobody could escape His penetrating gaze. Hard to placate, He systematically used conscience as His scourge to admonish and punish sinners. Such methods sometimes seemed cruel and unjust, as when children were made sick or even had to die for their parents' sins. However, people could always console themselves with the thought that God, by resorting to them, showed how much He cared.

Much as other reformers might differ with Luther over other questions, in respect to conscience they invariably followed his lead. Conscience, wrote the influential Swiss reformer Heinrich Bullinger (1504–1575), was 'the knowledge, judgement and reason of a man, whereby every man in himself and in his own mind, being made privy to everything that he hath committed or not committed, doth either condemn or acquit himself'.[66] Conscience, wrote the English reformer William Tyndale (1492–1536), obliged a person to resist even the

Pope.[67] Other Protestant luminaries described conscience as an 'internal punishment', 'inflicted on the soul while still in the body in the form of anxiety, penitence, fears, pangs and stings'. Second only to Luther in his advocacy of conscience was John Calvin (1509–1564). In his *Institutes* he used the term many times, often linking it to such adjectives as good/bad, pure/impure, peaceful/fearful and free/bound. It was the 'innate power to judge between good and evil' that enabled humans to 'discern between good and evil' actions, motivations and dispositions.[68] It separated what we ought to do from what we ought to avoid. Created by God, rooted deep in the heart, by right it should escape the jurisdiction of the laws designed by human institutions to control moral behaviour and faith.[69]

Briefly, the Catholic Church remained firmly opposed to freedom of conscience and remains so to the present day. Not so Protestants, who made their version of it take the place of both the Church – in theory, any Church whatsoever – and its priests. Much like Augustine, they freed it from the link with reason that some had tried to forge. Instead they turned it from a precondition for grace into one of the latter's effects. Above all, they lifted it from the centuries-old debris of ritual and superstition under which it had been all but buried. By so doing they made it into the ultimate guarantor of moral right-eousness, one each person carried within him- or herself. In matters great and small, conscience was what prevented persons from sinning. From the time of Paul on, no greater claim has ever been made on its behalf. The price to pay was constant 'anxiety, penitence, fears, and a "thousand pangs and stings"'. Opponents claimed, as they still do, that it 'killed the soul' and led to self-destruction.[70] However, some proponents considered it too heavy a burden. Here and there men such as the Lutheran theologian Andreas Osiander (1498–1552) made half-hearted attempts to turn back the clock by reasserting priestly control over it, but to no avail.[71]

To this day Protestant theologians like nothing better than dis-cussing the precise meaning of conscience, its relationship to God, its implications and its place in human life in general. Their endless and highly repetitive ruminations are enough to make one sick. The most important twentieth-century representatives of the species included Albert Schweitzer (1875–1965), Karl Barth (1886–1968),

Reinhold Niebuhr (1892–1971) and others too numerous to list. So great was the emphasis on *bad* conscience in particular that, in the end, having one was almost turned into a duty. As pastor Dietrich Bonhoeffer (1906–1945) once quipped: 'His conscience was pure – he never used it.' Unlike some others, Bonhoeffer was as good as his word. Using his work for the German Military Intelligence Service as his cover, he participated in the plot against Hitler. Arrested, he ended up being executed.

Meanwhile, and not for the last time, the rise of the individual conscience as the ultimate guide to private behaviour also gave rise to problems of coherence and organization. Embarking on his career, Luther took it for granted that Scripture was 'clear, simpler, and more certain than any other writing'.[72] Such an approach followed naturally from his original intention, which was to bring about religious reform by means of a return to the sources. However, it also pointed to a certain naivety on his part. Starting around 1525 he changed his mind. Increasingly he worried lest the vast role he had allotted to the individual conscience would lead to endless disputes and ultimately anarchy. As he told his circle of intimates, 'nowadays everyone thinks he is a master of Scripture; and every Tom, Dick and Harry imagines he understands the Bible and knows it inside out.'[73] The genie he had created, or at least liberated, from the bottle in which the Church had imprisoned it for so long now threatened to devour him.

To counteract this threat he began to publish binding articles of faith designed for the mass of the theologically untutored. The best known of these were the two catechisms of 1529. Both were popular documents expressly designed for those who did not have the time, inclination and/or ability to read the Bible, even his Bible, on their own and draw the conclusions Luther thought followed from it. The importance of the catechisms cannot be exaggerated. The 'small' one in particular spread until it came to form the basis for religious instruction in every school in every Lutheran country. Generations of children were made to study it until they could recite them in their sleep.[74] Both documents are still widely used by pastors all over the Lutheran world.

The systematic indoctrination of the young, undertaken to shape their conscience before it could really gain understanding and become independent, was only one step. Very much against his original intention, Luther found himself compelled to break with the mighty organization represented by the Catholic Church. Having done so, his followers had nothing to put in its place. Occasional attempts to set up a comprehensive Protestant hierarchy in possession of binding powers were made. However, being oxymoronic they never amounted to much – and still don't. As a direct result, Luther's fears proved to be well founded. He lived to see quite some other reformers, several of whom were his bitter rivals, spreading their own doctrines and organizing their own communities. A few, especially those who created Anglicanism and Episcopalism, did not go as far as he had and are perhaps best understood as seekers of a compromise between Catholicism and Protestantism. Others, to the contrary, went much further still. One source puts the number of denominations at 33,000 and counting.[75]

Nor was religion the only field in which anarchy threatened. Four years after the encounter at Worms the Peasants' Revolt broke out. Their leaders appropriated for themselves the same right Luther had claimed: to read the Bible according to their consciences unless and until somebody proved their interpretation of it wrong. In the last of the so-called Twelve Articles of the Black Forest, an enormously popular document that was reprinted 25,000 times, they explicitly said as much.[76] Faced with anarchy even while being threatened by the mighty, centuries-old organization that was the Church and its greatest supporter, the emperor, Luther had no choice but to turn to the German princes. It was they who saved him from the fate of previous reformers. In return he and his supporters, endlessly quoting Mark 12:17 ('render unto Caesar what is Caesar's'), had to accept the full power of secular government. Previously religion had been the province of the Church which, in severe cases, would call on the secular authorities for help in punishing transgressors or, if there were many of them, organizing a crusade. Now even some of the best-known Protestant confessional documents, notably the Heidelberg Catechism of 1563, came to be commissioned by secular rulers. To write them they harnessed university professors of theology who were not even necessarily priests.

In 1555 the Peace of Augsburg, by establishing the principle of *cuius regio eius religio* ('to whom political power, to him control over religion'), turned the system into a cornerstone of contemporary government. Catholic states soon started to follow the Protestant lead. True, they stopped short of turning priests into civil servants as Protestant ones did. The ecclesiastical organization, with its centre in Rome, remained largely intact. The Church also retained many of its privileges, particularly in such fields as the right to maintain its own system of education, exemption from various forms of punishment and not being obliged to pay taxes. However, in these countries too the more important decisions concerning religion were increasingly made by royal councils on behalf of the king. The French Revolution accelerated the process. Claiming to act in the name of reason, the Revolutionaries stripped the Church of its remaining secular power as well as much of its property. Even more important, they separated state and religion. During the nineteenth century their example, as well as the somewhat earlier one set by the United States, was widely imitated.[77]

Thus the Protestant house was built of three elements. At the centre stood a wide-awake, highly vindictive God. Having endowed man with a sinful disposition, He was always prepared to inflict severe punishment for the slightest transgression. The framework was formed by secular law, 'the scourge of evil', as Luther once called it. Within that framework, freedom of conscience was granted, but only as long as it did not clash with secular law. To quote Frederick II of Prussia (1712–1786), who as we shall see had a lot to say about the matter, 'my subjects are free to think what I want and I, to do what I want.' The glue holding the parts together was a guilty conscience. To repeat, Protestant consciences are guilty by definition. The sinner's broken heart both opened the way to repentance and caused God's anger to melt away. No other religion seems to be using the guilt/conscience complex to nearly the same extent.

The outcome has long been, and still is, an exceptionally effective method of social control. As if to emphasize the point, subsequent German Protestants invented *Geswissenspflicht*, literally 'conscience-duty'. Dutch Calvinists use the term *gewetensplicht* even more often. Still not content, they speak of *dwingende gewetensplicht*, 'coercive-conscience-duty'. It is applied to everything from the need to keep one's word through a physician's duty to his patients all the way to the duty of a divorced parent to pay child support. Admittedly such attitudes are hard to measure. Yet their impact on the societies in question is enormous. In the words of Melanchthon, 'if any of [the princes'] commands are tyrannical, the magistrate is to be suffered for charity's sake in all cases where change is impossible without public commotion and sedition.'[78] For charity's sake! Countries such as Germany, the Netherlands, Switzerland and those of Scandinavia have gained quite a reputation for the highly disciplined, even obsequious way in which their peoples conduct themselves in the face of what the Germans call *Obrigkeit* and the Dutch, *overheid* (Authorities, with a capital A). The terms themselves pre-date the Reformation. However, they acquired their popularity during the sixteenth and seventeenth centuries.[79]

Even more paradoxically, several of the countries in question managed to combine submissiveness with some of the earliest and best forms of democracy known to the modern world. In them democracy did not mean and still does not mean weak government, let alone the absence of government. Rather, it meant very strong government along with the right to periodically throw out one bunch of politicians and usher in another. Democratic or not, from the end of the Thirty Years War, which put the final seal on these countries' religious identity, not one of them has experienced a large-scale civil war or a major revolution involving great bloodshed. Unlike their Catholic and Pravoslav neighbours, they did not breed anarchist doctrines or movements of any importance. There was neither a German Bakunin, nor a Scandinavian Kropotkin, nor a Dutch Sorel. The very idea is enough to make one smile. Attempts to assassinate rulers, while they did take place, were very rare.

One outcome was that until very recently, many of those rulers were often able to do with less protection and lead more normal lives than anywhere else. The above-mentioned Frederick the Great once made a telling comment on this. The truly wonderful thing about his army, he said, was neither the precision with which the troops manoeuvred, nor the speed with which they reloaded and fired their muskets, nor their steadiness under fire. It was the fact that he and his generals could stand in the midst of tens of thousands of heavily armed men, many of whom were serving against their will, without the slightest danger to themselves. He certainly succeeded in disciplining his subjects. As the Jewish-German poet Heinrich Heine, a native of Dusseldorf – which after the Napoleonic Wars was made part of Prussia – wrote, so straight did they stand that they might as well have swallowed the stick with which he beat them.

Later on, the Batavian (Dutch) Revolution of 1795 claimed no casualties. The Swiss Civil War of 1847 lasted for three days and ended with fewer than a hundred dead. What few exceptions there were prove the rule. The most important one was the German Revolution of 1848–9; notoriously it failed. It did so because, once Friedrich William IV of Prussia had rejected the offer of the German Crown, the professors left Frankfurt and tamely went home. From then on all that was left to the king's troops was to mop up. As Marx wrote, if German revolutionaries ever stormed a railway station they would buy a ticket first. Not even the events of 1918–19, which followed upon Germany's defeat in the greatest and most deadly war in history until then, changed things. In Berlin, even at the height of the disturbances, life went on as usual. Streetcars kept running, services such as gas, water, electricity and telephones continued to function, and crowds besieged the department stores. In legend if not in fact, the left-wing Spartacists in their attempt to seize power were careful not to step on the grass; on being told to pay his men by taking money from the Reichsbank, Captain Hermann Ehrhardt, a notorious Freikorps commander, answered that he was no bank robber. A decade later Christmas of 1932, just days before Hitler was appointed chancellor, was the most peaceful in years.[80] The Nazis' fear of a Communist uprising in the wake of the Reichstag Fire in March 1933 also proved to be entirely unfounded.[81]

As we shall see, during the Third Reich 'conscience' even played an important role in making many Germans cooperate with the Gestapo. When Field Marshal Erich von Manstein, one of the Führer's most brilliant commanders, was asked to join the June 1944 plot against him, he is supposed to have answered that 'Prussian officers don't mutiny.'[82] The Lutheran peasants who, in 1945–6, invaded the Junkers' Estates in the Soviet-occupied part of Germany did so in a highly disciplined manner. First the land was formally confiscated. Next they followed the orders of Communist Party functionaries who had supplanted the Nazi ones and who had the mighty Red Army to back them up. The movement was anything but a *Jacquerie*. There was little destruction and even less rape and killing; though admittedly one reason for this was the fact that the owners, or at any rate those whom the NKVD had not arrested, had mostly fled.

German reunification in 1989 was also achieved without bloodshed. As Erich Honecker's 'People's Police' was first challenged, then swamped and pushed aside, there were moments when the outcome hung by a hair. For example, in Potsdam near the Glienicke Bridge, which marked the border between West Berlin and the 'Democratic' Republic, a mechanized battalion stood ready, the guns of its armoured personnel carriers loaded. Much later, its commander gave me to understand that he would have obeyed his orders if such had arrived. Still, in the end not one demonstrator was shot, not one East German official killed or executed. Unification was celebrated with beer, not blood. If all this came about, or did not come about, then it was due in large part to the way secular authorities and the Church, enlisting conscience in their service over several centuries, had somehow succeeded in incorporating it into what can only be called a single power structure.

It is hardly an accident that, among the world's supposedly ten most corruption-free countries, nine are Protestant.[83] To that extent, the building of which Luther and his fellow reformers laid the foundations still stands.

III

From Machiavelli to Nietzsche

The Great Divide

An outstanding feature of the development of conscience, not yet mentioned in this study, is the almost total absence of a dividing line between the high and the low, rulers and subjects, the public sphere and the private one. True, the late second-century AD Roman jurist Ulpian had laid down the principle, long since self-evident in practice, that *salus respublicae summa lex* (the good of the republic is the supreme law) and *princeps legibus solutus est* (the ruler is absolved from the law). Others often repeated the phrases, but they were referring to the law, not to conscience. Centuries before anybody hit on the idea that all men were created equal, in respect to conscience and its wished-for results – that is, certain kinds of behaviour to adopt and to avoid – everybody was supposed to be exactly that.

A very good example is Aurelius' *Meditations*. At the time he wrote it he was one of the most powerful rulers in history. He could do anything to anybody at any time and for any reason or none at all. Nevertheless, whatever he has to say about conscience, and indeed about practically everything else, could just as well have come from a philosophically inclined private individual. The same is true of the kind of attitude and behaviour he advocates. Lines such as 'never allow yourself to be swept off your feet', 'in your power at all times and places there lies a pious acceptance of the day's happenings' and many others applied, and were meant to apply, to every human being regardless of class, position, creed and nationality (today we would no doubt add sex). Nor does Aurelius differentiate between the ruler's public life and his private behaviour. Both are supposed to be spotless.[1]

The kind of treatise known, generally, as mirrors for princes similarly fails to distinguish between rulers on the one hand and ordinary people on the other. As a literary genre, such mirrors go back at least as far as the fourth century BC.[2] Their purpose is to teach rulers and their heirs how to conduct themselves. Those originating in the Middle Ages bore such titles as *The Duties of a Prince*, *On the Training of Princes*, *On the Government of Princes* and the like.[3] Almost all the authors agreed that the best form of government was hereditary monarchy. All argued that princes should stay within the law, in which respect they differed from the Roman tradition. Yet they also understood quite well that princes had it within their power to do almost anything they wanted regardless of the law. The technical term for this situation, against which they railed, was 'tyranny'. Without exception, they denounced it so as to prevent it from taking hold. In doing so, their only choice was to appeal to the rulers' ethic sense, in other words conscience (joined, it is true, with religion). Conscience alone could prevent a prince from abusing his power and surrendering to the temptations to which that power exposed him.

Princes, says Martin of Bracara (d. AD 580), should be examples of the four cardinal virtues: prudence, magnanimity, constancy and justice. They should, adds Isidore of Seville (AD 570–636) also be chaste, humble, moderate, kind, merciful and always mindful to return good for evil. They should lead a good and moral life, set an example to everyone, keep faith and in general be kind, merciful, just, truthful, patient, generous, devoted to all, moderate in taste and dress and upright in manners and morals as well as humble, affable and generous in giving alms (Alcuin, 737–804). They should be unequalled in their patience, truthfulness, love of learning and avoidance of evil thought. All this will only be possible if they surround themselves with advisers who possess similar qualities. Otherwise they will easily be corrupted. Again no distinction is drawn between public and private life; not only the rulers themselves, but their wives too should be rich, noble, chaste, prudent and god-fearing, women who would take care of their children and sacrifice themselves for their husbands if necessary.

One of the best-known treatises of this kind was penned by our learned friend Desiderius Erasmus. The work is dated 1516. The title of the modern English edition, *The Education of a Christian Prince*, is misleading. Most of the essay advises a prince who is already on the throne, not one destined by birth to occupy it. Hence a better translation would be, 'The Ways of a Christian Prince'. The volume bristles with sentences such as 'the first duty of a good prince is to desire the best things possible; the second, to see by what means all things that are evil can be avoided or removed.'[4] 'Whenever the prince picks up a book,' runs a typical homily, 'he should do so not with the idea of gaining pleasure but of bettering himself by his reading.'[5] Useful advice, no doubt, but it could apply equally well to any of the prince's subjects.

To accentuate the problem, by Erasmus' time little remained of the power of the Church to coerce rulers by applying sanctions such as interdict, excommunication and the like. Gone were the days when Emperor Henry IV went to Canossa and had to wait for three days in the snow before being received back into the Church. No longer could a pope such as Boniface VIII in his Bull *Unam Sanctam Ecclesiam* (1302) proclaim that secular power should be exercised 'at the command and sufferance of the priest'.[6] All the more reason, as a modern scholar has noted, to stress 'Christian goodness' as the key to everything else.[7] The outcome was to render the gap between theory and practice – always very large – unbridgeable. All the former still had to offer the latter was pious platitudes. In some ways it was more suitable for schoolchildren than for adults, let alone adults bearing heavy political responsibilities.

The man who finally set out to expose the hypocrisy and close the 'gulf', as he called it, between theory and practice was Niccolò Machiavelli (1469–1527). Unlike most of his predecessors Machiavelli had never been an ecclesiastic. The son of a middle-class lawyer, early on he discovered he was more interested in *affari*, best translated as politics, than in *negozii*, commerce. While still a young man he found himself occupying important political, diplomatic and military posts during the period when his native Florence was a republic (1494–1512). He was a member of the *stato*, a term he often uses. However, it is best rendered not as a state but as the power structure through which rulers exercise their rule.[8]

With the return of the Medici rulers Machiavelli was dismissed from office. He spent the rest of his life on his modest estate, not far from the city, devoting himself to studying what today we would have called political science but also producing some plays that were successfully performed. His best-known work, The Prince, was written in 1513, three years before The Education, but never printed in his lifetime. In many ways it is typical of the long-lived genre to which it belongs – that is, mirrors for princes. Where it differs is that it aims to act as a guide to what Machiavelli calls *effectual* conduct and action – action directed, in this case, towards either the greater glory of his native Florence or the unification of Italy (the issue has never been quite cleared up).[9] Throughout, the emphasis is on providing effective, 'how to' advice concerning concrete action towards concrete goals. By following it a prince, especially a newly established one who faced the greatest difficulties, would be able to become safe and secure in his government.

This approach led to the assumption, nowhere explicitly stated but present from beginning to end, that conscience may have its place in the private lives of ordinary people. However, in the field of politics – and here Machiavelli is very explicit indeed – it is suicidal. Rulers, surrounded by others of their own kind, simply could not afford to let themselves be guided by conscience, as so many previous authors had believed or, perhaps, pretended to believe.[10] In reality, the force that presided over the world of politics was not conscience but *necessità*. By using this key term Machiavelli meant the need to do whatever it took to maintain, and if possible expand, the power both of the prince himself and of the polity for which he was responsible.

Machiavelli's own private morals were probably neither more nor less elevated, neither more nor less lax, than those of most of his contemporaries. As he once wrote, he had always been 'honest and good'. By that he meant that he had served the Florentine Republic faithfully to the best of his ability and without taking bribes.[11] Nor is there any sign that he was trying to play the revolutionary. Instead of inventing all kinds of imaginary communities that had never existed and could not exist, he simply described the art of politics as he saw it practised by rulers: biblical, classical (mainly Roman Republican) and those of his own day.

One friend to whom he showed the manuscript told Machiavelli that it did not really contain anything new. In a way that was true enough. From Julius Caesar down, history has known plenty of men, sometimes women, who knew how to combine the lion with the fox. But that fact did not save our author from his posthumous fate. Quite soon after the publication of The Prince he came to be seen as the Devil incarnate. Had Machiavelli been able to reply to his critics, no doubt he would have said that the opprobrium was undeserved. All he had done was tear away the centuries-old veil of hypocrisy so evident in countless other works claiming to advise princes to get at the tough reality underneath. Judging by what they did rather than by what they said, that was a reality most thinking men understood perfectly well. But they did not care to admit as much.

To be sure, princes would do well to adopt outward forms of behaviour more or less in accordance with conventional morality. In other words, the best Machiavellian was the one who kept his Machiavellianism under cover.[12] Doing so would help him mislead those he wanted to and help keep his subjects in their place on a day-to-day basis. Talk of peace and truth, but prepare for the opposite and practise them when necessary.[13] Unlike his well-meaning predecessors, Machiavelli wanted princes to be judged not by their goodness but by their virtù. Skipping over the Christian centuries, it was a term he took directly from classical Latin. The root of virtù is vir, man. It is also linked to vis, force.[14] The best translation is 'prowess' of the sort needed to overcome one's enemies, rise to the top of the social heap, stay there and depart this life with a reputation, if not for goodness then at least for ability. As such it has little if anything to do with either morality or conscience. Instead it includes courage, determination, foresight and leadership as well as cunning, trickery of every sort, double-dealing and breaking one's word. In Machiavelli's works it often goes hand in hand with ferocità, no translation needed, which the ruler could and sometimes should use in order to intimidate both friend and foes.

As has been said,[15] Machiavelli drove a sword into the flank of the Western understanding of human life, causing it to shriek and rear up. Using brilliant prose, he provided the theoretical justification for driving conscience out of political life, striking it the heaviest blow it has ever received. His works were put on the index and banned in several countries. Before long he was being called by every bad name anybody could think of. While it is probably untrue that the expression 'Old Nick' is derived from his name, the attempt to form a link between the two is itself worth noting. Taking a different tack, legions of well-meaning if mostly mediocre authors have tried to tone down his doctrines and find ways to better reconcile them with conventional morality. Either way, neither has his voice been silenced nor the chasm he created closed. The idea that *ragione di stato*, reason of state, had and should have priority over everything regardless of what conscience might say was born and embarked on its long and, many would say, inglorious career. Nowhere was this truer than in Machiavelli's own homeland. One author alone, Federico Bonaventura (1555–1602), distinguished between six different kinds of *ragione di stato*.[16]

By then the cultural pre-eminence Italy had enjoyed during the Renaissance was being lost. Individual rulers, using the most underhanded methods to maintain their positions, may well have been as conscienceless as anywhere else. However, the peninsula was divided and most of it was ruled by foreigners from Spain, Austria and, on occasion, France. Hence these rulers only played a minor role in European politics, let alone the affairs of the much larger world created by the geographical discoveries from 1492 on. Far from the main scene of action, they were sometimes derisively known as *principini*, 'princelings'. Their own subjects and immediate neighbours apart, few people paid close attention to what they did or did not do. The smaller a state, the harder it was to distinguish the villainy its rulers exercised on behalf of themselves, their relatives and their mistresses from the kind motivated by reasons of state.

Yet no sooner did this begin to change than the questions Machiavelli had raised resurfaced. Could statesmen afford to have a conscience, and how far were they allowed to go when serving their country's interests? By this time, what was at stake was no longer merely the ability of some petty ruler to hold on to his *stato* or even to expand it at his neighbour's expense. Instead it was the fate of a nascent national state of some 22 million people. Take Camillo Benso, count of Cavour (1810–1861), the Piedmontese statesman who took the leading role in the unification of Italy. As he is supposed to have said, 'had we done for ourselves what we do for our country, what rascals would we be.'[17] That included bribing newspapers and rigging elections, and, to crown it all, a most unholy alliance with Napoleon III that led directly to an aggressive war against the Austrian Empire. In Cavour's favour it must be said that he always retained his sense of humour. As he once explained, he had discovered the art of deceiving diplomats. All you had to do was to tell them the truth, and you could be sure they would never believe you.

Some decades later still yet another Italian expressed the idea in what is perhaps the most extreme form it has ever been given. He was Antonio Salandra, prime minister from 1914 to 1916. Like Cavour, personally Salandra was as respectable a bourgeois as any. Yet this did not prevent him from coining the term *sacro egoismo*.[18] The context was another sordid deal then in the making. In return for promises of money and booty, Salandra undertook to stab his country's German and Austrian allies in the back and enter the war on the side of the Entente. The man who arranged the deal was Salandra's foreign minister, Sidney Sonnino. Ironically his personal motto happened to be *aliis licet, non tibi* (what others are allowed to do, you are not). Among those who picked up *sacro egoismo* was a fiery, 31-year-old newspaper editor by the name of Benito Mussolini.[19] In 1932, by which time he was his country's undisputed ruler, he was reported as saying: 'everything within the state, nothing outside the state, nothing against the state'.

Outside Italy the reception Machiavelli got was initially more circumspect or, as he himself would no doubt have said, hypocritical. People were not sufficiently brazen to accept the radical separation of politics from morals he advocated; instead they made his name synonymous with anything wicked. The fact that to them he was a foreigner helped. In France he was made to carry the blame for the crimes, real or alleged, of Catherine de Medici (1519–1589), the Florence-born-and-bred wife and later widow of Henry II. In 1572 she had helped organize the massacre of the Huguenots known as St Bartholomew's Night. Thereupon she was called the Devil's chosen instrument for spreading Machiavellianism in France, no less.[20] Never after did she shed her sinister reputation as a schemer and a poisoner always ready to resort to the most underhanded means. Shakespeare for his part wrote of the 'murderous Machiavell' (Henry VI, Part III, 2). He also accused the Duke of Alençon, a son of Catherine, a suitor of

Elizabeth I and an unsavoury character, of being a 'notorious Machiavell' (*Henry VI*, Part I). Many of his followers agreed. Indeed between 1585, the year when the first English translation of *The Prince* was published, and 1660 or so there was hardly an English playwright who, when portraying a villain, did not seek some way to link him with the famous Florentine.[21]

The first half of the seventeenth century witnessed the rise, in most countries, of absolute government. With it came attempts to use reason of state in order to justify the endeavours of such governments to stamp out internal resistance and secure the existence of the state – by this time the modern meaning of the term had become well established – amid similar states whose objective was the same as theirs. It is true that Machiavelli's own name was not often mentioned except, as before, to denounce him as a double-dealing, devilish scoundrel. People, it almost seems, were ashamed to openly admit how much they had learnt from him. Still there is no doubt that this was how Thomas Hobbes (1588–1679) and Baruch Spinoza (1632–1677) looked at things.

Both Hobbes and Spinoza were esentially atheistic and could not derive morality from God's command, as so many before them had done. Instead, they sought to anchor it in reason. The objective was to prevent men from literally eating one another and force them to live in peace; the means, giving state ethics (or to be honest, as those ethics were not, lack of ethics) absolute priority over private ethics. This was something even Machiavelli, who was less concerned with presenting a systematic account of the problem than with telling the prince how to behave and act, had not done. Hobbes, indeed, questioned whether conscience, being an expression of 'inner truth' and thus unique to each person and likely to give rise to endless contention, could have any kind of natural basis at all. He suspected it was merely a name men 'vehemently in love with their own new opinions, however absurd, and obstinately bent to maintain them' gave those opinions so as to increase their authority. The most the two of them were prepared to concede was that, in keeping order and maintaining itself, the state should not proceed arbitrarily but should follow the dictates of reason so as to achieve its goals all the better.[22] In the harsh world of power politics, in other words, reason of state *was* ethics.

In a way, both Hobbes and Spinoza had an easy time of it. Like many of their predecessors, and their successors too, they were private persons. The former was employed as a private tutor to young aristocrats. The latter made his living as a grinder of lenses. Neither had authority over or responsibility for anything or anybody really important. As if to emphasize the point, both were lifetime bachelors. So, interestingly, were quite some others, both lay and ecclesiastical, mentioned in the present study: think of Antigone (who died before her wedding), Plato, Kant and Nietzsche.

By contrast, persons who were not philosophers and did carry responsibility sometimes found the clash between the demands of conscience and the necessities of politics much harder to deal with. Originally reason of state was used to release kings, and from time to time queens too, from the need to listen to their consciences when necessary. Soon, however, things were turned upside down. Putting one's conscience aside became a *duty*. The best-known example of this approach was none other than Frederick the Great. As he wrote, '[I am] the first servant of my state.'[23] Originally Frederick was an intelligent and rather sensitive youth. Growing up in a corner of Europe long considered relatively backward, he was strongly influenced by the Enlightenment ideals of humanity, justice and progress. In his own words, 'to show sympathy with the weaknesses of men and to have a feeling of humanity for everyone – that is the way in which a reasonable man should act.'[24] In spite of having been almost literally beaten and kicked into shape by his father, Frederick William I, he was never quite able to reconcile these attitudes with the need, which he saw as built into the very nature of the state, to defend and expand it by every available means.

Another reason why Frederick was obsessed by the problem was because, in his father's and his own time, Prussia was launched on the course that would turn it from a negligible principality into the second strongest German state and eventually one of the most powerful states the world has ever known. The process made the relationship between private and public ethics more urgent and more problematic than ever. In 1739, aged 28, Frederick penned the *Anti-Machiavel*. In it he attacked the Florentine precisely for the immoral methods he had advocated. Possibly he was preparing to protect himself against himself. Whatever the purpose, no sooner had he ascended the throne the following year than he grasped what wonderful ammunition he had provided his enemies with. He tried to recall the published copies, to no avail.

By this time the combination of standing armies, powerful bureaucracies, submissive ecclesiastical organizations that had lost their independence and, in Protestant countries, conscience had caused the absolutist state to become well established everywhere. Internally this stabilization enabled Frederick to dispense with some of the more barbaric methods Machiavelli had advocated, such as having troublemakers murdered and leaving their mutilated corpses in the marketplace *pour encourager les autres*. However, in his role as his own foreign minister cum commander in chief Frederick was as unscrupulous as any other ruler. He claimed and invaded lands that were not his, broke promises and repeatedly betrayed allies when it suited him – all, as he explained, in the name of 'adverse necessity' and reason of state.

The greatest political 'crime' Frederick committed came towards the end of his life when he took part in the partition of Poland. He justified himself by citing 'unfortunate necessity' and the fact that his colleagues, Catherine the Great of Russia and Maria Theresa of Austria, shared in the outrage. Of the latter he said that 'she wept but took'. He was, so to speak, a Machiavellian with a conscience. Repeatedly he suggested that the ruler 'sacrifice himself' in doing what had to be done. Still he never gave up hope that 'posterity . . . will distinguish the philosopher in me from the ruler, and the respectable man from the politician.'[25] In the *Political Testament* of 1752 he conceded that Machiavelli, the bogeyman who had haunted his youth, had been right after all. A power trying to stay honest in the midst of others would surely come to grief.[26]

Modern, politically correct German commentators have often presented Frederick as almost a pure *Machtmensch*, one concerned exclusively with his own power and that of the Prussian state he claimed to serve. If that is true it is hard to see why as late as 1775, three years after the first partition of Poland, when he was 63 years old, the problem continued to haunt him. To deal with it he wrote yet another one of his essays. In it he listed the circumstances under which rulers were justified in breaking treaties and abandoning their allies.[27] On occasion the inescapable gap between private aspiration and the duties of government made him feel self-pity. As he once complained, he was condemned to make war in much the same way as dolphins were condemned to swim in the sea. It also explains why he became a cynic. Having ascended the throne with high hopes, the would-be benefactor of humanity ended up as a misanthrope. He spent hours walking the park at Sanssouci ('Free of Care') in the company of his dogs, which he preferred to men and with which he was finally buried.

Given how important the problem of relieving conscience – a *guilty* conscience – in the face of realpolitik was to Protestants, it is not surprising that the person who set out to free rulers from the dilemma was himself one such: I am referring to Georg Wilhelm Friedrich Hegel (1770–1831). From the time of his death to the rise of destructivism and postmodernism a century and a half later, nobody has been more influential in shaping the modern view of the role of history, the way it operates and what could and could not be learnt from it. All three great twentieth-century political ideologies – that is, liberalism, socialism/communism and fascism – were heavily in his debt. Around 1900, even in England, a country not generally given to theoretical speculation, his name was said to 'stir the imagination of our youths of both sexes, even as the name of Jerusalem moved the hearts of men in centuries behind us'.[28]

Hegel, a native of Stuttgart in southwestern Germany, was brought up to follow his father as a Lutheran pastor. In typical Protestant fashion, he considered conscience something that both implied a moral obligation and was rooted in that obligation.[29] However, while studying theology he lost his faith in a personal God. Following a long intellectual development, he replaced Him by the impersonal world-historical spirit, or *Weltgeist*, of which he himself was the principal priest. *Weltgeist* was characterized by two things above all. First, since everything that existed had to exist (or else it could not have existed), it was the embodiment of reason. This held true regardless of how cruel, tortuous and inscrutable its manifestations often appeared. Second, it steadily drove humanity towards the perfect society of the future. In that society all contradictions would be resolved and a sort of secular paradise regained.

Driving history along its predetermined path towards greater perfection, *Weltgeist* did not work through individuals. For this there were two reasons. First, individual people were puny creatures characterized by all the inherited weaknesses of their biology. For the most part they were concerned almost exclusively with their own likes, dislikes and interests. Even within that narrow field their reasoning was by no means infallible. Second, being subject to the law, without which no orderly community could exist, and thus lacking sovereignty, their ability to realize their full selves was necessarily limited. Much the same applied to the many kinds of organizations they built and which, in their actions and interactions, were collectively known as civil society.

Of all human organizations, or corporations as Hegel called them, the only ones able to escape these limitations and fully realize themselves were states. Thanks to their sovereignty, states had no superior over themselves. This quality gave them the potential to become what they could be and what the infallible *Weltgeist* had meant them to be. They did not do so consciously – all each state did was to pursue its own interests. Driving them was a sort of invisible hand not too different from the one Adam Smith had made famous. Nevertheless states had it within their power to both create and reflect a unity far transcending the individual self-interest of rulers, the ruled or both. Outside the family, which operated on an entirely different level, they and they alone were not instruments to an end but ends in themselves. Partly as a result of this fact and partly in order to prove it, they demanded and often received blood-sacrifice from their members. Conversely war provided individuals and civil society with an ethical meaning, a cause greater than themselves, which otherwise they did not and could not have. Not only was *salus respublicae summa lex* (the state is the highest law), but the state was a *moral* creature: in Hegel's own phrase, 'the echo of God's footsteps on earth', no less.[30]

Thus the problem Machiavelli had been the first modern author to raise, that Spinoza and Hobbes put in a more abstract form, and which had given so much trouble to Frederick, was finally 'solved'. It was as if a bastard everybody admitted was strong, clever and obstreperous had been legitimized. One outcome was that reason of state, being taken for granted, tended to disappear from the literature. The process involved two separate steps. First, as Frederick's career shows, sovereignty was transferred from the ruler to the state. Being the 'servant' of that state, it was his 'duty' to 'sacrifice himself' when necessary. Second, as states ceased to be merely self-seeking organizations but came to embody the mechanism by which the *Weltgeist* made its way towards perfection, almost anything a statesman did, provided he was seen to act in good faith on behalf of his state and not as simply trying to fill his own pockets, became ethical by definition. The criterion by which he would and should be judged was not ethics but the success of his state as measured primarily in terms of power and wealth. To these Hegel added the ability to provide a favourable environment for the growth of culture, a point that his successors often overlooked. Thus success was equated with ethics not merely in practice, as it had long been, but in theory too.

Still there was an important reservation. Hegel was well acquainted with the kind of *principini* that Germany, even after its consolidation at the hands of Napoleon and the Congress of Vienna, still had by the dozen. He knew just how tyrannical, petty and stifling their rule could be. He had neither sympathy nor patience for *Kleinstaaterei* or particularism.[31] Consequently he applied his ideas only to large and powerful states; those, in other words, which seemed to stand for something more than their rulers' private interests. Indeed, the larger and the more powerful a state, the easier it was to separate the two. To some Hegel was, and remains, the great bully of international relations, always ready to bulldoze 'delicate flowers', as he called them, in favour of what he took to be the direction in which the *Weltgeist* pointed. To others his message, coming as it did during a period when the movement towards the unification of Germany was starting to gather steam, could not have been more welcome and more timely.

At the time of Hegel's death, Prussia – in whose capital Berlin he spent the last thirteen years of his life and whose government he extolled – was still a small but rapidly increasing power. For such a state to maintain itself, let alone grow, among the sharks circling all around it would obviously take a lot of extremely sophisticated statesmanship combining the power of a steamroller with the guile of a Machiavelli. In the end, the man who had what it took to mobilize and use that combination was found: Otto von Bismarck (1815–1898). Based on his doctrine of 'iron and blood', Bismarck invented a new theory of parliamentary government, used it to tame the Prussian Parliament or Landstag and went on to unleash the wars of 1864 and 1866. Next he goaded Napoleon III into starting the one of 1870–71. The upshot was the German Reich.

Later still Bismarck did whatever he could to chicane his country's Catholics and Socialists, each of whom he regarded as threats to the new Germany he had built. Whether Bismarck's public life was more or less scrupulous than that of other men in similar positions – whether Lord Acton was correct in claiming that all great men are bad men – is not the issue here.[32] All that can be said is that he was more honest than many of the historians, especially but by no means solely German ones, who traced his career. Blinded by nationalism, they sometimes rose to mystic heights of obfuscation in their attempts to justify the course he took. He himself summed up the politics of his own age, and probably those of all ages, succinctly enough: the only way a statesman can keep his conscience clear, he is reported to have said, was not to use it.

The Death of God

Throughout the Christian centuries conscience and religion marched together. Starting with Paul, with whom conscience took the place of the Jewish Law, so closely intertwined were they that separating them became all but impossible. Saints and lesser ecclesiastics might argue whether God had implanted conscience in the minds of every man or woman, even including those who persecuted and crucified Christ, or just in those of the select few. The relationship between conscience and God's omniscience and omnipotence, conscience and reason, conscience and law, the methods by which a guilty one might be relieved, the individual conscience and the teachings of the Church, were examined closely and often repeatedly. Until 1500 or so, most of the debates were limited to a small number of well-educated theologians. However, at that point the rise of print gave them far wider currency, enabling them to take their place at the very heart of the Reformation. The outcome was the peculiar Protestant approach to the problem. As Luther and Hegel, each in his own way, showed, it somehow succeeded in fusing coercion, freedom and conscience into a single complex.

Whatever the precise solution to these problems, invariably they were discussed in the context of a world that had been created by God and was closely governed by Him. Here, too, the first important author to cry out that the king was naked was Machiavelli. Machiavelli hated the Church, which he saw as hypocritical and as primarily responsible for the fact that Italy, unlike the France and the Spain of his time, remained divided and occupied by 'barbarians'.[33] This fact did not prevent him from being a good Catholic, dutifully going through the motions. Though The Prince has a lot to say about ecclesiastical principalities, it barely mentions religion. Of all Machiavelli's heroes, ancient and modern, the only one who owes his achievements to it was Moses. 'He alone merely executed what God had commanded [and] must be praised for the grace which made him worthy of speaking with God.' That is why the Florentine prefers not to 'reason' about him in detail.[34]

At the opposite pole from Machiavelli stood Calvin. Throughout his career, Calvin did his formidable best to enlist a guilty conscience in the service of morality and, through the latter, political life among the elect. What was called for was lifelong, unending and above all sincere contrition. Along with conscience went the certainty that an all-powerful, all-seeing God did in fact exist. If provoked, He would visit sinners with swift and terrible punishment. Illnesses, accidents and natural phenomena such as droughts were all interpreted in this way. Popular verse, widely distributed and recited, never ceased to reinforce the message.[35] There are some similarities to Judaism here, except that the latter put a much greater emphasis on practice as opposed to guilt and accordingly spelt out the various dos and don'ts in much greater detail.

Still, in the long run there was only so much godliness people could take. The first reason for this was the extremely destructive nature of the wars of religion. Starting in 1546, with some interruptions they went on for a century. First France, then Germany and finally much of Central Europe were devastated. When the wars finally ended in 1648 the population of some of the countries in question may have been reduced by a third. Relative to the size of that population, in the whole of history few armed conflicts have been as deadly. Yet they failed to produce a decision as to which Christian creed was the right one. The lesson was quite clear. If some kind of civilized life was to continue at all, then some other principle to base it on had to be found. The Peace of Westphalia, by reaffirming the principle of *cuius regio*, did just that.

The second reason for the decline of religion, and the kind of conscience that was part of it, was the emergence of a mechanical world-view as part of the so-called Scientific Revolution.[36] It was created by the likes of Johannes Kepler (1570–1631), Galileo Galilei (1584–1642) and, above all, Isaac Newton (1642–1727). By the 1650s it was well on the way to separating philosophy from religion; after 1690 or so it rapidly took over among the well educated in particular. The mechanical world-view demonstrated how reason could be used to explain natural phenomena. Consequently the distance between the world of God and that of men increased. Some discarded the Christian God altogether, turning towards deism instead. By 1675 the term was sufficiently current to be included in an English dictionary.

Understood as 'natural' rather than as the result of revelation, the most important Deistic postulate was that the world was a sort of gigantic clockwork. As the marvellous order increasingly being discovered in nature seemed to prove, a Supreme Being did indeed exist. However, having created the world, wound it up and set it in motion He threw away the key. Whether He kept close watch over His creation was moot. Certainly He did not interfere with the way it operated, let alone upset the laws He Himself had established by allowing them to be disturbed by miracles. For generations past a good Christian was one who believed that incidents such as the infertility of one's wife, the death of one's cow or the failure of one's crops had been brought about by God (or perhaps by the Devil) in response to one's sins. Now an enlightened person was one who ridiculed such ideas and dismissed them as superstitions.

Some went further still, declaring themselves atheists. Nor was it solely a question of changing one's religious beliefs so as to marginalize or abolish God. Since time immemorial, one of the most feared natural phenomena of all had been lightning. Caligula,

Suetonius tells us, hid under his bed during thunderstorms.[37] The Catholic response to it had long been prayer, the ringing of bells, the burning of candles, the distribution of incense, good deeds and the like; the Protestant one, penance and contrition. Some Protestant theologians, indeed, argued that God's purpose in creating lightning and thunder was precisely to remind Christians of their duty to repent. Along came Benjamin Franklin, himself a deist. In 1752 he discovered that lightning is an electric discharge and devised the lightning conductor for rendering it harmless.[38] At about the same time experimental attempts to inoculate people against smallpox, a dread disease that killed a third of those exposed to it and left the rest disfigured for life, got under way. Better illustrations of the way science started taking over from religion, providing practical solutions to problems and thereby helping change people's beliefs, could hardly be imagined.

Deism and atheism caused conscience to lose its anchor, which throughout the Christian centuries had rarely been completely absent, in the form of divine approval and reward, disapproval and punishment. By so doing they left the individual to his own devices. They made conscience, now increasingly decoupled from any kind of metaphysics and understood as an 'inhabitant of the breast, the man within, the great judge and arbiter of our conduct' (Adam Smith) even more important than it had been.[39] How does one do away with the anchor without allowing the ship to drift?

To contemporaries, the answer was education. Not merely of the kind that would liberate people from superstitions and make them more intelligent and more rational, but such as would improve them from a moral point of view. Much the greatest educator of all was considered to be Jean-Jacques Rousseau (1712–1778). Like so many others who have written about the subject, certainly he could not have gained his reputation because of any example he gave. The son of a watchmaker in Calvinist Geneva, Rousseau at one point converted to Catholicism. Allegedly his purpose in doing so was to protest against the Calvinist dogma that man was depraved by nature.[40] His own life was an itinerant one. Rising from domestic servant to literary celebrity, he was nevertheless often without a penny in his pocket. On the way he had numerous liaisons with women, some rich, others poor. With at least one of them he had children. However, claiming that their education would suffer from the fact that the mother, Thérèse Levasseur, was herself not well educated, he persuaded her to give them to a foundlings' hospital. As he must have known, mortality at such institutions, caused by malnutrition, disease or neglect, was running at anything between 50 and 90 per cent.[41] So much for his own conscience.

Rousseau's shortcomings as a human being are one thing, his books another. Unlike so many of his contemporary Enlightenment writers, he consciously appealed not to his readers' rational mind but to their heart. For good or ill, that was one reason why his work has acted as a beacon for all subsequent educational theory.[42] Rousseau's masterpiece in the field was *Emile; or, on Education* (1762). The purpose of education was not, as had previously been supposed and is still sometimes supposed, to break down the child's personality (especially the male personality, since boys had long been seen as more obdurate and more obstreperous than girls) so as to make it amenable to the demands of God, parents, the authorities and society at large.[43] Such education, which sacrificed the present for the future, Rousseau regarded as 'barbaric'.

A good education should not attempt to thwart a child's unruly desires in order to turn it into an adult as soon as possible. Doing so would only 'produce precocious fruits which will be immature and insipid and will not be long in rotting'.[44] Instead the objective should be to foster its innate tendencies, abilities and sentiments. If any sentence in the long book sums up the author's philosophy, it is the following: 'By never doing anything except what suits him, [Emile] will soon do only what he ought to do.' The outcome would be a person so faithful to what benevolent nature had made him, so much at one with himself, as to be capable of leading a simple, happy life while effortlessly resisting the corrupting influence of society.

As one might suppose, conscience played a cardinal part in the enterprise. There is, says Rousseau, 'In the depth of the soul, an innate principle of justice and virtue according to which, in spite of our own maxims, we judge our actions and those of others as good or bad. It is to this principle that I give the name conscience.'[45] It 'persists in following the order of nature against all the laws of men'.[46]

References to it are scattered throughout the text. But nowhere does the author provide a coherent explanation of the mechanism whereby it is developed. Like so many others before and after him, he had some doubts as to whether it had its origins in 'nature', in which case at least the potential for it was present in every individual from the moment of birth on, or in quid pro quo reasoning that only developed at a more mature age.

However that might be, Rousseau in his book provides a detailed account of the way he thought conscience should be engraved on a young person's mind. On the one hand it could only be based in reason. On the other, it involved an overcoming of that reason. Conscience, indeed, could be defined as that part of the mind that recommended not doing, or else regretted having done, that which reason suggested. The clear implication was that moral education should only get under way after the child had learnt to think: that is, while it was in its late teens.[47]

In part IV of Emile Rousseau delivered his famous final blast of the trumpet on the subject. Speaking through the mouth of an imaginary Savoyard vicar, he has the following to say:

> Conscience! Conscience! Divine instinct, immortal and celestial voice, certain guide of a being that is ignorant and limited but intelligent and free; infallible judge of good and bad, which makes man like unto God; it is you who make the excellence of his nature and the morality of his actions. Without you, I sense nothing in me that raises me above the beasts, other than the sad privilege of leading myself astray from error to error with the aid of an understanding without rule and a reason without principle.[48]

Thus Rousseau is best described as a sentimental deist. Indeed sentimentality, or sensibility as his contemporaries called it, was his greatest strength as a writer.[49] It was in line with this attitude that, throughout his life, he never ceased writing hymns to the Supreme Being. They were meant, he explained, to express 'admiration and contemplation rather than request'.[50] The older he became, the more he tended to take this road.

Rousseau's best-known book, *The Social Contract* (1762), was published almost simultaneously with *Emile*. In it he paints a portrait of an ideal society. In that society, so closely fused together are the individual and the community in which he spends his life as to render government itself all but unnecessary.[51] As the fact that both books were quickly banned shows, contemporary reality was very different. Practically all eighteenth-century countries had absolute government, a growing fiscal-military-police state headed by a sort of hereditary despot. Another pillar of absolute government was the altar, in turn supporting it and being supported by it. As the reader will recall, in Hellenistic antiquity such government, taking the place of the older city states, had helped give rise to Stoicism. With it there arrived the kind of conscience Zeno, Cicero, Seneca, Epictetus and Marcus Aurelius cultivated.

The problem facing the increasingly secular society of the late seventeenth and eighteenth centuries was in many ways similar. Declining belief in God required new soil in which to root conscience, yet a clash between that conscience and the powers that be had to be avoided. Achieving this was the self-imposed mission of Immanuel Kant. Like Rousseau (and Hegel), Kant came from a Protestant background. However, there any resemblance ends. Having lost his mother when he was nine days old, Rousseau was practically fatherless from the age of ten on. He hardly ever attended a regular school but picked up his education from the men and women who gave him shelter instead. Starting as a Protestant, he converted to Catholicism and then, late in life, back again. Kant grew up in an intact middle-class household. His father, a harness-maker, and his mother were Pietists, members of a Lutheran faction that stressed lay participation in religious life. Studying religion as closely as possible was everybody's duty. This intellectual penchant came on top of the usual Protestant emphasis on a literal interpretation of the Bible, strict discipline, personal humility and intense devotion. Except that he never married, Kant was the perfect bourgeois. He spent his entire life at Koenigsberg, now Kaliningrad, in East Prussia, probably never moving more than 15 km away. This somewhat restricted existence did not prevent him from developing many different interests. They included astronomy, geology, art, the way our senses perceive the world, politics and much else.

To the reader, Kant presents a paradox. On the one hand his works are very difficult, full of those long, complex sentences with which Mark Twain in 'The Awful German Language' was to have such great fun. On the other, nobody has ever been better at putting his finger on the most important philosophical questions of all. As he explained in his best known work, The Critique of Pure Reason (1781), at bottom there were only two such questions. The first referred to the origins and workings of the 'starry skies', meaning the vast and awe-inspiring world that we can see all around us; the second, to the way each of us ought to regulate his or her conduct during the time we spend in that world.[52] Concerning the former, Kant claimed that, while the existence of a divine creator could not be proved, He was a necessary postulate of the human mind which cannot explain the world without it.

Concerning conscience, the most important passage Kant ever wrote runs as follows:

> Every human being has a conscience and finds himself observed, threatened, and, in general, kept in awe by an internal judge; and this authority watching over the law in him is not something that he himself makes, but something incorporated in his being. It follows him like his shadow when he plans to escape. He can indeed stun himself or put himself to sleep by pleasures and distractions; but he cannot help coming to himself or waking up from time to time; and when he does, he hears at once its fearful voice. He can at most, in extreme depravity, bring himself to heed it no longer, but he still cannot help hearing it.[53]

Unlike Luther, who linked it to faith in God, and unlike Rousseau, who appealed to nature and thus to the innate goodness of man, Kant believed that he could base conscience on reason – in other words, logic. It was a sort of self-regulating mechanism that proclaimed as follows: 'Act only according to that maxim by which you can at the same time will that it should become a universal law.'[54] The name he gave to this was the Categorical Imperative. There is not a word here about a divine instinct or a celestial voice, let alone a God, either strict or benevolent, who watches over the universe and navigates it along. Nor a word about good and bad either. Instead, what seems to matter most is regulating one's behaviour in such a way as to allow an orderly social life to exist and flourish.

Kant did indeed concede that obeying the Imperative might contribute, if not to happiness, then at any rate to inner and of course outer peace and sound sleep. However, he argued that the primary reason why one should do so was because it was one's *duty* to the community and one's fellow citizens.[55] Duty, described as a 'sublime and mighty name', neither charmed nor insinuated. Instead, it 'require[s] submission'; in front of it, 'all inclinations are dumb'.[56] What follows is an example Kant himself uses:

> Suppose somebody has a deposit that was entrusted to him and whose owner is dead. The dead man's relatives know nothing about it, nor can they ever learn of it. One could ask a child of eight or nine the following question: Suppose the person in charge of the deposit, through no fault of his own, is in deep trouble. He can save his unfortunate family, wife and children, from penury by appropriating the deposit; suppose, moreover, he himself is a lover of humanity and a philanthropist, whereas the dead men's heirs are so rich, so hateful, and so inclined to waste that adding this sum to their fortune is equivalent to throwing it into the sea. Is he entitled to use the deposit to meet his own needs? Undoubtedly the child would answer: 'No! Because it is unjust, *and because it conflicts with one's duty.*'[57]

Probably only a person who, coming from a Lutheran-Pietist background, served as a tenured professor, and thus as a civil servant, in a state that, perhaps more than any other in history, put duty at the very core of its being, could have conceived of such an idea.

Above all, the Categorical Imperative was supposed to operate *within* the law. It did not act as a substitute for it, as with Paul; or against it, as with Luther; or in its absence, as in Rousseau's ideal community where the fusion between the individual and the 'general will' was so complete as to make laws superfluous. It is true that Kant was not necessarily in favour of the absolute monarchy under which he and most of his contemporaries lived. But he was certainly an advocate of strong government and, even more so, the need to obey so as to enable communal life and culture to flourish. 'Evil', he says at one point, means 'contrary to the law'.[58] In this, as well as the role he assigned to reason, there are obvious parallels between Kant's thought and that of the ancient Stoics. No wonder he was interested in those 'valiant men', as he called them; including also the way in which some of them, unable to face the authorities and maintain their consciences as they thought was their duty to themselves, committed suicide.[59]

Kant's definition of conscience proved to be well attuned to modern life, especially its bureaucratic aspects, of which his own Prussia, and later Germany as a whole, provided such a prominent example. To be sure, the language he used was often highly complex. Even the most important term he coined, the Categorical Imperative, was made up of a mixture of Greek and Latin, thus providing a direct link to his academic background. Yet Kant explicitly opposed Stoic elitism, which looked at most of mankind as hopeless fools.[60] He did his best to reach, if not every clodhopper, at least the educated bourgeoisie of contemporary towns. Following the reforms of 1807–12, that was precisely the class that now began to form the backbone of the Prussian state as it rose like a phoenix from its 1806 defeat at the hands of Napoleon.

Throughout the nineteenth century, on both sides of the Atlantic, the middle classes created 'progress' and progress, the middle classes. The members of this class liked to think of themselves as virtuous. It was Kant, more than anybody else, who taught them what virtue meant and how to practise it. Moreover, as Hegel pointed out, the 'Categorical Imperative' could readily be seen as an attempt to protect the most precious of all bourgeois possessions – property – against those who did not have it.[61] Does not the above-mentioned 'case study' provide an example of precisely that? One way or another, throughout the century the river of popular works, whether in German or in other languages, trying to explain Kant's thought on the matter never ceased.

Right from the beginning of the Christian centuries, conscience had usually gone hand in hand with repentance in front of God.

Among Catholics that repentance was often ritualistic and symbolic, aiming to obviate the sins of the past and set the sinner's mind at rest. Among Protestants, a greater emphasis was put on instilling a feeling of guilt, changing the penitent's behaviour and thus providing some kind of guarantee for the future. The nineteenth century by no means abandoned religion; to adduce but one example, Kant's younger colleague Friedrich Schleiermacher (1768–1834) could still describe conscience as 'the voice of God'. Yet as time went on, the more secular reasoning tended to take the place of the religious approach to such problems.

One very important reason for this was the incipient use, towards the end of the eighteenth century, of prisons not just to arrest criminals and hold them until they could be tried but to punish them. They thus took the place of fines, public shaming, caning, mutilation and, of course, the death penalty. In some ways prisons simply continued the drive towards education we have mentioned before. Modelled on the shelters many cities had built for orphans, the indigent and the mad, increasingly they provided the bureaucrats in charge with something their predecessors with their once-for-all methods did not have: namely time in which an attempt could be made not merely to punish the guilty but to provide them with the consciences they did not seem to have.

Along with prisons came similar institutions such as poorhouses, workhouses, institutions for the mentally ill and schools which, as part of the growing bureaucratic state, started appearing in large numbers.[62] There was much variation from one institution to another and from one country to the next. But everywhere it was a question of patiently, persistently and systematically instilling reason, good behaviour, order, thrift and industry until they became, in Kant's words, 'incorporated into [people's] being'. How successful was the enterprise in moulding nineteenth-century society at large? Gertrude Himmelfarb, an American historian, has sought to answer precisely this question. Himmelfarb, who was born in 1922, is married to Irving Kristol, 'the godfather of Neoconservatism', as he has been called. She spent much of her career at the City University of New York systematically lambasting contemporary American 'values', which she regarded as lax, by comparing them with the 'virtues' of the 'Victorian' age.

The titles of Himmelfarb's works tend to speak for themselves. One is *On Looking into the Abyss: Untimely Thoughts on Culture and Society*; another, *The De-moralization of Society: From Victorian Virtues to Modern Values*. Behind both titles there is a tale, partly inspirational, partly sad, of a long-gone time when people, including above all middle-class people, still had a conscience rooted, ultimately, in the belief in God. It made them respectable, hardworking and willing to postpone immediate gratification in exchange for future gain. Their lives were marked by 'moral earnestness . . . military heroism . . . social service . . . [and] religious piety'.[63] Christie Davies, a former professor of sociology at Reading University, England, in *The Strange Death of Moral Britain* (2006), has painted a similar picture of that region. It explains, or claims to explain, how 'a once respectable and religious Britain became a seriously violent and dishonest society, one in which person and property were at risk, family breakdown was ubiquitous, and drug and alcohol abuse was rising'.[64]

Never mind that almost one-third of nineteenth-century rural English brides went to the altar pregnant. Never mind that, among the upper classes on both sides of the Atlantic, marriage between cousins, based not on love but on the desire to keep the family property together, was very common.[65] Never mind that, among the working classes, sexual initiation often took place at thirteen. Never mind that, though divorce was rare, one reason for that was because countless lower-class couples never bothered to formalize their liaisons, entering and leaving them as they saw fit. Not to mention the fact that, by one contemporary estimate, one in twelve unmarried English women above the age of puberty was a prostitute.[66] Judging by the diary of that unknown Victorian gentleman, Walter, in England finding a woman, single or married, professional or amateur, for occasional sex was as easy as drinking a glass of water and only a little more expensive.[67] The situation in the U.S. was no better. When the German sociologist Max Weber visited Chicago in the early 1890s he noticed how prostitutes were arrayed in windows, each one with her, sometimes his, price displayed.[68] While men enjoyed themselves, well-to-do women flocked to doctors to have their clitorises stimulated, first manually and later with the aid of specially designed machines.

Never mind that in reality crime rates were much higher than they are today.[69] Never mind, too, that most of those who worked were very poor and that many of those who were rich did not work. As the mystery writer Agatha Christie (1890–1976) wrote of her father, Frederick Alvah Miller, they spent their lives visiting their clubs and being 'pleasant'. At a time when money was stable – it was, after all, linked to gold – and prices, thanks to industrialization, kept going down, saving for the future made much better sense than it does now. Finally, remember that the much-admired Victorian age was also that of colonialism, leading to the death of innumerable non-Europeans who had the effrontery to try to resist, and of the robber barons. Enough said.

So far as anyone can determine, the Victorian virtues so loudly trumpeted by Himmelfarb, Davies and others were little but a hypocritical myth similar to the one that ten centuries' worth of medieval mirrors for princes sought to propagate. In part this myth was deliberately fostered by the upper classes to provide an example to the lower ones. Their purpose was to maintain their own right to stay in power and enjoy its privileges. In practice the members of the upper classes, provided they were discreet, did much as they liked.

Storming the Heavens

Not everybody was happy with Kant's attempt to anchor conscience in duty, especially if that duty was understood simply as the imperative to assist the state and the *Obrigkeit* that governs it in enforcing the law. Let alone with the kind of education that was meant to implant a conscience, rooted in what was considered useful for society, into those who did not seem to have it so as to turn as many people as possible into performing poodles. Perhaps surprisingly in view of what has been said about Protestantism, the most important opponent by far was himself a German and a Protestant by birth. He was Friedrich Wilhelm Nietzsche (named after Friedrich Wilhelm IV, who reigned from 1840 to 1861). Perhaps it was this contradiction that caused Nietzsche to claim, quite spuriously, that his ancestors had been Polish noblemen. As many passages in his work testify, for 'mere Germans' he had nothing but contempt.

Born in 1844, Nietzsche was four years old when his father, a Lutheran pastor, died. He grew up with his mother, two unmarried aunts and a younger sister. Recognized early on as a brilliant student, he gained admission to Schulpforta, reputedly the best Gymnasium in the German-speaking world. There he received a solid grounding in classical languages and music in particular. Originally his chosen field was theology, which naturally caused him to reflect on the problems of good and evil. Later, though, having lost his faith in God, he changed course and spent several years studying classical philology at some of Germany's best universities.

In 1869, when he was not yet 25 years old and before he had completed his doctorate (he never did), he was given a position at the University of Basel. There he stayed until 1879, when ill health forced him to retire. Later he wrote that, for those as passionately interested in great ideas as he was, universities, with their day-to-day routine and tendency to compartmentalize knowledge, provided the wrong environment. From then on, sustained by a small pension, he led the life of an itinerant scholar, constantly moving between Germany, Switzerland and Italy until he collapsed in 1889. Right from the beginning, though, Nietzsche disappointed his former teachers by neglecting philology in favour of philosophy. Even as a philosopher he almost immediately caused eyebrows to rise. Systematically unsystematic, he regarded 'systems' as opposed to what he always called 'life'. The latter he characterized as *essentially* disorderly and all but impossible to mould, guide and control.

All this makes Nietzsche into an enormously difficult thinker to summarize. Convinced that the idea of objective truth itself is an error, he floated like a butterfly, stung like a bee. He drew his ideas from some and directed well-aimed darts at others, all the while questioning existing philosophy, laughing at its pretensions and either shattering its ideas or spoofing them. Compounding the problem, he dressed much of his work not in straightforward prose but in aphorisms, maxims, metaphors, allegories, short sketches and even poems.

As he himself said, if there is any single clue to his thought it is provided by his view of himself as 'a psychologist who has not his equal'.[70] This quality, a largely intuitive ability to look into the souls of men (like so many other philosophers we have met on these pages, Nietzsche had little use for women; he saw them as 'cats', amoral creatures standing beyond conventional good and evil and only interested in using men for their own ends, the most important of which was having children), enabled him to identify *ressentiment* as the dominant characteristic of contemporary civilization. In tracing its origins he proceeded more as a psychologist than a historian.

Having put the need for 'scientific' history aside, Nietzsche could focus on *ressentiment* – he always uses the French expression – proper. *Ressentiment* originated in a combination of envy and impotence. An impotence, to be sure, brought about not so much by objective circumstances as by cowardice and the self-hatred it both generates and reflects. It was what the weak and sickly felt in respect to the strong and healthy members of the aristocracy (from the Greek *aristos*, meaning excellent or superior).[71] Blissfully unaware of good and evil, of morality and conscience, as they subsequently evolved, throughout antiquity those superiors, as exemplified above all by the Homeric heroes and, much later, the Roman nobility, had ruled over the multitude. They overpowered it, suppressed it, stamped their own marks on it, exploited it and governed it. If necessary they also killed its members in large numbers and without feeling any compunction about doing so. Their proud spirit, untrammelled by either conscience or its close companion, guilt, enabled them to create what is known as classical culture and make it the highest that had ever existed.

It was to bring down this aristocracy that Christianity was first introduced. As we saw, by turning 'knowledge with oneself' into a substitute for the Jewish commandments, Paul had immensely increased the importance of whatever notions of conscience existed before his time.[72] To Nietzsche, the reason why he was successful was because his version of Christianity, which incidentally had little to do with that of Jesus, chimed with and gave voice to *ressentiment*. It provided the multitude – now led by priests, some of whom were themselves renegade aristocrats – with a way to avenge itself. It did so not by virtue of its strength; that was a feat beyond its ability, perhaps even its imagination. Instead it appealed to its own abject weakness, so long held in contempt. Had not Jesus Himself, in the Sermon on the Mount, blessed the poor in spirit and the meek, calling them the salt of the earth and promising them heavenly rewards?

Specifically the tool the priests used to transform weakness into strength, and strength into weakness, was moral judgement, or conscience. It was 'the favourite revenge of the spiritually limited on those who are less so'.[73] Rising from the underworld of classical civilization, murky depths where the light of aristocratic culture had hardly penetrated, Christianity managed to do what brute force could never have accomplished: to wit, make the members of the elite put on shackles and wear them out of what, on the face of things, was their own will. Instead of glorying in their strength, they learnt to feel guilty about it and turn it against themselves. In the whole of human history, no other 'achievement' was nearly as great and nearly as harmful to everything healthy, powerful, great, beautiful, creative and, above all, free.

Like its root, *ressentiment*, the Christian conscience started out as a dagger directed by the self against the self. To paraphrase, my weakness prevents me from doing what the strong do and what I really want to do. The outcome is a sick mixture of envy and rage. Therefore let me adopt and internalize 'moral' barriers that will explain why I don't do it. Next I shall seek to extend those barriers to the strong as well. Thus I shall draw their sting, weaken them and ultimately bring them down to my own level. That which does not conform to those barriers I shall give the name 'bad', that which does, 'good'; as Nietzsche saw it, the invention of evil preceded that of its opposite.

Close behind conscience came sin, guilt, remorse, pity and charity – the last two, Nietzsche says, are dangerous to the agent and humiliating to the recipient – self-abnegation and self-flagellation. Not to mention any number of empty rituals, foolish superstitions and degrading practices. Classical civilization, which had been built from the top down, saw such things as signs of impotence and despised them as they deserved to be. No Achilles, no Democritus, no Zeno and no Marcus Aurelius would have dreamt of stooping so far. Christianity, turning the world on its head, raised them, extolled them and made them into the greatest 'virtues' of all. Yet nothing could change the fact that they were at bottom suicidal. Spreading like rot in an apple barrel, wherever the Christian conscience triumphed it was accompanied by sickness, degeneration and death.

Perhaps worst of all was the Pauline contention that no human being can achieve salvation (supposing that such a thing does exist, and supposing people need or even want it) by their own efforts and at their own risk. Jesus Himself had never said as much, but this idea was adopted by all Christian denominations with hardly any exception. Instead they depend on he who has sacrificed Himself on their behalf. The very idea, Nietzsche said, amounted to a prohibition on thought. Had not the second-century AD writer Tertullian once said that belief – he was referring to the resurrection of Jesus – was necessary *because* it affirmed what reason could not accept?[74] Worse still, it required that men give up what, in his last and never completed book, he called their will to power. No other idea had ever been more humiliating, more destructive to free development and thus to 'life' than this one.

To 'brand' this idea on the human mind – so insensate, Nietzsche says, often so foolish, so unstable, always so ready to distort and to forget – the Church, often working through the secular authorities, resorted to the most frightful forms of torture. Depending on fashion, among them were stoning, breaking on the wheel, impalement, quartering, boiling in oil and flaying. Perhaps worst of all was the consciousness of owing God a debt. Growing not out of what people had done but out of what they were, and not out of some agreed-on and mutually beneficial contract but out of a pure act of unilateral grace, the debt (as Nietzsche points out, in German the same term, *Schuld*, can mean either debt or guilt) could never be discharged. Man was tuned into an animal that 'tears, persecutes, gnaws, disturbs, mistreats itself . . . rubs itself raw against the bars of its cage'.[75] In the end the only possible outcome was madness.

Somehow or other a few 'free spirits', motivated by the 'piety of the search for knowledge', managed to maintain themselves.[76] With them in the lead, towards the end of the fifteenth century belief in God began to decline and the doors of the madhouse opened a little. It was this process that led to the statement, repeated several times in Nietzsche's works, that God is dead.[77] Contrary to the popular interpretation and the occasional jokes to which it has given rise, that 'fact' did not mean He had physically died as other creatures do. How could He, given that He was but a figment of the imagination, an entity man had invented and set up over himself? Rather it meant that belief in Him had waned and ceased to play a great role in human affairs. The idea, which subsequent historians were to call 'secularization' and about which they eventually wrote entire libraries, was hardly original. It may be found in the works of Hegel, and during the first half of the nineteenth century it became commonplace.[78]

In Germany at any rate, the factor that had brought about the death of God was the sheer stubborn industriousness of generations of middle-class people in particular. The lives they led, wrote Nietzsche, were of such a kind as to leave them with little time or inclination to think about anything but their business and their pleasure, not to mention their families, the papers and 'the fatherland'. Outside the theological faculties, in institutes of higher learning, making thinking people take God seriously had become practically impossible. To this day, any scientist or scholar so rash as to mention divine intervention in his or her work will immediately be branded as 'unscientific' and subjected to a torrent of ridicule, as happened to Francis Collins, longtime Director of the National Institutes of Health in the U.S., after he wrote that, to him, the existence of morality was 'the strongest signpost of God'.[79]

As the churches grew empty the entire vast net of fables, such as the one about the existence of 'another' world, that generations of priests, theologians and similar 'learned cattle' had woven around Him started collapsing. No longer was God able to provide moral guidance, let alone promise reward and threaten punishment for paying or not paying obeisance to Him. In the words of the madman in The Gay Science (1882):

Where has God gone? . . . I shall tell you. We have killed him – you and I. We are his murderers. But how have we done this? How were we able to drink up the sea? Who gave us the sponge to wipe away the entire horizon? What did we do when we unchained the earth from its sun? Whither is it moving now? Whither are we moving now? Away from all suns? Are we not perpetually falling? Backward, sideward,

forward, in all directions? Is there any up or down left? Are
we not straying as through an infinite nothing? Do we not
feel the breath of empty space? Has it not become colder? . . .
How shall we, murderers of all murderers, console ourselves?
That which was the holiest and mightiest of all that the world
has yet possessed has bled to death under our knives. Who
will wipe this blood off us? With what water could we purify
ourselves? What festivals of atonement, what sacred games
shall we need to invent? Is not the greatness of this deed too
great for us? Must we not ourselves become gods simply to
be worthy of it?[80]

Mankind stood in need of a new compass to guide it through life.
What was it to be? For Hegel it had been the state and the duty to
serve it to the best of one's ability, even if doing so meant sacrificing
oneself for it in the bloody mayhem called war. Nietzsche rejected
that solution out of hand. It was simply not true that the state represented an ideal, let alone an ethical one. In reality it was 'the coldest
of all cold monsters'. Both when dealing with its fellow states and
when treating its own people, it never ceased lying, bribing, entrapping,
assaulting, torturing and murdering. It did everything it prohibited
others from doing, not accidentally but continuously and by reason
of its very nature.[81] Hegel's view of conscience as rooted in duty the
individual owed to the state was not simply wrong: it was grotesque.

For Rousseau, whose importance Nietzsche acknowledged even
though he characterized him as *canaille*, rabble, the answer had been
man's nature.[82] To become good, all he needed was a proper education.
Nietzsche strongly dissented. The idea that man was essentially good
and gentle was rejected as nothing more than sentimental nonsense.
In fact man, having started as an ape, remained more of an ape than
any ape.[83] As Charles Darwin had recently shown, nature was based
on the most ferocious competition. To Nietzsche, as to countless
others of his generation, that meant not the survival of the fittest
through reproduction and adaptation but an everlasting physical and
mental struggle for power.[84]

By Nietzsche's day universal compulsory schooling had become
well established in the most advanced countries. Perhaps this helps

explain why he, a born contrarian, did not put his trust in education to nearly the same extent as Rousseau and others had done; after all, he could see its results, or lack of them, wherever he went. Much education consisted of foolish rote learning and was more likely to close the mind than to open it. Too often all it did was produce 'learned cattle'. The more education expanded, the more it was made to serve either the happiness (read, prosperity) of the 'stupid, dull masses' or the power of the state. As it did so it became devalued, so much so that it lost its ability either to confer privileges or to command respect.[85]

Having dealt with Hegel and Rousseau, Nietzsche turned on Kant as the most important proponent of conscience. In all essential points, Nietzsche charged, Kant had retained the Christian moral framework in which he had been brought up. All he did was to build, or try to build, a new foundation for it to stand on. However, that foundation was no more certain than the one it sought to replace. 'Kant', Nietzsche wrote, 'believed in morality not because nature and history demonstrate it, but in spite of the fact that nature and history continually contradict it.'[86] The Categorical Imperative was just another name for the dagger men were pointing at their own essential nature. Worse still, it had not been put in place by some awesome and all-powerful God, or even by the self-serving and mendacious priests who had invented Him and claimed to serve Him. Instead it owed its existence to the most 'enlightened' philosopher of his age and some would say, all ages.

Consciously or not, Kant spent his entire life working for 'the coldest of all cold monsters'. His unfortunate influence happened to be in accordance with the spirit of the time. However, the Imperative's very claim to universality condemned it. Putting an end to any kind of independent thought it put a fool's cap on the head of anybody who accepted it, 'Old Kant' himself not excepted.[87] Ostensibly its purpose was to make a civilized life possible. In reality it took deadly aim at the essence of humanity – people's unity with themselves, their freedom and their unending quest for more and more power. It prevented people from becoming all they were, could be and should be. Kant's cardinal tenet, Nietzsche wrote, was 'I know how to obey – and so should you.'[88] As with all attempts to make people internalize their morality, in other words develop a conscience, a 'whiff of cruelty' was by no means absent.[89]

Regardless of whether its origins were religious or secular, a bad conscience meant one of two things. A person might not have the courage to do all that his nature required for its own development; or else, having transgressed in trying to do so, to confront the consequences of his or her deeds. Not many criminals have what it takes to be proud of their crimes and, instead of concealing them or denying them or trying to minimize them or begging for mercy for having committed them, boast of them in court. The few who did so, however, had been 'carved out of about the best, hardest, and most valuable timber of all'.[90] If anybody approached his ideal of the *Übermensch*, best translated as 'more-than-man', it was they. He had met some such men in Machiavelli, who had rightly celebrated Cesare Borgia. Others populated the pages of *The Brothers Karamazov*. Of Dostoevsky, its author, Nietzsche wrote that he was the only psychologist from whom he had anything to learn.[91]

The problem was that most people were too weak both to avoid committing deeds that went against their consciences *and* to live with those consciences later on. Split in two, they had turned to Christianity. Christianity created conscience as we understand it. For centuries on end it also provided people with some methods, however ridiculous and however unhealthy, to cope with these problems. The death of God caused those methods to lose whatever efficacy they had ever had. The outcome was the most profound crisis in human history. Its manifestations were mental conflict and hypocrisy, including the kind of hypocrisy that made some call themselves 'the first servants of their states' and claim that they were working 'for the common good'. Ultimately it led to degeneration.

Wearing their consciences like fake jewellery, such people turned pity, or perhaps one should say 'sensibility', into a secular religion. They were

> in sympathy with whatever feels, lives, suffers (down as far as animals, up as far as 'God') . . . in mortal hatred for suffering in general, in their almost feminine incapacity to remain spectators of suffering, to *let* suffer; at one in their

involuntary gloom and sensitivity . . . at one in their faith in the morality of mutual pity, as if it were morality in itself and the pinnacle, the attained pinnacle of man, the sole hope of the future, the consolation of the present and the great redemption from all the guilt of the past.[92]

They also displayed an insufferable combination of moralizing, airs of superiority, constant meddling in other people's business and a tendency to humiliate those they pretended to help. Not to mention fear of anything great, powerful, proud and confident that might upset their petty lives. A really good psychologist, such as Nietzsche considered himself to be, could identify *ressentiment*, the emotion that stood at the root of all this, by its characteristic stench.[93]

Thus it was Christianity that had given birth to conscience, man's self-inflicted wound and the enemy of everything in him that was strong and great. Kant put it on a secular basis, but he left its foundations intact. Nietzsche's self-imposed task, which he proudly says was the most important and highest ever undertaken by anyone, was to go beyond good and evil and reunite man with himself. That meant uprooting conscience and draining the morass, made up of a sickly combination of cowardice, fear and *ressentiment*, from which it had sprung. The person who was always stumbling over his own conscience was to be replaced by the one to whom not even the highest and most arduous tasks are impossible. *Ecrasez l'infame*, crush the monster, were his final words on it.[94] Providentially, if perhaps accidentally, they were also among the very last ones he wrote before darkness enveloped his mind.

IV
Life without God

From Liberation to Dressage

From Sophocles to Kant, many different figures of speech have been used to describe what conscience threatened to do, or did, to the minds of those who were about to incur or had already incurred feelings of guilt by transgressing against it. To list but a few, they included 'knowing' (the term Oedipus used and from which all subsequent names for conscience were derived), 'disturbing', 'judging', 'gnawing', 'stinging', 'haunting', 'afflicting', 'punishing', 'tormenting' and finally 'driving mad'. That was what Shakespeare's Richard III, a multiple murderer who did not even stop at killing his nephews, innocent children, meant when he said that his conscience had 'a thousand several tongues, and every tongue brings in a several tale, and every tale condemns me for a villain' (v:iii). Arguably it is this passage above all which reminds us that, morally monstrous though the king may be, in the end he is a human being like the rest of us.

As the play draws to its end, though, the king provides us with another view of the matter:

Let not our babbling dreams affright our souls;
Conscience is but a word that cowards use,
Devised at first to keep the strong in awe;
Our strong arms be our conscience, swords our law.
March on, join bravely, let us to't pell-mell;
If not to heaven, then hand in hand to hell (v:iii).

Nietzsche, who greatly admired Shakespeare,[1] would have subscribed to every word. If necessity compels you to perform the deed, go ahead. If it doesn't, don't. Whatever your decision, don't hide behind it or deny it or fret over it or, even worse, apologize for it. Rather, be man enough to enjoy it, stand by it and repeat it if necessary. Giving way to remorse merely meant piling a second stupidity on top of the first.[2] The outcome would be to straighten his back, which Christianity and Kant in particular had bent, and restore his pride in preparation for the great tasks ahead. These included above all the ability to storm the heavens; live without a God to tell him what was and was not permitted; and create new values that would be entirely and uniquely his own.

The man who had the greatest influence on the study of human psychology during the twentieth century, and perhaps in all centuries, was Sigmund Freud (1856–1939). From an early age, Freud always sought to emphasize his own originality. This caused him to deny that a close connection with Nietzsche existed.[3] Yet some of the evidence suggests otherwise. At one point he said that Nietzsche had been the ideal of his youth; in 1900 he bought all of the philosopher's books. A direct link between Nietzsche and Freud also existed in the person of an intellectual Russian woman, Lou Andreas-Salomé. In the 1880s she had befriended Nietzsche, who admired her intellect and at one point proposed to marry her. Later she joined Freud's circle, was analysed by him, participated in his Wednesday-evening meetings and started to work as a psychoanalyst herself.[4] Accordingly, examining Freud's ideas on conscience in the light of Nietzsche appears to be sound, methodologically speaking.

As Nietzsche once wrote, 'if there were gods how could I endure not being a god? *Therefore* there are no gods.'[5] Writing some four decades later, Freud likewise argued that God was a 'higher being' man had created out of his imagination for his own purposes. Chief among those purposes, he added, was the longing for a substitute for the dead father.[6] However, the idea that He might 'really' exist was a leftover from a superstitious, pre-scientific age, a blot on the intelligence that was both childish and foolish.[7] Each of the two men had his own reason for rejecting religion. Nietzsche did so because it prevented men from becoming all they could be; Freud because, like Kant, he thought that there was no 'scientific' proof of its truth. What Freud and Nietzsche had in common was that by rejecting religion, they automatically cut any link that might have existed between it and conscience. Holy voices entering the soul from above, divine sparks and the like were definitely ruled out, hopefully for all time to come. Those who heard them were more likely to end up in the madhouse than in the temple.

Another assumption Nietzsche and Freud shared was that, whatever Kant, Hobbes and the Stoics might have said, the essence of man was not reason but any number of drives whose nature remained eternally the same. Wild, uncontrollable and often conflicting, the drives had their origin in man's soul and ultimately his biological being. A close analogy would be various different liquids being forced through a narrow gorge by the pump behind. Some of the liquids are pure, others mixed. They can interact with each other and produce different and often surprising, even explosive, compounds. Should the gorge be dammed, the pressure will start building up until it threatens to demolish both the dam and everything around it. To Nietzsche the most important drive, over-arching all the rest, was the will to power. To Freud, who started his career by treating female hysterics, it was the sexual one. In his *Three Essays on the Theory of Sexuality* (1905) he compared it to hunger.[8] Yet since the two drives sprang from the same source, they were to some extent interchangeable. Now one predominated, now the other. Both often manifested themselves in the form of aggression.

At this point Freud started to leave Nietzsche behind. To Nietzsche aggression, leading to overcoming and to growth, was the essence of life. As against this, conscience was an invention put in place by the weak and the sickly, of whom Kant was the latest and most influential representative. Their purpose in doing so was to avenge themselves on the strong and the healthy, reducing them to their own level and threatening to destroy the basis from which all human culture arose. Freud was not quite as radical. In his most important work on the subject, *Civilization and Its Discontents*, he did indeed recognize the inevitability of aggression and the centrality of its role in human life. Writing a decade after the Great War, however, he put a much stronger emphasis on its disruptive, destructive character.

If a civilized life were to be possible at all, it had to be restrained, canalized and provided with outlets other than those available in the trenches.

What methods did society use, Freud asked, in order 'to hold in check the aggressiveness that opposes it, to make it harmless, perhaps to get rid of it'? He answered that

> the aggressiveness is introjected, *internalized*; in fact, it is sent back where it came from, that is, directed against the ego. It is there taken over by a part of the ego that distinguishes itself from the rest as a super-ego, and now, in the form of *conscience*, exercises the same propensity to harsh aggressiveness against the ego that the ego would have liked to enjoy against others.

'The tension between the strict super-ego and the subordinate ego', he added, 'we call the *sense of guilt*; it manifests itself as the need for punishment. Civilization, therefore, obtains the mastery over the dangerous love of aggression in individuals by enfeebling and disarming it and setting up an institution within their minds to keep watch over it, like a garrison in a conquered city.'

The most remarkable thing about guilt was that it was experienced not just by those who had committed a 'bad' deed but also by those who had merely intended to do so or thought of doing so. Often 'the more righteous a man is, the stricter and more suspicious will his conscience be, so that ultimately it is precisely those people who have carried holiness farthest who reproach themselves with the deepest sinfulness.' This could reach the point where people sinned *in order* to draw punishment on themselves. But how could such feelings rise in the first place? 'It is easy', Freud wrote,

> to discover the motive in man's helplessness and dependence upon others, it can best be designated the *dread of losing love* [original emphasis]. If he loses the love of others on whom he is dependent, he will forfeit also their protection against many dangers, and above all he runs the risk that this stronger person will show his superiority in the form of punishing

him. What is bad is, therefore, to begin with, whatever causes one to be threatened with a loss of love; because of the dread of this loss, one must desist from it. That is why it makes little difference whether one has already committed the bad deed or only intends to do so; in either case the danger begins only when the authority has found it out, and the latter would behave in the same way in both cases.

Both for the individual and for the human race as a whole, initially all we see are transgression, guilt and fear of punishment. While Freud conceded that such fear does not deserve the name of conscience, he saw it as providing the soil in which the latter can grow. Conscience proper develops

> as soon as the authority has been internalized by the development of a super-ego. The manifestations of conscience are then raised to a new level . . . At this point the dread of discovery ceases to operate and also once for all any difference between doing evil and wishing to do it, since nothing is hidden from the super-ego, not even thoughts.

Welcome back to the omnipresent, all-seeing, vigilant and vengeful Judeo-Protestant God. Except that He now exists not in heaven but inside the soul, as an integral part of the super-ego which directs and chastises the ego.

The blocking of one's drives, originally imposed by society, causes the ego, understood as the conscious element in man, to break up as part of it turns into the super-ego. That part in turn directs itself against the ego. True, there is no precise match. Instead, the interaction between 'constitutional factors' and 'the actual environment' can cause a lax upbringing to result in a strict conscience, or vice versa. Still there is no question that the process soon becomes self-reinforcing, with no clear beginning or end. In it, Freud believed, are to be found the origins of human civilization. The latter could never have arisen or developed without it. However, the self-reinforcing damming of the drives could also escalate and be carried to excess. In this process was contained the seed of much if not most human suffering. Often it extended into various forms of anxiety, neurosis and even psychosis. Physical symptoms, such as bedwetting and trembling, were not lacking either. The more advanced a society and the greater the restrictions it imposed, the worse the problem.

Some of the differences between Nietzsche and Freud have their roots in the two men's social backgrounds, personalities and objectives in life. Nietzsche was an unmarried, rather abstemious philosopher, always fleeing from one city to another and hopelessly unable to form part of any organized effort. His true preoccupation, derived above all from his background in ancient Greek history and culture, was the quest for human excellence. Freud was a good bourgeois with a large family to look after. He was also a physician who early on shifted the focus of his enquiries from the physical symptoms of disease to the psychological ones. Until the last years of his career, when *The Future of an Illusion* (1927) marked his growing focus on philosophy, his main concern was to diminish suffering by helping the patient break the self-reinforcing cycle. To do so it was necessary to make him or her grasp its origins.

However, the material he was trying to dig up was located in the unconsciousness of each individual separately. This could apply even to the feelings of guilt themselves.[9] How could one reach into the individual and drag out what he or she had suppressed? As Freud explained in his *Autobiographical Study* of 1924, early on his instrument for the purpose had been hypnosis. Finding it inadequate, he switched to the interpretation of dreams. Later still he combined the latter with free association.[10] Free association came complete with the famous couch and the analyst whom the patient was unable to see. An absolute prerequisite was a comfortable, confidential and uncensorious environment in which the patent would feel so much at ease that he could dissolve himself, so to speak.

Such surroundings would enable the flow of words, uttered without any attempt at thought or direction, to gush forth without bringing on either approval or punishment. In the flow were supposed to be hidden truths, which it was the function of the analyst to note, bring to light and interpret. On the assumption that people spent a lifetime repeating the experiences of their childhood, special attention was devoted to bringing suppressed memories of that period to light.

The philosopher Aurel Kolnai (1900–1973) provides an excellent description of the way things were supposed to work: 'the essential object . . . is to lift to the level of self-critical judgment the patients who have remained fixed in the stage of repression.'[11] Once the patient understood the inner conflict that caused his suffering, he would be able to reconcile himself with himself. Nineteen hundred years earlier, the Evangelist had put it more simply: 'the truth will make you free.'[12]

Under this method patients were neither supposed to submit to sermonizing nor to receive absolution from their sins. Indeed Freud once called the latter idea 'absurd'. All they were supposed to do was examine themselves as closely and as honestly as they could. Having understood *why* they had acquired the symptoms that were giving them trouble, they might be able to rid themselves of them. Looking back, it appears that therapy often had a liberating effect on patients. If Freud's consulting room became famous, especially among upper-class ladies, then this was in large part because it provided an opportunity for airing problems that had previously been considered taboo. Prominent among them were sexual ones. Precisely because psychoanalysis was liberating, many theologians saw it as an all too easy method of ridding people of their feelings of guilt and cleansing their consciences.[13] Well aware of the accusation, Freud did his best to counter it.[14]

As the number of psychoanalysts as well as psychologists and psychiatrists grew, inevitably the field became institutionalized.[15] Tirelessly working to spread his message, Freud himself played an important role in this process. The outcome was any number of professional associations complete with publications, steering committees and training courses. Growing longer and more demanding, the courses in turn made necessary some kind of written doctrine, or at least guidelines. Passing through those courses, taking the exams and becoming members in the associations were made prerequisites for acquiring a licence and practising. Practice itself was regulated by ethical codes and professional courts. The incipient rise of the welfare state in the 1930s, followed by the outbreak of the Second World War, also played a role in this. Growing numbers of psychiatrists and psychologists were drafted into the ruling bureaucracy, including the military bureaucracy. Soon they became an integral part of it.

In the U.S., the number of psychiatrists and neurologists per 100,000 of the population increased tenfold between 1950 and 1980. From 1966 to 1977 alone, the number of psychiatric nurses almost doubled.[16] All this altered the background against which treatment took place and, to some extent, its nature too. Early on it was simply a question of the therapist working with his or her patients. They formed a purely private, purely voluntary relationship that both sides were able to enter and terminate if and when it suited them. Ultimately it was the patient himself who decided whether he wanted to be treated and whether the treatment he was receiving suited him. As if to emphasize the amount of freedom involved, Freud himself sometimes disregarded his own methods. Not only did he treat patients for free, but he might even take them for walks in the streets of Vienna. Such informality may still persist in some cases. However, in many others institutionalization meant that freedom was circumscribed or lost.

Take the case of Sándor Ferenczi (1873–1933), an early psycho-analyst who had an exceptional capacity for empathy. He coddled his patients, embraced them and even kissed them as a mother does her child.[17] Today such behaviour would quickly cause him to be not just barred from practising but imprisoned as well. Given the rumoured habit of Carl Gustav Jung (1875–1961), the only disciple whose intel-lectual brilliance approached that of the master, of sleeping with his female patients, what would have happened to him almost defies the imagination. Therapists are no longer allowed to treat their relatives, as they regularly did in the early days (Freud himself analysed his daughter, Anna).[18] As the prohibition of these and other practices shows, increasingly analysts came to represent not just themselves but their associations, or society, or even the state. They came to function as the practitioners' collective conscience, the first directly, the other two indirectly.

Considered both as a method of treatment and as a theory of human nature, the influence of psychoanalysis peaked between 1930 and 1970. During those decades it pervaded not only mental health but culture and education too. Later, various factors caused it to come under growing, often vicious and often unjustified attacks that were launched at it from many different directions.[19] Yet one should not allow the baby to be thrown out with the bathwater. Acting almost single-handedly, Freud invented what used to be called 'the talking cure' and is now known as psychotherapy. For this reason alone his place in history is secure. Whatever one may think of his theories, so far no replacement nearly as comprehensive, self-consistent or fertile has appeared on the scene. Hence reports of their death are considerably exaggerated.

The relative decline of psychoanalysis caused the already fragmented mental health industry to break up into a thousand contending schools, all proclaiming their own originality and independence. Here and there a rebel might try to make a complete break with the establishment and start operating entirely on his or (rarely) her own. Particularly important in this respect were Roland Laing (1927–1989) and Thomas Szasz (1920–).[20] But such attentats, even including the most famous one made by the historian Michel Foucault in Madness and Civilization (1961), did not get far beyond the margins. Most states were all too happy to delegate the treatment of various difficult citizens to 'experts'. If only for that reason, the existence of the psychological establishment in general, and the psychoanalytic one in particular, was not seriously threatened. In the end what counted were not ideas, which remain as numerous and often as short-lived as berries, but organization and the backing it received.

Organization meant that mental health workers, whatever their precise profession and the school of thought to which they belonged, were selected, trained, licensed and regulated. If and when they violated the growing professional ethic they could also be disciplined. On the way they were equipped with an agenda that was to a large extent dictated to them from outside. This has reached the point where such workers are often obliged to turn in patients if they confess to transgressing certain parts of that agenda, such as engaging in what is called sexual child abuse.[21] Agendas were especially important in the growing number of cases when the therapist's fees were paid not by the patient himself but by some third party such as an insurance company or a government-run health service. Either way, in such cases 'curing' often meant simply making the patient accept the agenda within the shortest possible time and at the lowest possible cost.

To revert to Freud's own terminology, originally he had hoped to liberate his patients by helping them to break the escalating conflict between super-ego and ego which laymen had long known as the guilt-feeling/conscience complex.[22] A true understanding of the burden would lead to unburdening, or at least make it possible. There was no question, he wrote, of producing '"normality" according to schedule'.[23] In the hands of his successors of all persuasions, though, too often therapy meant trying to do exactly that. It became a question of dressing the ego until it met the demands of society in much the same way as wild animals are trained for the circus. Patients had to be conjured into 'voluntarily' assuming a new burden, not helped to discard it. The more highly institutionalized the profession to which therapists of all kinds belonged, and the less autonomy it enjoyed *vis-à-vis* society, the state and their instrument, the law, the greater pressure both on them and their patients.

As the growing use of non-medical terms such as 'deviance', 'disturbance', 'disorder' (as opposed to order), 'adjustment' (as opposed to 'maladjustment') and 'functional' (as opposed to 'dysfunctional') shows, the emphasis changed from relieving suffering to inducing conformity. Possibly this had something to do with the fact that the centre of psychoanalysis, as of psychology and psychiatry as a whole, moved to the United States. As Alexis de Tocqueville noted, nowhere is the pressure towards conformity as strong as in democratic America.[24] In 1929, 90 per cent of the world's analysts spoke German, thought in German and dreamed in German. Twenty years later, 70 per cent did so in English. Of some 800 analysts who conferred in Zurich in 1949, over half were American.[25] The Americans adopted a pragmatic – as opposed to cultural-philosophical – approach.[26] 'A Calculating People', as they have been called, could hardly be expected *not* to try and set up 'objective', if possible quantifiable, standards against which the 'effectiveness' of treatment could be measured.[27]

In the process patients (from the Latin *patiens*, one who suffers or endures) were turned into 'clients' or 'users' of care, and therapists into the latter's 'providers'. Freud himself expressed his fear lest caretakers, trained and licensed and working in such an environment, would either reject his ideas or, worse still, stifle them by embracing them and devising standards for implementing and controlling them.[28] His fears proved well-founded. The mother of all the standards is the *Diagnostic and Statistical Manual of Mental Disorders* (DSM). It is published by the American Psychiatric Association (APA), the largest and most prestigious of its kind. The DSM's importance in telling mental health workers which disorders will and will not be covered by insurance, and therefore how to label their patients, can hardly be exaggerated. When it first saw the light of print in 1952 it listed just 60 such, which were spread over 132 pages. By 2012 the number of pages had grown to 886 and that of diseases to 341. Thanks to a process of amalgamation, as when Asperger's lost its independence and was reclassified under the autism spectrum, the latest edition, which was published in May 2013, has only added a few more. As if to compensate for this, however, it contains no fewer than 992 pages.

Is this expansion the outcome of improved methods of diagnosis and treatment, as the manual's authors and other mental health workers keep saying? Or does it reflect changing fashion as well as a variety of social, economic and political pressures? The latter is suggested by the fact that even as many new disorders were added, others somehow disappeared.[29] The best example is homosexuality. The initial push to remove it from the list of mental disorders was provided by the gay rights movement, which mounted demonstrations and disrupted the meetings of psychiatrists, psychologists and other mental health workers. Thus it was not the dog (psychiatry) which wagged the tail (the nature and the meaning of homosexuality), but the other way around. The actual decision was taken by a majority vote. Applied to politics, such an approach may have its merits. However, as Freud himself wrote as long ago as 1924, it strongly suggests that psychiatry has nothing to do with science.[30]

Another example is transsexuality: men who feel they would like to be women or women who believe they are really men caged in a woman's body. Long considered pathological in the West, but not in some other cultures, it has been quietly dropped from the list of disorders. Whatever the prevailing standards at any given time and place, therapists of all kinds were asked to deploy their magic to make patients meet them. Unofficially or officially, they would be evaluated by their success at doing so. Severe cases who did not respond and were considered dangerous to themselves and/or others were incarcerated either in prisons or in mental hospitals. Another 'solution' was to try and influence their brains by surgical, electrical or chemical methods. On this, more later.

To sum up, Freud's idea was that the guilt-feeling/conscience complex, which so often manifested itself in neurosis and led to endless suffering, was caused by conflicts between different forces inside the soul. In some ways following Nietzsche, but reluctant to acknowledge the fact, his purpose was to lift the conflicts out of the unconscious, break the cycle, bring about liberation and restore people so they could exercise a greater part of their capacities and drive satisfaction from doing so. This may still be possible in some cases, especially those that are based on purely voluntary cooperation between independent people who have complete trust in one another's integrity and goodwill. Such trust, of course, presupposes ample time, an environment that is confidential and safe and a certain degree of financial comfort on both sides.[31]

Gradually, though, things changed. The sheer growth of the mental health industry and the pervasive influence it developed on many aspects of society and the state led to professionalization. Professionalization in turn required some kind of common agenda, and vice versa. In the opinion of both the administrators and the practitioners surveyed, many parts of the agenda in question did not originate within the profession as a result of 'disinterested' research. Instead they sprang from every kind of social and political pressure coming from outside. Often, too, researchers anticipated the results their employers wanted.[32] Another cardinal factor was the fact that many treatments were no longer paid for by the patients themselves. The more health services, private and public, got involved, the greater the pressure to produce tangible, if possible quantifiable, results, and the more pronounced the limits on the most essential element of conscience – freedom – became.

The parallels between this process and those that governed the evolution of conscience first under the Catholic Church and then in the hands of Luther and his followers are obvious. In each of these three cases the starting point was formed by a fresh and even startling idea concerning the origin, nature and function first of *syneidēsis* and then of *Gewissen* (both Luther and Freud, remember, wrote in German). The intention was to achieve liberation, even if doing so meant breaking with the accepted social norms. That, however, was only the beginning. The very success of the idea, as measured by its widespread acceptance, soon put an end to spontaneity. It required the establishment of some kind of organizational framework, consisting of people, agendas, regulations and ceremonies, to guard it and apply it in practice.

With organization came the question of how scarce resources should be distributed. Next the framework in question developed its own momentum. It kept redefining the limits of conscience, often changing it out of all recognition and often all but burying it under itself. Voluntarily or involuntarily, sooner or later it also found itself in touch with the law, opening the way to its own subjection. In the end it reached the point where it virtually invited rebellion against itself, causing the cycle to start all over again. That is how things have worked in the past. And that is how, unless some miracle happens, they will continue to work in the future.

Alternatives to Conscience: Japan

Starting with Seneca in the first century AD, and perhaps as far back as Antigone in the fifth century BC, conscience has usually been understood as the innermost voice. Embedded in the individual, himself understood as a unit that enjoys a fair amount of autonomy, it is supposed to be based on the critical distinction between good and bad. Equally important is the fact that it does its work even when there are no witnesses. In fact its presence under such circumstances is just what sets it apart from considerations concerning approval and disapproval, reward and punishment. Christians added that conscience had been implanted into man by God. Using it as a substitute for the law, they combined it with faith and turned it into a necessary condition for redemption. They then spent centuries arguing whether non-Christians could have a conscience and also about the precise ways in which all these factors were linked. Kant put duty in God's place; next, Nietzsche claimed that there was no God and Freud agreed with him in this respect.

Previously I used the example of the Judaic tradition to show that conscience is by no means universally considered a part of the human soul. Even as late as the first decades of the twentieth century, Hebrew still did not have a term for it. The one that was finally adopted represented a translation from some European language (the same, incidentally, applies to Yiddish). Another society that managed to do without conscience as it is understood in the West is Japan. Throughout history, the Japanese have tended to see the Chinese as some sort of elder brothers and borrowed much of their culture from them. That includes Confucianism, Buddhism and Daoism.

None of the three has any use for a personal god. Daoism in particular is said to have important affinities with Japan's native religion, Shinto. While the literal meaning of Dao is 'the way', that of Shinto is 'the way of the gods', or kami. Having become deeply fused with the other three, which were grafted onto it, the essential function of Shinto is to provide a link, by means of ritual and worship, between people, the land they inhabit and the kami. The last are best understood not as corporeal beings but as spiritual essences. Some kami are the spirits of departed people. Others are identified with such natural phenomena as grass, mountains, rivers, waterfalls, waves, trees, rocks, the moon – briefly anything considered beautiful, noble, and/or awe-inspiring. Following the Meiji Restoration of 1868, the emergence of 'State Shintoism' caused special attention to be paid to the kami of state and emperor. However, the defeat of 1945 put an end to this.

Whether the kami dwell inside the above-mentioned objects or are identical with them is not entirely clear.[33] Be this as it may, they are believed to exist not separately from, but in the same world as, ordinary mortals do. Though their presence is stronger in some places than in others, people are always surrounded by them. Thus the Western separation between the 'real' world and the metaphysical one does not exist. The practice of religion consists of elaborate rituals which are believed to express, maintain and reinforce the link.

By far the most important kami is the sun, Amaterasu. But even the sun does not amount to a personal god always on the watch to punish sinners or else to forgive them on condition that they believe, repent and promise not to transgress again.[34] Indeed it would be true to say that, whereas in one sense there are myriad gods, in another there are none at all. Nor is there any supernatural being either to implant a conscience in people's minds or relieve it when necessary. As a result, what one author has called 'the culture of confession', which from the time of Augustine on has served Christians as the method for relieving guilty consciences par excellence, never took hold either in the Shinto temple or in the Japanese psychoanalyst's consulting room.

Japanese psychologists were first introduced to psychoanalysis during the last years before the First World War. Right from the beginning, they questioned whether neuroses were really the outcome of a conflict between the ego and the super-ego. Instead they came up with the idea that it was a question of people focusing too much on themselves, as opposed to their surrounding society. Thus they 'interrupt[ed] the flow of normal life'.[35] Later on, when psychoanalysis finally did get a foot in the Japanese door, it became mixed up with all sorts of Buddhist notions that seriously altered its character. They even affected that most central of all Freudian myths, the Oedipus complex. The latter was something that Japanese culture could only accept with some difficulty.[36]

During the 1930s two collections of Freud's writings were published in Japan. Nevertheless most scholars seem to agree that Japanese psychiatrists either failed to fully comprehend the way psychoanalytical therapy was supposed to work, or, if they did understand it, rejected it.[37] In the words of the most prominent psychiatrist in question, Shoma Morita (1874–1938), what mattered were symptoms, not more or less suppressed childhood memories.[38] At least one American psychoanalyst who visited the country in the late 1940s came back convinced that Japanese psychoanalysis was not psychoanalysis at all. The reason, he wrote, was the powerful pressure society brought to bear on the individual. It doomed any attempt at achieving individual autonomy.[39] The French psychoanalyst and philosopher Jacques Lacan (1901–1981), who from about 1950 on was probably the most important of all Freud's followers, agreed.[40] Psychoanalysis in Japan was neither possible nor necessary. It was not so much a question of being unwilling to confess as of being unable to do so.[41] To this day, it has been claimed, what passes as psychotherapy in Japan does not focus on emancipating the patient from the unconscious, as originally at any rate psychoanalysis sought to do. Instead it is a question of renouncing one's selfish preoccupations and surrendering oneself to society.[42]

So what mental mechanisms *did* Japanese society develop to guide its members? In the literature, societies that centre on guilt-feeling/conscience are often contrasted with those that are built on shame. The idea is traced to a collection of essays from 1937 edited by the American anthropologist Margaret Mead (1901–1978).[43] Mead's former teacher, Ruth Benedict (1887–1948), provided a classic definition of the difference. 'True shame cultures', she wrote in 1944–5,

> rely on existential sanctions for good behaviour, not, as true guilt cultures do, on an internalized conviction of sin. Shame is a reaction to other people's criticism. A man is shamed either by being openly ridiculed and rejected or by fantasying to himself that he has been made ridiculous. In either case it is a potent sanction. But it requires an audience or at least a man's fantasy of an audience. Guilt does not. In a nation where honor means living up to one's own picture of oneself, a man may suffer from guilt though no man knows of his misdeeds and a man's feeling of guilt may actually be relieved by confessing his sin.[44]

Since then, the literature that has been written about the issue has grown far beyond the ability of any individual to master. Many authors admit that the distinction between the two kinds of society is anything but absolute.[45] Yet the fact that much of the world is grey, and that grey itself has 50 shades and more, does not prevent us from recognizing the existence of black and white either. Benedict herself used the contrast between guilt and shame as the theoretical basis of her book *The Chrysanthemum and the Sword* of 1946. Originally it was written for the Office of War Information at the Pentagon. The idea was to analyse the Japanese national character and, as far as possible, predict future Japanese behaviour. The strange thing about it was that Benedict did not know Japanese and had never visited Japan; nor did any of her previous work deal specifically with that country. To use modern language, in no sense could she be said to be a Japanese 'expert'. Yet once it had been published it became an absolute bestseller. In Japan alone it sold over two million copies.[46] It is still listed in almost any discussion of the subject, often as the oldest item by far.

'Shame' (haji), Benedict wrote, 'is a thing bitterly felt in Japan.' However, and herein lies the difference, it can be the outcome not only of what one had said or done but of what has been said or done to one's 'unworthy' self.[47] Conscience does not distinguish, or is not supposed to distinguish, between a transgression committed in private and one that becomes known to others. Shame does make the distinction, with the result that as long as the deed remains secret the person in question does not need to feel troubled.

> [For the Japanese] a failure to follow their explicit signposts of good behaviour, a failure to balance obligations or to foresee contingencies is a shame. Shame, they say, is the root of virtue . . . Shame has the same place of authority in Japanese ethics that a 'clear conscience' 'being right with God', and 'the avoidance of sin' have in Western ethics. Logically enough, therefore, a man will not be punished in the afterlife.

'The primacy of shame in Japanese life', continues Benedict, 'means, as it does in any tribe or nation where shame is deeply felt, that any man watches the judgment of the public upon his deeds. He need only fantasy what their verdict will be, but he orients himself towards the verdict of others.' This is the exact opposite from Marcus Aurelius, who understood *syneidēsis* as the quality that made a person indifferent to and independent of that verdict. It also contradicts Luther's idea that conscience meant standing up against the verdict when necessary. In Japan,

> those who do respect themselves chart their course, not between 'good' and 'evil' but between 'expected man' and 'unexpected man' and sink their own personal demands in the collective 'expectation'. These are the good men who know shame (haji) and are endlessly circumspect. They are the men who bring honor to their families, their villages, and their nation.

The demands all this makes on the individual are both very great and inescapable. No wonder education aimed at making children understand them, internalize them and conform to them starts at a very early age. As one would expect from a follower of Freud, Benedict believes that this has something to do with toilet training. Once the training has begun it never ceases. '"Children", the Japanese say, their eyes smiling benignantly, "know no shame". They add, "that is why they are so happy."' The first sanction used to instil shame is laughter. Others will follow. As in any other society, formal sanctions do exist and are applied if necessary. Yet the worst imaginable one is to have one's family turn against one. Nothing, the Japanese believe, could be better proof of the fact that a person has failed to maintain his *giri*, the duty to keep one's reputation unspotted.

As late as 1992, two anthropologists claimed that everything written in the intervening decades had done little but add footnotes to Benedict's work.[48] Another sociologist added that 'cultural portraits contrary to the tenaciously normative template constructed by Benedict . . . can only always be "alternative" or "other" as opposed to un-acknowledged facets of the complex, composite, and integrated whole of "Japanese culture".'[49] Countless publications have contrasted American individualism with Japanese 'groupism', egalitarianism with hierarchy, contract with 'kintract' (a system whereby blood ties, not formal contracts with strangers, govern social relationships), private with public, openness with closure and, yes, 'guilt' with 'shame'.[50] 'The ideal solution of a conflict', wrote Professor Ben Ami Shillony, '[is] not a total victory for one side and a humiliating defeat for the other, but an accommodation by which winner and loser could co-exist without too much loss of face.'[51] In Japan, two other experts say, 'majorities do not simply outvote minorities in parliament. Those who can win the vote [pretend to] allow their opponents to influence the final outcome.'[52]

A fourth expert tells us that the system hinges on 'the cultural traditions of shaming wrongdoers, including an effective coupling of shame and punishment'.[53] One curious outcome of the emphasis on shame, as opposed to guilt, is the role played by apology. As the proverb *qui s'excuse, qui s'accuse* implies, in the West a person who apologizes is thereby assumed to have a conscience that makes him or her admit guilt. Strangely enough, in Japan one can apologize *and* insist on one's innocence at the same time. People, it is said, apologize not for what they have done but for having allowed themselves to be suspected of wrongdoing and thus casting shame on those around them. A reference to one's unworthiness (*futoku*) allows one to express modesty or humility. Often, though, it has nothing to do with either feelings of guilt or contrition.[54]

Conscience, including even conscience understood as a duty as with Protestantism, Kant and Hegel, always presupposes an individual who has a fair measure of independence and freedom of choice. On the contrary, the Japanese culture of shame – and, as we shall see, the Chinese one of reverence – requires a society that is much more closely knit. Interpersonal relationships centre on harmony, cohesion, cooperation, obligation and obedience. Not only do such values require a certain degree of uniformity, but they explain why, in the country of the rising sun, the kind of conscience which whistleblowers small and large have has always been rather rare.[55] Fortunately seven decades of sociological study have given us masses of quantitative evidence on these subjects, evidence that Benedict did not have. On the whole, it seems to show that in Japan such uniformity and such cohesion do indeed exist.[56]

Minority peoples in Japan are few in number and any political power they exercise is negligible. Though Japan is one of the world's most heavily industrialized countries, and in spite of the way society emphasizes hierarchy, gaps between rich and poor are much smaller than in other developed countries. Geographically speaking Japanese people are, or at any rate used to be, much less likely to move from one home to another than either Americans or Britons.[57] This in turn both reflects the social demand that children care for their aged parents and ensures that such care should be a practical proposition.[58] The recession that started in 1990–91 and still continues has caused guaranteed lifetime employment to decline. Nevertheless labour mobility still remains lower than in Western countries.[59]

A survey shows that the more socially integrated a Japanese person is, the more internal gratification he or she feels.[60] The overriding objective is not autonomy but security. Conversely the family, neighbours and employer are in a position where they are able to keep individuals firmly in their place with relatively little resort to the police and the courts. Since the shame that overtakes the individual extends to the group to which he or she belongs, surrogate apology – apologizing on behalf of somebody else – is very important and can reach extreme proportions. Conversely the group in question may also try to cover up any transgressions its members commit by engaging in what is usually called corruption. All this is very much part of expected, hence tolerated, behaviour.[61] As a result Japanese visitors to countries where such social discipline does not apply are said to feel like fish out of water.[62]

To end this chapter I would like to share with the reader something that happened to me as I was researching it. Ben Ami Shillony, I am proud to say, has been a close friend of mine for over 40 years. His unrivalled knowledge of Japanese history and culture has brought him a medal at the hands of the emperor himself. So nothing was more natural than to ask him whether the Japanese have a word for conscience and just what it meant. He has kindly allowed me to quote his answer: 'Of course there is a word in Japanese for conscience. It is: ryoshin. Ryo means good and shin means heart, in the sense of feelings. There are also other words near that, like honshin (basic heart) or dogishin (moral heart).' Later he explained:

Conscience is a basic element in Japanese culture. It evolves around the tension between one's moral inner conviction and one's social duties. Sometimes the tension is irreconcilable and the solution is suicide or retirement to a monastery. Conscience was especially strong among the warrior (samurai) class, where both duty and inner conviction were stressed.

To help me, as a non-Japanese speaker, understand what it was all about Ben Ami recommended Ivan Morris's The Nobility of Failure (1975) and Paul Valery's Warriors of Japan (1994). The first thing I noticed was that neither volume mentions conscience even in the index. In the case of Warriors of Japan this is because only proper names are listed. That, however, does not apply to The Nobility of Failure, which does have entries for haji as well as 'loyalty' and 'sincerity'. As the title indicates, The Nobility of Failure deals with the lives of samurai, many of them more or less legendary. It concentrates on tales concerning the ways in which they prove their nobility in situations where they and their lords are about to be defeated. In the process they are exposed to conflicts between formal and emotional loyalty (loyalty based on the 'pathos of things', as the Japanese say), loyalty and death, dignity and death, life and obedience.[63] They may act in order to relieve the sufferings of the people, as the early nineteenth-century rebel Oshio Heihachiro did, but this is rare indeed. All the stories tell of the protagonists' almost superhuman effort and courage. However, their very sincerity dooms them from the outset. As Morris says, being Japanese they unerringly choose the losing side. They thrive not on victories but on difficulties and disasters.[64] In the end, defeated and looking death in the face, they give one final proof of their nobility. That is precisely how the tales or plays acquire their tragic character.

The most popular tale is the one of Minamoto no Yoshitsune. Many of the details are legendary, but unlike some others he was a historical figure who lived from 1159 to 1189. A scion of one of the two principal aristocratic clans of the time, he started as a melancholy boy who wandered about playing the flute. Later he grew into a cour-ageous but warmhearted warrior endowed with all the qualities needed to inspire men with fierce loyalty even unto death. At first Yoshitsune went from one victory to the next. However, lacking political acumen and deceitfulness he was betrayed by his brother Yoritomo. Ultimately he found himself in a situation where, with eight followers, he had to fight off 30,000. Cool and self-possessed to the end, he died by *seppuku*. The way the legends tell it, during his life Yoshitsune was admired both as a commander and as a human being, as indeed his great qualities entitled him to be. But it was his misfortune, defeat and stoic death that turned him into the hero of countless legends.[65]

Valery in *Warriors of Japan* is less concerned with the literary impact of the legends and more with using them in order to get at the under-lying historical reality. His is mainly a story not of nobility but of endless political manoeuvring, alliance-forming and betrayal that would have made Machiavelli blanch. We also learn of the most incredible atrocities, often committed on peaceful men, women and children. As the wood-and-paper towns in which they lived were set alight, their 'shrieks . . . could not have been surpassed by the sinners in the flames of hell'.[66] On one occasion alone 40,000 people lost their lives. Nevertheless the qualities that made some samurai infamous and others famous – in the latter case especially after their deaths – emerge clearly enough. Infamous men 'did not obey the rule of their old lords or former sovereigns, led dissolute lives, ignored admonitions, were not aware of the world's disorders, and were blind to the suffering of the people'. Famous ones were loyal – the most important quality of all – both to others and to themselves. They were also courageous and self-possessed unto the very end.

If the two works are representative, as Ben Ami says they are, then it seems to me that Japanese ideas of morality in many ways are much more like the Homeric *aidos* than like the subsequent *syneidēsis* and the modern conscience. As with Homer, the ideas in question are those of a warrior society where life and death are never far apart. As with Homer, the warriors compete with each other for excellence. They seek the most dangerous spots in battle and sometimes deliberately court death in their efforts to outshine everybody else. As with Homer, too, the choice facing them is not so much between evil and good as between advantage on the one hand and loyalty/honour/ sincerity on the other. Indeed it would be true to say that evil is advantage and good, loyalty/honour/sincerity. With rare exceptions, the nature of the cause for which the heroes fight only takes second place, if any. The more a hero stands to lose by giving up the former in favour of the latter, the greater the victory he wins through defeat and the more popular the legends that have been woven around him.

Alternatives to Conscience: China

To repeat, Shinto is not the only 'religion' that does not have a personal god. The latter is a characteristic it shares with the great Chinese systems of thought with which it is inextricably entwined: Confucianism, Daoism and Buddhism. These three have long been the dominant influences among about one-fifth of the world's population and certainly not the fifth whose future prospects, at the moment, appear the worst of all. To focus on Confucianism as the first and perhaps the most important, so great is its impact that several present-day

East and Southeast Asian governments have tried to 'hijack' it. They harnessed it to their own chariots and modified it as they did so.[67] Here our purpose is not to survey all religions but merely to show how a society without conscience can function. Hence we may use it as an example.

True enough, there is heaven. Transcribed as Tien or Tian, it is the friendly blue sky that covers 'all under heaven'.[68] To misuse Winston Churchill's words about the late unlamented Soviet Union, for those used to monotheistic religion, everything about Tian is a riddle wrapped in a mystery inside an enigma. It is neither God nor not-God, but contains aspects of both. Only one thing is certain: it is not dead matter but a living, sentient being. Nevertheless Confucianism does not recognize revelation, holy books, miracles or any kind of divine interference in human affairs.[69] While opinions about the exact nature of Tian have varied, generally it is understood less as a personal God and more as an impersonal power.

That in turn explains why occasional attempts by missionaries to identify Tian with the Christian God have been rejected by Chinese scholars. The latter even claimed that they were unable to understand what that God meant. In the absence of a personal God as the source of creation, people owe their existence to their parents and, through them, their ancestors and extended family into which they have been born and of which they remain a part for as long as they live. Stories are told of families comprising up to nine generations, including many collateral descendants and unrelated persons such as concubines and servants, all living together in the same compound.[70]

In theory there is no limit to the family's size. Ultimately it is identical with 'all under heaven', meaning the entire empire (barbarians do not count) and everybody in it. The Jewish, Graeco-Roman and Christian traditions all put a person's given name first. Not so the Chinese (and Japanese) ones, where surnames come first and proper ones last; thus the family, and through it society, is everything whereas the individual counts for very little. Confucius himself repeatedly pointed out that without society a human being did not exist. To this day, so strongly embedded is the tendency to put 'we' ahead of 'I' that Chinese who move to the West often find breaking the pattern very difficult.[71]

Apparently able to survive the ravages of both communism and modern capitalism, ideally the Confucian society is governed by five distinct sets of relationships. The strongest relationship is supposed to be that of king to subject. Next, in descending order, come father to son, husband to wife, elder brother to younger brother and friend to friend. Some sources provide slightly different lists. Note that none of the five is based on equality; that even applies to the one between friends, which is usually construed as senior to junior. All are mutually beneficial but they are also asymmetrical.[72] Since the idea of individual rights is unknown, inside each pair the superior party had extensive power to command, discipline and punish the inferior one. That is just why each superior is urged to exercise mildness and benevolence. Mildness and benevolence from above are supposed to be reciprocated by loyalty, respect and obedience from below. But for all these qualities life would be utterly chaotic and society could not exist.

Under this system there can be no single ethical standard such as the one Kant, basing himself on reason and seeking a single, universal paradigm, thought he had found. That even applies to the most basic rule of all, the Silver Rule, as formulated by Confucius himself: do not impose on others what you do not want to be imposed on yourself.[73] Instead social ties are seen like ripples in a pond. The further from the epicentre they spread, the weaker they become. Seeking to illustrate this idea, Confucius, while responding to a comment made by one of his disciples, referred to a situation in which a son turns in his father, who has stolen a sheep, to the authorities. He is recorded as saying that 'in our village those who are straight are quite different. Fathers cover up for their sons, and sons cover up for their fathers.' 'Straightness', Confucius added, 'is to be found in such behaviour.'[74] It is only fair to add that this is not the same as 'my father, right or wrong'. Gentle remonstrance is permitted and obligatory. Yet even if the remonstrance goes unheeded, one should still not become disobedient but remain respectful.[75]

Outside the family the same principle applies. Since standards of behaviour are not uniform, they keep changing just as people's social position in the community does. Confucius himself was always careful to calibrate his behaviour to the rank of his interlocutors.[76]

This relativism, which is said to distinguish Confucianism from any other religion or philosophy from either East or West, is sometimes known as role ethics.[77] Yet excellence does not consist of preferring one relationship to the rest. Rather it is to harmonize them all, not only at any one moment but flexibly as circumstances change over time. Obviously this is a supremely difficult task, but one which must nevertheless be performed both with joy and elegance.

The ethics of the masses are governed above all by their relations with the members of their families and the communities in which they live. Not so those of government officials. For them, putting their own house in order is but the first step in a long journey that lasts throughout life. But they must also serve the emperor and, through him, the empire and everything in it. A prerequisite for this was acquiring wide knowledge of everything. Much more than in any other country, in China government officials have always represented the educated elite. So great was their role in Confucius's scheme of things that subsequent generations, Mao and his Communists included, sometimes accused him, not entirely without reason, of addressing himself solely to them.[78]

As the reader will have noticed, the contrast with Machiavelli, Hegel and other Western proponents of 'reason of state' could not be greater. For those proponents, politics were incompatible with ethics as ordinarily understood. The higher ranking a statesman, the more he was *obliged* to ignore questions of conscience such as the ones other people confronted in their daily lives. Failing to do so was akin to treason, if it did not actually amount to it. In China the situation was just the opposite. No true Confucian would have expressed anything but contempt for a Cesare Borgia, that multiple murderer and occasional rapist. Such a sage would have looked at Frederick II as a foolish bleeding heart; he would never have agreed with Sonino that *sacro egoismo* can justify everything and anything. Instead the higher one's rank, the greater one's moral obligation, culminating in the emperor's own person.

True, the emperor should be as much concerned with the welfare of his empire as any Western ruler or statesman. But he could only maintain this welfare by supporting a moral burden far heavier than the one carried by any of his subjects. Should he fail in his duty towards Tian, then the outcome would be the withdrawal of the latter's mandate, or ming. There would be floods, droughts, earthquakes and similar natural disasters, leading to death for some and hunger for others. Hunger in turn might lead to uprisings among the peasantry who, throughout Chinese history, have formed the overwhelming majority of the population. As a famous proverb had it, when the peasantry is discontented all under Tian trembles. In extreme cases the emperor might lose his throne. He and his relatives would be killed and his dynasty come to an end. Even the empire itself might fall – either by being split into warring states or by being overrun by foreign barbarians, as happened several times in Chinese history.

In all this no distinction is made between private behaviour and politics. Dissolution, excessive drinking and engaging in orgies could lead to the same consequences as breaking treaties and betraying allies.[79] Thus China never introduced the Great Divide characteristic of so much Western political and ethical thought from Machiavelli on. Whether the outcome has been greater honesty or merely greater hypocrisy is moot. Be this as it may, the absence of a personal God capable of reading human minds caused a much greater emphasis to be put on outer behaviour as opposed to inner emotion.[80] The ideal to be aimed at, if those are the right words, is not spiritual redemption, let alone of the kind that takes place in the next world, as is the case in the Christian West.

Nor is the ideal a tragic if spectacular dénouement, as among the samurai and, through them, the rest of Japanese society brought up on their example. On the whole Chinese culture has little patience either with the person who wallows in remorse or with the failed hero who, sincere and faithful to the end, crowns his career by killing himself. Confucius himself did not take his leave of this world in a blaze of glory like some martyr or samurai. Reputedly he died of heartbreak following the death of his son and some of his leading disciples. What counts is ren, best understood as exemplary perfection. As with the Greek agathos, originally it may have referred to a quality that aristocrats reserved for themselves alone.[81] Later its meaning was extended downward until finally, at least in theory, it was within the reach of common people as well.

The outward manifestation of *ren* consists of performing a complex series of ancient rituals collectively known as li.[82] That is not to say that all rites are automatically approved of simply because they are old. According to legend Confucius himself persuaded his contemporaries to end human sacrifice. Broadly, though, the rites must be performed strictly as they had been transmitted by one's ancestors. They are not means to an end but ends in themselves; it is the spirit in which they are performed that matters. In Confucius' own words, if benevolence is lacking then of what use are the rites?[83] Ritual in turn must infuse life, transforming the whole of the latter into an extension of the former. Whether or not other people are watching is immaterial. There are many stories about hermits who distinguished themselves – the words form an oxymoron, but no better ones are available – by living the ideal, despite the isolation and sometimes extreme poverty to which it led. Confucius in the *Analects* expressed his admiration for some of them.

The Western idea of conscience, especially the Protestant one, often looks as if it takes positive delight in being 'troubled'. Not so Confucianism, which leaves little room either for agonizing before taking action or for remorse after doing so. Such agonizing and such remorse, far from being understood as indications of a high moral character, are seen as signifying weakness and imprudence. From the stories that have been woven around him, Confucius himself emerges as someone who made decisions carefully and deliberately. Once they had been made he rarely went back on them. On one occasion, told that a disciple by the name of Chi Wen Tzu always thought three times before taking action, he responded: 'twice is quite enough'.[84]

From beginning to end, the Confucian idea of conscience, if that is the word, does not involve a choice between good and evil as in the West. Nor was it one between honour/loyalty/sincerity and advantage as in Japan and other aristocratic warrior societies. One reason for this is because in China it was scholars who occupied leading positions and were expected to set the example. By contrast, soldiers tended to be regarded with some contempt. For the Confucian, what makes society tick is not conscience but reverence (*ching*).[85] It is that which causes us, each according to his or her station, to slip into and remain faithful to a way of life that will promote harmony first inside the family and then in society at large; self-interest and disruption must be avoided. No person can ever have just cause to act otherwise, not even by mistake. That is why traditional Chinese law did not recognize the distinction between murder and accidental homicide. Both Confucius and his most important student, Mencius, say that there are circumstances where even suicide is preferable to giving up Ren.[86]

The similarities to Stoicism, including also a certain kind of elitism, are obvious. Western missionaries, especially the great Matteo Ricci (1519–1612), noted them centuries ago.[87] Just as Stoicism had helped smooth the way to Christianity, they believed, so Confucianism might do the same. By and large their hopes were disappointed. What keeps the two creeds or philosophies apart is the fact that the Stoic individual, coming as he does before society, is perfect and unchanging. Not so the Confucian one; inextricably linked with society as he is, his Ren consists partly of his ability to adapt as his position in it changes.

To Confucians, the fact that even very young children respect their elders shows that the inclination towards such respect is innate. Potentially it is present in everybody. All that is needed is to foster it gently but firmly from the moment of birth on, starting with little things. If this is done the way it should be, then ultimately the bigger ones will take care of themselves. Confucius's followers have sometimes compared self-interest to clouds that obscure the sun; blowing them away would enable the light of the latter to be fully extended until it filled everybody and everything, leaving no dark spots.[88] As the Master himself put it in his succinct way, the best society is one in which the courts have nothing to do.[89] Using our own, more abstract terms, we might perhaps say that it is nothing less than a perfect fusion between the individual, society and Tian.

V

Conscience in the Third Reich

Those Who Commanded

To many who are familiar with the savage cruelty of Nazism and the unspeakable horrors of the Holocaust, the fact that Adolf Hitler understood himself as a good, even kindly person and certainly not as a wicked one may well come as a shock. Yet one only needs to delve a little into the sources to discover that such was indeed the case.

Reminiscing about his youth, repeatedly Hitler referred to himself as a 'scamp' among scamps. At school he and his chums could be unruly. However, the tricks they played did not involve ill-will, let alone evil intent.[1] In a letter to the Linz Municipality, written early in 1914 to excuse himself for not reporting for military service, Hitler claimed that 'despite cruel poverty in what were often dubious surroundings, I have always kept my name decent and completely spotless before the law and before my own conscience.'[2] If, during his four years at the front, he was any more vicious towards the enemy than was normal at that time and place, then none of those who knew him at the time said so.[3] There is no evidence that he ever used the dog-whip he liked to carry wherever he went. The First World War over, he never killed or assaulted anybody. On one occasion at Bayreuth in 1937, when told how shy people felt in his presence, he laughed and said that he had yet to see anybody who was afraid of him.[4]

From the emperors Caligula and Nero onwards, many absolute rulers have used their positions to engage in orgies of drunkenness and debauchery. Hitler, who always presented himself as 'a man of the people', did not live as modestly as he liked to pretend. However, unlike some of his paladins, especially Hermann Göring, who accepted bribes right and left and built a huge fortune, he was neither corrupt nor extravagant. There was no money stashed away in foreign countries, no stables full of mistresses, not even a bejewelled Madame de Pompadour who took an active role in shaping policy. Probably the worst sin he committed was commandeering works of art. They were meant for a museum he intended to build in Linz, the city where he had spent the happiest years of his youth and which he hoped to turn into a rival of Vienna. Shortly before his suicide he still was busying himself with the building plans. Briefly, in comparison with some others both before and since, his private life was a model of probity.

Compared with the rest of us, absolute rulers enjoy greater freedom because concepts such as law, reward (they can reward themselves) and punishment do not apply to them in the same form. That was precisely why Hitler, talking to his generals, said that he felt responsible only to his own 'conscience and sense of duty'. One of the best sources for his thought are the so-called 'Secret Conversations', a body of informal talks to close collaborators and occasional guests delivered at Headquarters between 1941 and 1944 and taken down in shorthand. They leave little doubt that he saw himself as a decent human being. 'I have a bad conscience when I get the feeling that I have not been quite fair to somebody.' 'I don't think a man should die of hunger because he has been my opponent. If he was a base opponent, then off to the concentration camp with him! But if he's not a swindler, I let him go free and I see that he has enough to live on.'

Discussing his chauffeurs and their responsibilities, Hitler said that 'I find it unpleasant when a car splashes mud on people lined up on the edge of the road, especially when they are people in their Sunday clothes.' Also that 'I've always avoided persecuting my enemies' and that he 'had never allowed anyone to resort to assassination in the political struggles'. No 'targeted killings', in other words. 'The method', he added,

> is generally inopportune, and to be recommended only in exceptional cases. In fact, it cannot lead to any important success, unless it enables one to eliminate the man on whose shoulders rests the whole organization and power of the

enemy. But even in such a case, I'd have refused to use this weapon.[5]

He conveniently forgot the dozens, perhaps hundreds, of victims killed during the Night of the Long Knives in June–July 1934. The way he saw it, however, probably most of them were not simply opponents but traitors. They were getting ready to mount an armed coup and were only stopped in the nick of time. As to the very numerous smaller fry who died of brutality in the camps, he can hardly have concerned himself with every case.

In late 1944 he told his doctor, Theodor Morel, that he was 'not an ungrateful person'.[6] None of this changes the fact that, in the whole of history, very few rulers have been responsible for the deaths of more innocent people than the Führer of the Greater German Reich, as it was known from late 1939 on. Did that realization leave him untouched, gliding off him as water glides off the back of a duck? Or did it bother him, at least occasionally and to some extent? The problem is best tackled by focusing on two issues: the deaths of several million German soldiers and civilians on the one hand and those of more millions of Jewish men, women and children as well as other 'undesirables' on the other.

Concerning the former, the evidence, though scant, seems to be fairly clear. 'If I am reproached with having sacrificed a hundred or two hundred thousand men by reason of the war', he is recorded as saying in 1941 not long after the opening of the Russian campaign,

> I can answer that, thanks to what I have done, the German nation has gained, up to the present, more than two million, five hundred thousand human beings. If I demand a tenth of this as a sacrifice, nevertheless I have given 90 percent. I hope that in ten years there will be ten to fifteen millions more of us Germans in the world. Whether they are men or women, it matters little; I am creating conditions favorable to growth.

And: 'I should regard it as a crime to have sacrificed the lives of German soldiers simply for the conquest of natural riches to be

exploited in the capitalist style.' Better ways to distribute the
would have to be found. In giving every man his chance, he cla
'[his] conscience [was] clean'.[7] Briefly, German soldiers' bloo
the most precious resource in the world. Accordingly the possi
that this might indeed have happened, or might happen, di
leave him indifferent.

At least one officer, who was in almost daily contact with H
is quoted as writing that he was too soft-hearted to be a good c
mander. According to this person, whose name we do not know
who may have been his chief operations officer Alfred Jodl, 'casua
which he was compelled to deal with personally, or of which he
given realistic descriptions, were a source of horror to him and ol
ously caused him as much suffering as the deaths of people he kne
'He was afraid of his own softness and susceptibility, which wo
have hampered him in making the decisions that his political v
demanded of him.'[8] One would be inclined to dismiss this, but oth
sources support this idea. Albert Speer recounts an episode wh
Hitler's train was accidentally standing on a parallel track next
another one filled to overflowing with the dirty, hungry wounde
coming from the Eastern Front. He could see them, and they wer
looking straight at him as he was standing at the window of hi
luxurious, well-lit cabin.

Based on his experience during the First World War, Hitler always
claimed to have a good understanding of and sympathy for the mentality of simple soldiers at the front: 'the poor worms', as he used to
call them. That was something not even the generals who were most
critical of his leadership cared to deny. In spite of this – perhaps
because of it – rather than taking the opportunity to visit them, he had
the curtains drawn. Repeatedly Goebbels suggested that he should
tour bombed cities as Churchill often did. Just as repeatedly Hitler
refused, saying he could very well imagine what it was like.[9]

If only because the matter was kept secret as far as possible, when
it comes to the extermination of the Jews the evidence is more ambigu-
ous. The idea, first raised by David Irving in the late 1970s, that the
Führer's subordinates kept him ignorant of the Holocaust has now
been firmly refuted.[10] The mass shootings of Jews in Russia was prepared ahead of time and started very soon after the invasion of that

country got under way on 22 June 1941. However, the 'Secret Conversations' do not have a word to say about this fact. In respect to German
Jews the situation is different. On the night of 8–9 August 1941 Hitler
said that

> if any people has the right to proceed to evacuations, it is we,
> for we've often had to evacuate our own population. Eight
> hundred thousand men had to emigrate from East Prussia
> alone. How humanely sensitive we are is shown by the fact
> that we consider it a maximum of brutality to have liberated
> our country from six hundred thousand Jews. And yet we
> accepted without recrimination, and as something inevitable,
> the evacuation of our own compatriots![11]

As a matter of fact, the evacuation of German and other Jews had not
yet begun but was only being considered as various people submitted
their ideas. Was Hitler testing the waters to gauge his listeners'
reaction, or was he genuinely concerned with the question of right?
In the event, the actual decision to evacuate, and then to kill, was
made on 16–17 September in a series of meetings involving Hitler,
ss commander Heinrich Himmler, foreign minister Joachim von
Ribbentrop and others. At that time the Führer optimistically assumed
that the Soviet Union would be defeated by 15 October.[12]

On 23 January 1942 he returned to the topic. One of the guests
was Himmler. By this time, with the Wehrmacht retreating from
Moscow and the u.s. joining his enemies, Hitler probably began to
realize that the war could no longer be won. This was also the time,
more or less, when the first extermination camps were starting
operations.

> One must act radically. When one pulls out a tooth, one does
> it with a single tug, and the pain quickly goes away. The Jew
> must disappear from Europe. Otherwise no understanding
> will be possible between Europeans. It is the Jew who prevents
> everything. When I think about it, I realize that I am extra-
> ordinarily humane . . . I restrict myself to telling them that
> they must go away. If they refuse to go voluntarily, I see no

other solution but extermination. Why should I look at a Jew through other eyes than if he were a Russian prisoner of war? In the POW camps, many are dying. It's not my fault. I didn't want either the war or the POW camps. Why did the Jews provoke this war?[13]

And again four days later:

The Jew must pack up, disappear form Europe. Let them go to Russia. Where the Jews are concerned, I am devoid of all sense of pity. They'll always be the ferment that moves peoples one against the other. They sow discord everywhere, as much between individuals as between peoples. They'll also have to clear out of Switzerland and Sweden. It is where they are to be found in small numbers that they are most dangerous.[14]

More light on the matter is shed by something else he said in late September 1941. Referring to another crime he intended to commit – the destruction of the 'Bolshevik capital' of St Petersburg which his troops were then besieging – he said:

Plainly I belong by nature to quite another species. I would prefer not to see anyone suffer, not to do harm to anyone. But when I realize that the species is in danger, then in my case sentiment gives way to the coldest reason. I become uniquely aware of the sacrifices that the future will demand, to make up for the sacrifices that one hesitates to allow today.[15]

All this sounds very much as if he were trying to justify himself – to himself first and foremost, or why bring up these subjects at all?

To me, these and other episodes – several of which involved 'gracious ladies' whom he liked and in whose eyes he did not want to appear heartless[16] – suggest that, when he claimed that the crimes he was ordering contradicted his real nature as a 'humane' person whom nobody needs fear, he may well have been giving voice to some kind of subjective truth. In 1940–41 he rejected the plans of Reinhard Heydrich, the second highest ranking officer in the machine in charge of extermination, whose nickname was 'the hangman', as too radical. To be sure, he did so for political reasons and not for conscientious ones. Proud of his intuition, which supposedly enabled him to gauge the mood of the German people better than anyone else, he felt that they were not yet ready for carrying out the proposed measures.[17] Still, the speech he delivered at Heydrich's funeral (Heydrich was assassinated in June 1942) is interesting. He called the deceased 'the man with the iron heart'.[18] That does not sound like a compliment.[19] The reader is free to interpret these incidents and any similar ones that have come to light or may still come to light in any way he or she wishes.

Occupying the key position between Hitler and Heydrich was Heinrich Himmler. In June 1934 he and Hermann Göring, the latter in his capacity as the founder of the Gestapo among other things, had been primarily responsible for organizing the purge of the SA. Göring on his part shrugged off the murders. By 7 July, a mere week after they had taken place, he was wining and dining those responsible in a beer garden specially constructed for the purpose at his country house, Carinhall. Captain Hawes, the British naval attaché who got to know him well, once described him as 'a mountain of egotism and pomposity'.[20] Not so Himmler who, true to character, felt obliged to justify himself. Speaking to a meeting of all Gestapo officials in October of that year, he described the Night of the Long Knives as 'the hardest day that can be visited on a soldier in his lifetime. To have to shoot one's own comrades, with whom one has stood side by side for eight or ten years in the struggle for an idea, and who had then failed, is the bitterest thing that can happen to a man.' He went on to put the blame on the Jews, Freemasons and Catholics. They had, he claimed, infiltrated the entourage of SA commander Ernst Rhoem and 'driven him to catastrophe'.[21]

Six years later, on 15 May 1940, Himmler prepared an interesting memorandum for Hitler. It had, he claimed, the Führer's 'full approval'.[22] The subject was 'racially pure children of foreign peoples in the east'. They would, provided their parents agreed and as a condition for receiving a good education unavailable in their native lands, be removed to Germany and brought up as Germans. 'Cruel and tragic as this may be in each individual case', Himmler reasoned,

'If from inner conviction one rejects the Bolshevik method of physical extermination as un-German and impossible, then this method is still the mildest and the best.' Presumably similar considerations applied to the Jews, or else it is hard to see why, in the same memorandum, Himmler mentioned the possibility of assembling them and sending them to 'Africa'.

That was not destined to be the last word on the subject. By July 1941, in the occupied Russian territories, what had previously been 'un-German and impossible', namely the execution not only of men but of women and children as well, had turned into everyday practice. Again the contrast between Göring and Himmler is illuminating. The fat, pleasure-seeking Reichsmarschal did what he could to avoid seeing and hearing evil, though less so because his conscience was bothering him than because he was terrified of what Hitler might say and do if he made a wrong move.[23] The abstemious Himmler took the exact opposite tack. His somewhat jejune style of leadership always made him insist on doing, or at least witnessing, everything his subordinates did in his name, big or small. Among other things, when aged over 40, he still insisted on honestly winning a physical fitness badge. Knowing their man, his subordinates responded by secretly lowering the requirements so as to enable him to do so.

On 15 August 1941, in one of his numerous journeys of inspection, he flew to Minsk. There Arthur Nebe, commander of Einsatzgruppe B, organized an *Aktion* for his superior's benefit. The details are known from the testimony of another SS General, Erich von dem Bach-Zelewski. His job was to fight partisans; however, no fine distinctions were drawn and the relevant documents often say that, in addition to 'bandits', so and so many Jews were shot.[24] The demonstration involved some 200 Jews, not a large number as such things went. Most were young men, but there were also some women and children. The location was a field where two trenches had been dug, each 8 m long, 2 wide and 2 deep. The victims were made to lie face down in the pits. Beside each one a twelve-man firing squad took up position.

Standing on the edge of the first pit, where he had a good view, Himmler commented that it was as well that he could watch it for himself for once. He came from a good middle-class family; he had never seen anybody being killed before. He jerked convulsively, passed his hands across his face and staggered, his face turning green. At one point he took out a handkerchief to wipe off pieces of brain that had splashed on to his cheek and coat, heaving as he turned away. Later he commented that 'I can tell you it is hideous and frightful for a German to have to see such things.' While those who carried out the Aktion would no doubt have seen how much he hated the bloody business, he added, he wanted them to do their duty, hard as it might be. Again the reader is invited to draw his or her own conclusions.

On their way back from the killing fields, von dem Bach-Zelewski told his commander that the members of the firing squads were now ruined for life, destined to become either nervous wrecks or ruffians. This problem was one of the reasons that caused Himmler to start looking for 'more humane' methods of execution. Others included the inefficiency of the process and the impossibility of keeping it secret. In his quest the Reichsführer and his subordinates could look back to the model provided by the T-4 euthanasia programme, which at that time was in full swing. In it, use was made first of the exhaust gas of internal combustion engines and then of the cyanide-based insecticide Zyklon B. Construction of the various camps, along with their gas chambers, began in the autumn and went on for several months. It was at this time that Himmler told his subordinates that 'he was making a superhuman-inhuman demand on them, but it was by order of the Führer.'[25] This does not sound like a man who was unaware of the moral difficulties that carrying out the most horrible of all orders involved.

On 4 October 1943 Himmler addressed the assembled ss commanders as well as some others.[26] First he surveyed the situation on the various fronts. Then he focused on the main point. 'I also want', went the crucial passage,

> to mention a very difficult subject before you here, completely openly. It should be discussed amongst us, and yet, never-theless, we will never speak about it in public. Just as we did not hesitate on June 30 to carry out our duty, as ordered, and stand comrades who had failed against the wall and shoot them. About which we have never spoken, and never will

speak. That was, thank God, a kind of tact natural to us, a foregone conclusion of that tact, that we have never conversed about it amongst ourselves, never spoken about it, everyone shuddered, and everyone was clear that the next time, he would do the same thing again, if it were commanded and necessary. I am talking about the 'Jewish evacuation'; the extermination of the Jewish people. It is one of those things that is easily said. 'The Jewish people is being exterminated', every Party member will tell you, 'perfectly clear, it's part of our plans, we're eliminating the Jews, exterminating them, ha! a small matter'. And then along they all come, all the 80 million upright Germans, and each one has his decent Jew. They say: all the others are swine, but here is a first-class Jew. And none of them has seen it, has endured it. Most of you will know what it means when 100 bodies lie together, when there are 500, or when there are 1000. And to have seen this through, and – with the exception of human weaknesses – to have remained decent, has made us hard and is a page of glory never mentioned and never to be mentioned . . . We have taken away the riches that they had, and I have given a strict order . . . we have delivered these riches completely to the Reich, to the State. We have taken nothing from them for ourselves. A few, who have offended against this, will be [judged] in accordance with an order, that I gave at the beginning: He who takes even one Mark of this is a dead man . . . We have the moral right, we had the duty to our people to do it, to kill this people who wanted to kill us. But we do not have the right to enrich ourselves with even one fur, with one Mark, with one cigarette, with one watch, with anything . . . Because at the end of this, we don't want, because we exterminated the bacillus, to become sick and die from the same bacillus. I will never see it happen, that even one bit of putrefaction comes in contact with us, or takes root in us. On the contrary, where it might try to take root, we will burn it out together. But altogether we can say: We have carried out this most difficult task for the love of our people. And we have taken on no defect within us, in our soul, or in our character.

Most historians agree that Himmler's purpose in delivering the speech was to warn his audience, both those who knew about the ongoing process of exterminating the Jews and the few who did not, that they had burnt their bridges. The choice they faced was between fighting on in the hope of gaining a (Nazi) heaven on the one hand and literally going to hell on the other. This interpretation is probably correct. Yet it is also true that some of what he said, especially about the need to stamp out corruption and avoid infection, cannot be explained in this way. Reacting against the rowdies of the SS parent organization, the SA, Himmler always thought of the former – the one he himself headed – as akin to a medieval order.[27] He did what he could to infuse his men with a sober, somewhat ascetic code of behaviour. In this he enjoyed the support of Heydrich as his highest-ranking subordinate.[28] There was supposed to be no swaggering, no drunkenness, no personal animosity towards the victims and no sadism. Orders were to be formulated and carried out in a spirit of cool, bureaucratic efficiency.

Not for nothing did the inscription on the SS men's belts run: *Unsere Ehre heisst Treue* (our honour is our loyalty), as if loyalty could justify even the most hideous crimes. Another key term Himmler often used in his speeches was *Anständigkeit*. He did so, for example, when he hectored Walter Schellenberg, the head of the SS Security Service, soon after Heydrich's assassination, and again when addressing armament workers immediately after the failed attempt on Hitler's life.[29] Best translated as an amalgam of decorousness, appropriateness, correctness, seemliness, honesty, integrity, frankness, respectability, reliability, loyalty (or rather, the opposite of disloyalty) and decency, *Anständigkeit* was to be maintained at all costs, even if doing so involved using brutality.[30] He also believed that the conflict between the need for 'decency' and the many horrifying orders he had to give and witnessed being executed cost him dear, resulting in severe stomach cramps that never left him throughout the war.[31]

By assuming that he had succeeded and that profiteering was, in fact, limited to a few cases, Himmler displayed a surprising naivety. As his Finnish masseur, Felix Kersten, who knew him as well as anybody did, later wrote, at bottom Himmler was a romantic. Not only was he proud of his own honesty in keeping his word, but he really thought his men, or most of them, would behave similarly. Knowing how seriously their boss took these things, many of those men abused their advantage to the limit of their ability.[32] When Himmler in the same speech said that exterminating the Jews, women and children included, was 'the most difficult task that we have ever had to undertake', he was not referring to any technical problems. Relative to running a world war, the latter were minor. For example, just *forty* SS men – of whom never more than twenty were active at any one moment – plus some Polish, Lithuanian and Ukrainian assistants operated the death camp at Treblinka. In it, some 900,000 people perished.[33]

The evidence regarding other top-level Nazi leaders is too meagre to allow any conclusions to be drawn. Goebbels in his diary at one point says that the process whereby the Jews were being eliminated – he must have been referring to the gassings – was 'pretty barbaric'. He consoled himself with the thought that 'they [had] brought it upon themselves'.[34] The claim that 'my conscience is called Adolf Hitler' has been variously attributed to Hermann Göring and to Labour Front leader Robert Ley. Supposing the words were ever uttered, they can be understood in two ways. Either they meant that the speaker intended to follow orders and act without any considerations regarding right and wrong or else that he was shaking off responsibility, putting it on the Führer's shoulders. The two possibilities are not mutually exclusive.

To return to Hitler and Himmler, the former talked of turning 'ice-cold'; the latter, of decency and the hardness needed both to carry out one's terrible duty and to avoid personal gain and corruption. Obeying Hitler's orders, he had always sought 'to do what was right', even if it meant acting against his inner convictions. Nevertheless he had 'always been ready . . . to examine individual cases on humanitarian grounds and, if at all possible, provide a generous response'.[35] Given the contexts in which they spoke, in neither case is there any reason to suspect hypocrisy. Hitler almost certainly, and Himmler among other things, were trying to justify themselves in the eyes of others as well as their own. Theirs, I dare suggest, is hardly the language people who do not know the meaning of scruples would use. Even less is there an indication that they rejoiced in killing for its own sake. As Himmler himself explained in his speech, his goal was to create a new sort of morality, one that Germans would apply in their relations with each other but to nobody else; not to make do without any at all.

To say this is not to exonerate either him or Hitler himself. As the greatest Modern Hebrew poet, Haim Nahman Bialik, once wrote, not even the Devil himself can avenge the pain inflicted on a small child. On the contrary, it makes them even more repulsive as well as explaining how the crimes they ordered, supervised and committed acquired the peculiarly perverted, twisted character they had and which will cause them to be remembered not just for a limited number of years but for all time to come.

Those Who Killed

If those who commanded were sometimes beset by doubts which made their crimes even more horrible, how about those who killed? Von dem Bach-Zelewski, the reader will recall, warned Himmler that the members of the Einsatzgrüppen who carried out the mass liquidations were 'ruined for life'. Is there evidence that this is indeed the case? Did men join the Grüppen because they were psychopaths? Or did participation in mass murder turn them into such? Did the executioners give rise to more than their fair share of disciplinary problems? And how about those who survived the war and returned home after it was over? Did they feel remorse, become criminals, find their way into insane asylums or turn to drink?

The literature about the perpetrators of the Holocaust is vast and growing. However, few scholars have approached the subject with these questions in mind. Perhaps the best place to start is a well-known work by Christopher Browning, *Ordinary Men* (1992). Based on the records of inquiries held in the 1960s as well as some other contemporary and subsequent material, it tells the story of the 101st Reserve Police Battalion and the 'final solution' in Poland. The battalion's home base was Hamburg, a well-established, wealthy and unusually cosmopolitan port city. Like most members of the Einsatzgrüppen, junior officers included, the men were ordinary people not previously noted for anything in particular. They did not volunteer for the unit, let alone the specific job, but were simply drafted into it. In other words, there could be no question of self-selection.[36]

The average age of the rank and file was 39 years. Thus they were old enough to remember life before the Nazis took over and the most virulent kind of anti-Semitism became the order of the day. Almost two-thirds were working-class people: sailors, dock, warehouse and construction workers, truck drivers, waiters and the like. Just over a third came from the lower middle classes – white-collar office workers, sales clerks and so on. About a quarter of them were Nazi Party members, though most had only joined after the 'seizure of power', presumably in an attempt to grab at whatever privileges doing so might bring. Himmler always expended considerable care in choosing his main subordinates. But that did not apply to the relatively junior officers who commanded the units that actually did the killings, few if any of whom held ranks higher than that of major – let alone to the rank and file. If anything the selection was negative. Reaching maturity during the Weimar years, the men had never received military training, and by this time they were considered too old to serve in the Wehrmacht. A forty-something reserve lieutenant or captain whose commission dated to the last years of the First World War did not exactly make promising military material either.

Nor did the men receive any special training for the task ahead. Officially they only learnt its nature at the last moment, though rumours about this may have started circulating earlier. The first time the battalion carried out mass murder was on 13 July 1942. The location was Józéfow, not far from Lublin. The commander of the 101st Reserve Police Battalion was a kindly 53-year-old major by the name of Wilhelm Trapp. Known to his men as 'father', upon receiving the order on the previous day he wept and complained bitterly. Moreover, he made no attempt to hide his distress so that his main subordinates were fully aware of it. Later he absented himself from the actual killings whenever he could.

Yet he also said that orders were orders. Explaining the mission to his men, Trapp explicitly gave them permission to step out if they felt they could not carry out his instructions. Only about a dozen out of 500 did so. The rest proceeded to round up and shoot the 1,500

Jews of the township, women and children included. Over the next year or so a series of similar *Aktions* resulted in the death of at least 38,000 Jews. Another 45,000 were assembled and marched to railway stations. During these marches any person who could not keep up owing to age, gender or sickness was shot on the spot. At the stations they were put aboard trains whose destination was the death camp at Treblinka. Directly or indirectly, the total number of victims the battalion claimed before it was recalled to Hamburg in May 1943 was about 83,000.

Browning, a careful historian, believes that the men could be divided into three groups. A few, some officers included, developed into sadistic killers who enjoyed their work. They regularly volunteered for 'special missions' and were always looking for better ways to kill their victims. Some even begged to be allowed to participate in the massacres. A somewhat larger number refused outright, often at the risk of being berated by their comrades, who blamed them for their 'cowardice' and 'weakness'. Also included in this group were those who found various ways to avoid participating in the actual killings, for example, by insisting on being detailed to cordon duty or simply by falling sick at the right moment. The third and much the largest group obeyed their orders without any particular protest. Liberal doses of alcohol, regularly issued after each action, helped.

At one point Helmut James von Moltke, a relative of the great nineteenth-century commander and a leading anti-Nazi, informed his wife of a conversation he had had with an unnamed nurse. She told him that a special hospital had been established for executioners who could no longer go on.[37] However, the story has never been verified. Whatever the truth, the battalion and its subordinate units, companies and platoons remained intact. Large numbers of desertions and disobedience, let alone a revolt, did not occur. The evidence does not allow the identification of even one occasion when disciplinary problems prevented the battalion or its subordinate units, companies or platoons from carrying out its mission. This is all the more remarkable because, throughout the period when they killed or rounded up an average of almost 300 Jews per day, apparently not one man was severely punished for refusing to play his part. It was always possible to find a way to exempt oneself, be assigned to other duties and the like.

Had resistance to orders or attempts to evade them become more widespread and assumed an organized character, things would have changed. In the five years from 1939 to the end of 1944, when the recording system broke down and the numbers shot skywards, the Wehrmacht is said to have executed at least 18,000 of its own men. Most were accused either of desertion or of the offence known as *Zersetzung der Wehrkraft* (undermining morale) by talking of Hitler's deficient leadership, the inevitability of defeat and so on.[38] Himmler, who commanded both the SS and the German police, was even more ruthless. Had resistance, let alone organized resistance, on the part of men of the 101st Reserve Police Battalion interfered with its operations to any noticeable extent, he would surely have resorted to harsh disciplinary measures.

Instead those involved in implementing the 'Final Solution' became used to their gruesome work.[39] One consequence was that whatever reluctance or resistance did exist at first tended to diminish rather than to grow. In fact it was so limited that Himmler probably never heard of it. A few of Trapp's men died during their time in Poland, mostly in encounters with Jews who had escaped, hidden in the forests and sometimes offered armed resistance when detected and attacked. Others were transferred to other units, front-line ones included. Others still were sent back to Hamburg. How many survived the war is unknown. During the 1960s, 210 were investigated for war crimes, thus providing the source material for Browning's research. But only a few were tried, and even fewer were convicted. Presumably many others who stayed alive understandably kept a low profile. They seem to have merged into the surrounding society without experiencing sufficiently severe emotional problems to attract attention. Some even built on their wartime record. They stayed in the police, turning what had originally been a temporary assignment into a permanent career.

During their investigations and trials the men often claimed they had acted under duress. As had also been the case during the trials of the major war criminals in Nuremberg, few if any spoke of regret or contrition. Whatever anti-massacre feelings they admitted to harbouring were based on physical revulsion, not on moral principles. Presumably the reason why conscience was left unmentioned was because speaking of it would have been tantamount to admitting that they did have a choice. Many also took care to emphasize that personally they did not have anything against Jews. This in turn may well have had something to do with the fact that, according to German law, one criterion for distinguishing between homicide and murder is the presence, in the case of the latter, of a 'base motive'.[40]

The trouble is that at the time they were investigated and charged, the men of the 101st Reserve Police Battalion were presumably prepared to say almost anything to save their hides. In so far as they may be reconstructed, the men's motives and feelings during the period when they were engaged in mass-massacring men, women and children are more interesting. Browning believes that anti-Jewish Nazi propaganda played a relatively small role. This is just the opposite of what other scholars specializing in the Holocaust have claimed. They also emphasize the uncanny ability of propaganda, provided it is sufficiently intense and sufficiently prolonged, to turn black into white and white into black.

Personally I tend to agree with Browning. To be sure, Himmler regarded himself as the educator of the German people in general and of the ss in particular.[41] He and his subordinates organized lectures, disseminated reading material and so on. In the case of the 101st Reserve Police Battalion, and presumably others as well, specific orders had been issued to the commanding officer to 'blot out' the terrible impressions of the day. The methods included comradely evening parties, music and lectures concerning the political necessity that allegedly drove the atrocities.[42] However, most of the propaganda material used for the purpose was of a very low quality likely to bore people – these, after all, were no rocket scientists. Nor do we know whether it did convince many of those who came in contact with it; if indeed they did come into contact with it at a time when, with the deprivations and horrors of war all around them, they were always driving in the mud from one godforsaken Polish village to another.

Along with Browning, I think that a much more important role was played by unit cohesion. Its very purpose, after all, is to produce men who will do what they are told. As military history shows, its importance in making them function even in carrying out the most difficult and perhaps dangerous tasks under the most appalling hardships cannot be exaggerated. Then and later, the Wehrmacht was famous for its ability to create and maintain cohesion. Probably no other factor contributed as much to its outstanding fighting power. If only because they looked up to the Wehrmacht and often modelled themselves on it, other German military and paramilitary organizations were not far behind. With Himmler at their head, they did what they could to prove that they, too, were 'soldiers'. As a result men, commanders specifically included, who objected, hesitated or shirked their 'duty' were certain to be resented or derided by the rest.

Much of the pressure in question was exercised by a man's comrades. However, it also enjoyed the powerful support of the command hierarchy. That hierarchy well knew how to wield the carrot and the stick. As the famous experiments by Stanley Milgram and Philip Zimbardo showed, turning ordinary people into sadistic executioners or prison wardens is much easier than is commonly thought.[43] As in those experiments, there were always some who resisted whatever pressure was brought to bear on them.

The reader will recall that, in Germany, the link between conscience and duty was a particularly powerful one. It went back to Kant, the Prussian monarchy (which ended up by imposing itself on the entire country) and ultimately Luther himself. Were the killers devoid of conscience, as people who contemplate the atrocities tend to think at first sight? Or was it precisely their conscience – a special kind of conscience, to be sure, but still a conscience – that made them carry out their 'duty' regardless of any personal feelings that at least some of them may have had? In 1998 the American historian Daniel Goldhagen published *Hitler's Willing Executioners*, a book specifically meant to refute Browning. In it he tried to show that many Germans went way beyond the call of duty. Drawing on a long tradition of what he calls 'exterminationist anti-Semitism', they were quite happy to abuse their Jewish victims whenever they could and as much as they could. Again I find myself siding with Browning. As the latter admits, undoubtedly some killers found their way into the Einsatzgrüppen because they were sadists to begin with. Others were turned into sadists by the work itself. The same was true of concentration camp guards.[44] But for the majority orders were orders. The more time passed, the more this tended to become the case. Apparently people become habituated to committing mass murder in the same way as they become habituated to so many other things, from smoking to writing books.

Close study of the most important killer of all, Rudolf Höss, seems to confirm this view. The son of a retired major in the German Colonial Army, Höss was born in 1901. As he recorded in the autobiography he wrote while being held in a Polish prison after the Second World War, he was brought up 'in deep feeling of duty. In my parents' home all instructions had to be executed exactly and with commitment.'[45] This kind of 'conscience', one that countless Germans and by no means only Germans shared, in many ways made him into the ideal subordinate: one who could be relied upon under the most difficult circumstances. Originally Höss had planned to become a Catholic priest. However, at the age of sixteen he tricked his way into the Army and saw action in the Middle East. After the war he returned home, joined a Free Company, or Freikorps, and saw more fighting in the Baltic. In 1923 he and some others were convicted for murdering a man suspected of having betrayed the saboteur Leo Schlageter to the French authorities during the occupation of the Ruhr. Though he was freed in 1928, his involvement did not exactly improve his chances of obtaining employment.

Several other luminaries of the extermination programme, such as ss generals Oskar Dirlewanger and Odo Globocnik, as well as the commander of the Treblinka death camp, Franz Stangl, had also been involved in crimes, or at least disciplinary problems. So, if one may believe Waffen ss general Georg Keppler, were some of the rank-and-file members of the Einsatzgrüppen.[46] This made them vulnerable to blackmail from above, a fact their superiors did not hesitate to use when necessary.[47] Freed just as the Great Depression got under way, Höss, with little prospect of employment, joined the ss in 1933. Next he made his modest way up by working in various concentration camps. He claims to have been deeply shocked by the first flogging he watched. Later, too, he felt 'compassion' for the prisoners. However, not wanting to admit his 'sensitivity' to his superiors and ask them for a transfer, he always put on a 'stone face'. In 1941 he was promoted to lieutenant-colonel. That summer he was put in charge of Auschwitz, a former Polish Army base. It was simply a concentration camp; there were no gas chambers yet.

Höss and quite some others of his kind glided into the role of mass murderers, so to speak. By his own testimony, he never doubted the 'need' to exterminate the Jews as the ultimate enemies of the Reich, which had been drilled into him for years. This very claim also enabled him, as well as many others from Eichmann down, to say that he personally had nothing against those Jews.[48] First he studied the best methods to carry out his mission by visiting the installations at which, at the time, the mentally ill and the disabled were being killed. Next he implemented those methods on a much larger scale. His sense of duty, alias 'conscience', drove him even when he presided over the murder and death of between two and a half and three million people (his own estimate at the Nuremberg War Crimes Trials).[49] Strange to say, this was the same sense that also drove some of the victims to obey the decrees ordering them to present themselves at the gathering points from where they were transported to the extermination camps.

Like any good commander, Höss took it for granted that 'the camp commandant is fully responsible for everything that happens in the camp.' In his autobiography he explains that, to the extent that his conscience bothered him at all, it was not because of the incredible crimes over which he was presiding day after day. It was because circumstances did not always enable him to meet each of the instructions Himmler and his staff had issued to regulate camp life. On other occasions the problem was the opposite. While he did obey orders, he could not help noting how some of them impeded efficiency.

In his cell at Nuremberg, Höss often talked to the prison psychiatrist, Gustave Gilbert. He said that, living in a villa (which still exists) near the camp along with his wife, Hedwig, their children, and some servants, he did not experience any particular psychological problems. That specifically included sexual problems.[50] His youngest daughter, Annegret, was actually conceived and born at the time when, not far away, millions were dying at his orders. How this can be reconciled with the claim, which can be found in his autobiography, that at one point she refused to go on sleeping with him is not clear. From time to time he would feel distress. To cope with it he would spend hours riding one of the horses he kept. In his last letter to his wife he plaintively wrote of the 'long-term, ironhanded training in the SS' he had undergone. It had turned him, originally a 'kind, pleasant, always friendly' person into 'a robot blindly following orders'.

Following his capture, the same kind of conscientiousness turned him into a model prisoner. Having been sentenced to death, just four days before his execution on 16 April 1948, Höss wrote to the Polish state prosecutor. He said that his conscience 'compel[led]' him to make a declaration. Alone in his cell, he had come to the 'bitter recognition' that he had 'sinned gravely'. As commandant of Auschwitz he had 'inflicted terrible wounds on humanity' and caused 'unspeakable suffering for the Polish people in particular'.[51] For that he would pay with his life and he could only beg God's forgiveness. Neither letter should necessarily be taken at face value. The one to his wife was almost certainly intended to shift the blame from himself to his superiors and the system they had built. The fact that, in the one he addressed to the prosecutor, he spoke of Poles rather than of Jews – for a long time thereafter, the Polish government refused to acknowledge the Holocaust as an event separate from that of their own people – is not without significance.[52] It may indicate that, even while facing the gallows, Höss was acting on some kind of instructions given him by somebody else. It is not impossible that he was hoping to gain a reprieve at the last moment.

Be this as it may, other killers did not even go that far. Among Höss's subordinates were three lowly SS men, Oswald Kaduk, Wilhelm Boger and Josef Klehr. All three had been born between 1904 and 1906. All three became SS men during the late 1930s, either volunteering for the organization or being drafted into it. Not being officer material, and too old to do front-line duty, almost accidentally all three found themselves at Auschwitz. The accounts of their sadistic deeds defy belief. Later all three returned to their wives and families. All found and maintained steady employment. Kaduk was active as a nurse in a hospital – one who, owing to his solicitude in looking after his patients, earned the nickname 'Papa Kaduk!' None is known to have suffered from any special psychological problems such as drunkenness and the like; if it had been Hitler's and Himmler's objective to rid them and many others like them of their 'Jewish' conscience, then clearly they succeeded all too well.

During the 1960s all three were arrested, tried, convicted and sentenced. Interviewed in prison after his trial, Kaduk said that right and wrong had been irrelevant. He had done as he had been told, and in any case could not have changed anything. No, Auschwitz did not figure in his dreams, because he had 'switched off'. No, he had not felt any scruples. And yes, on some points he had refused to testify so as not to compromise other ss men. He did, however, agree that 'if everything the prosecution witnesses say of me were true, then I would not be worthy of having the sun shine on me.'[53] Klehr on his part said that having to describe the way he killed people by means of injections to the heart was very painful to him. However, he too insisted that he had no choice and that he was just following orders. That was why he only felt 'a little guilty'.[54] Duty was duty. Of Boger, we know that he ended his days – he died in 1977 – as a broken old man. His suffering did not stem from contrition but from the fact that his family, having disowned him, refused to let him see his grandchildren. Other former guards also went on to lead normal lives.

Looking back, clearly whatever conscience these and other men (and women: there were some female concentration camp guards)[55] may have had was not strong enough to prevent the atrocities from taking place or even to interfere with them to any considerable extent. This may have been due to a combination of 'iron discipline' (Höss's expression) and peer pressure, as Browning claims, or else to indoctrination. At times all three were mixed with a strong dose of sadism, as Goldhagen, and even more so some recent psychological studies, emphasize. In the case of some medium-level commanders, conscience, assuming it did in fact exist, apparently never stood a chance. It was overruled by a not so subtle kind of blackmail: either do as you are told, or . . .

Neither, apparently, did pangs of conscience cause those who survived any great difficulties, at any rate not sufficiently so to make them draw attention to themselves. There is hardly a trace of 'anxiety [except, of course, the anxiety of being caught], penitence, fears, pangs and stings'. Yet to say that conscience did little if anything to interfere with the atrocities does not mean that it was not present at all. Some of the members of the 101st Reserve Police Battalion felt they could no longer take it and succeeded in obtaining a transfer.

Many others were demoralized. Early in 1942 even Bach-Zelewski, who in his post as chief of anti-partisan warfare on the eastern front was responsible for killing any number of Jews and others, was struck down by an incapacitating psychosomatic illness.[56] According to the SS doctor who treated him and reported to Himmler, he had hallucinations linked to the people he had ordered shot.[57] This was the same man of whom Hitler once said that he would 'happily wade through a sea of blood without the least scruple'. As with Heydrich, the words do not sound like a compliment. The breakdown did not last for very long. Having recovered, Bach-Zelewski asked for a transfer. He was refused and resumed his duties.[58]

At times conscience, twisted out of all recognition, operated in reverse. It made men do what they believed to be their duty – that word again – in spite of the considerable unpleasantness which it involved, especially at the beginning. As, for example, when members of the 101st Reserve Police Battalion took care to distract Jews whom they had known at home in Hamburg before they went on to shoot them. As when Stangl told the journalist who interviewed him in the cell, in which he lived as a convicted war criminal, that 'everything I did out of my own free will . . . I had to do as best I could'; and as when the commander of one of the Einsatzgrüppen, Otto Ohlendorf, boasted of how his 'humane' and 'efficient' methods minimized the sufferings of the victims.[59] This particular claim was made at the Nuremberg War Crimes Trials. But it accorded with the spirit Himmler had always wanted to instil in his SS.

Several of the psychiatrists who ran the euthanasia programme, which as mentioned above served as the model for the gas chambers in Auschwitz and elsewhere, had previously been well known for introducing new and humane methods of treatment. At least one, Professor Hermann Nitsche, who was later executed for his crimes, had actually been described as 'a thoroughly good man' by one of his fellow workers.[60] Explaining themselves during the Second World War, or called upon to do so after it had ended, they used reasoning similar to that of Ohlendorf. True or false, the traditional view has long been that conscience is what makes men different from beasts. Unfortunately the Nazi experience, but by no means only the Nazi experience, seems to show that, when it is misunderstood and misinterpreted, it is equally capable of turning men into something much worse than any beast has ever been or could be.

Those Who Resisted

Resistance under the Third Reich took many different forms. It started with so-called 'inner immigration', meaning adopting passive behaviour and making an effort to withdraw from society as much as possible, and clandestine listening to enemy radio broadcasts. There is no way to check on the first but the second appears to have been very widespread in spite of the draconian penalties. It reached all the way to the systematic refusal of Jehovah's Witnesses to use the 'German Greeting' or serve in the armed forces. Especially at the beginning of the war, there were also cases when opponents of the regime passed on information to Germany's enemies specifically in the hope of frustrating Hitler's plans.

Here I shall focus on two of the most extreme forms of opposition: assisting Jews on the one hand and conspiring to overthrow the regime on the other. Both in Germany and in every occupied country there were some people who risked their lives in order to help save Jews from the Nazi machinery of terror. Both in Germany and in every occupied country such people formed a small, even very small, minority. Given that, both in Germany and in every occupied country, the resources at Himmler's disposal were limited; in many places the extermination programme could never have been carried out without the assistance, even the active assistance, of the local civil service, police and/or population.

The most comprehensive programme aimed at identifying, classifying, researching and commemorating the so-called 'Righteous among the Nations' has been established and run by the Holocaust Museum (Yad Vashem) in Jerusalem from 1963 on.[61] As of early 2012 it listed the names of over 24,000 people in 44 different countries. However, the criteria those in charge have adopted in order to decide whom to include and whom to leave out are rather strict. On the other hand, not every rescuer survived, stepped forward and was in possession of the witnesses and/or documentation needed to prove his or her claim, or else was brought to the attention of Yad Vashem by others. Consequently that figure would seem to present little more than the tip of the iceberg. The true one is more likely to be anywhere between 50,000 and 500,000.[62]

Those who assisted Jews included city dwellers and farmers, professors, teachers, physicians, clergy, nuns, diplomats, labourers, a zoo director and a circus director. The vast majority of rescuers were at least nominally Christians of all denominations. But in the Balkans they also included some Muslims. Some lived in societies where anti-Semitism was virulent, as in much of Eastern Europe. Others came from those in which it was muted to the point of non-existence, as in Bulgaria and Italy. Perhaps because rescue work could be quite expensive, members of the upper and middle classes were more numerous than their proportion in the population would suggest. Rescuers were also more likely to have attended a university.[63] Some rescuers probably reached the decision to help over a period of time and in consultation with the Jews whom they had known as relatives by marriage, friends, neighbours, employers or employees. Others had to make the decision, which could well involve life and death, practically on the spot.

This was particularly the case when Jewish strangers came out of the blue, knocking on the door and asking for help. On other occasions, witnessing the horror of some Nazi-organized action directed against the Jews, the rescuers, feeling they just could no longer stand by and watch, took the initiative and decided to act. In the words of one unnamed man who helped save my uncle: 'I do not like Jews and do not mind them being chicaned a bit. However, this is going too far.'[64] Overall fewer than half had previously been acquainted with the people they decided to help. Quite some had previously had little contact with Jews, if indeed they had any at all. In two-thirds of cases people waited to be asked before taking action. Often the decision was made on impulse without thought of the future. Yet as many as two-thirds of those who did make it eventually found themselves becoming involved in more or less continuous rescue operations. That of course does not necessarily mean that from this point on they always helped the same people. Whether because of fear of discovery or for other reasons, both the rescuers and the rescued were constantly changing.[65]

The kind of assistance extended depended on circumstances and varied considerably. Many, including some German soldiers, simply looked away at the right moment. Others offered to take over and conceal the property of those about to be deported and look after it until the end of the war. A few did the same with children. Some provided false papers and some helped Jews to escape from the places where they had been incarcerated. Another important form of assistance, seldom noted, was to maintain contact among different members of the same Jewish families who found themselves widely scattered. Other things being equal, people who hid considerable numbers of refugees for considerable periods of time, which naturally also involved the responsibility for feeding them and looking after them in general, probably took the greatest risk of all. Such activities were hard to conceal. There was always a danger that somebody would blunder or turn traitor. In the West the normal penalty for those who were caught was deportation to some concentration camp. In the East, where the Nazis allowed themselves greater liberties, the outcome could easily be the death penalty not only for the rescuers but for their entire families. As a result, helping Jews was actually seen as more dangerous than general resistance activities.[66]

Given the tremendous risk many rescuers incurred, pointing out that the decision to help either acquaintances or strangers was not always based purely on ethical motives seems highly unfair. Nevertheless, to gain understanding, it must be done. Some of those who, whether acting on their own initiative or because they were asked to, agreed to take over property almost certainly hoped to retain it in case the Jews they were 'helping' did not return from wherever they were being evacuated to. Others expected and received some kind of payment for their services, which is why Yad Vashem did not include them in its list.[67] Especially during the last years of the war, there also seem to have been cases when families one or more of whose members had collaborated with the occupation authorities took care to have somebody in the other camp too. After all, the more Germany's defeat loomed over the horizon the easier it became to foresee a time when having saved some Jews, instead of being a crime, would become an honour and might earn one kudos in the community.

At times this ambiguity applied not only to individuals but to entire organizations. Take the case of Admiral Wilhelm Canaris, a strong nationalist – in 1919 he was a member of the court that tried, and acquitted, most of those involved in the murders of the socialist leaders Rosa Luxemburg and Karl Liebknecht. But for these qualities, as well as his proven excellence as an intelligence operative, he would hardly have been appointed head of the military intelligence/counter-intelligence. Though Canaris was never a Nazi, until 1937 he saw Hitler as Germany's only bulwark against Bolshevism. Later he changed his mind. This did not prevent him from maintaining his friendship with Heydrich and weeping at the latter's funeral.[68]

However that may be, in December 1941 Canaris told his chief subordinates that his organization would have nothing to do with the persecution of the Jews. The timing may have been an accident – some of his fellow officers mentioned his 'well-known humane feelings'.[69] Or it may have had something to do with the fact that the first death camps were just then beginning to gather steam. But it may also have reflected the fact that, in front of Moscow and in North Africa, the Wehrmacht was suffering its first serious defeats. In any case he proceeded to save the lives of some Jews by getting them to Spain. His subordinates helped others to cross the border to Switzerland by brazenly presenting them as their own agents.[70]

An even better example is provided by the government of Sweden. In the spring of 1944, bowing to U.S. pressure, it agreed to send Raoul Wallenberg to Budapest. Wallenberg was a member of the wealthy banking family which had close ties to the royal family. Like much of the Swedish establishment, they had done business with both sides throughout the war. They may have helped some leading Nazis conceal their assets, launder money and the like.[71] Raoul's mission was to save as many Jews as he could. Provided with funds, he quickly started establishing safe houses, clinics, soup kitchens and so on. He also issued 'letters of protection' left and right. With his associates in the Swedish Embassy, he probably saved more Jews than any other individual. His reputation as a hero is fully deserved. But that does not change the fact that some others, pulling the strings, may well have had different considerations in mind.

Many other considerations, including patriotism and sheer hatred of the Nazis, were also involved. Especially in the occupied territories, one did not have to have much of a conscience in order to resent the situation of one's country and one's self. Taking all this into account, whether it is really possible to single out an 'altruistic' type of personality, as some scholars have claimed, is doubtful. Is it really possible to separate 'elements of empathy' from 'normocentric considerations', 'principled behavior', 'self enhancement' and people's wish 'to preserve their sense of integrity and identity'?[72] This is all the more doubtful because some non-rescuers, far from putting their conscience aside, acted on it in the belief that other people deserved to be given priority. Others felt that their duty to their own relatives, whom they did not want to put at risk, came first. As far as they are concerned, let he or she who is without sin cast the first stone! Complicating the issue is the fact that some rescuers, interrogated after the war, tended to emphasize the role played by their consciences at the expense of any other less lofty motives they may have had – whether consciously or unconsciously.

In the end, all one can really say is that in some – perhaps many – cases, conscience, meaning a disinterested act based solely on the distinction between right and wrong, was indeed one of the factors involved in the decision to take a risk and do something. The war having ended, some of the people in question tried to save Nazis from being lynched.[73] Conscience might be rooted in religion. The latter stressed the duty to help the needy, or took a positive view of the Jews as God's chosen people, or both. However, in a continent that had been growing steadily more secular for several centuries past this was by no means always the case.[74] Great as the courage and the sacrifice of some individuals may have been, it must be admitted that, when everything is said and done, conscience could do little to impede the fearsome extermination machinery that Hitler and Himmler had built.

Much the same applies in regard to those who opposed the regime and tried to do something about it. As already stated, resistance assumed many different forms, some minor, some major. Many attempts to help Jews and other victims of National Socialism could themselves be constructed as acts of resistance. That was certainly the way in which the regime understood them. Other forms of resistance were more organized and had more far-reaching goals. I shall not dwell on the attempts of the remaining leaders of the banned Communist Party to mobilize and activate its former members, given that they were almost entirely politically motivated. The same applies to the resistance of socialists and trade unions, such as it was. Such people may have been somewhat more likely to help Jews than others, but there is no indication that the wish to do so played a large role in their decision to resist.[75] More important in the present context, in the spring and summer of 1938 a few members of the Army General Staff and the Foreign Ministry joined forces in the hope of toppling the Nazi government, deposing Hitler and putting him on trial. The objective was to prevent the outbreak of war. In the conspirators' view the latter could only end in Germany's defeat as its enemies husbanded their superior strength, just as they had done in 1914–18.[76]

Take General Ludwig Beck, the Army Chief of Staff. In the mid-1930s he did as much as anyone to rebuild his country's military might. Next, however, he started to question Hitler's expansionist policies. Thereupon he joined the plot and, though forced into retirement, continued to support it right until the end. Apparently the later the date, the more significantly moral as opposed to political motives coloured his reasoning.[77] Soon after the victory over France another General Staff officer, the then lieutenant-colonel Henning von Tresckow gave it as his opinion that, in the event of Churchill succeeding in dragging the U.S. into the war, in the end all that would be left of Germany would be the Electorate of Brandenburg.[78]

The remaining conspirators of this group were similarly motivated. Germany, after all, was Hegel's country par excellence: nowhere else was the idea of the state as incorporating the highest ethical ideal available to man on earth as strongly entrenched. They themselves were very much part of that state, which they had served for decades. The soldiers among them had even sworn a personal oath of allegiance to Hitler, one which many of them found it hard to violate. As their repeated attempts to get in touch with the Allies and obtain the most favourable terms possible for their country show, at first their motives were as much political as they were moral. More than a few hoped to retain some of Hitler's conquests, including Alsace-Lorraine,

Eupen (in Belgium), Austria, the Sudetenland, the Memelland and parts of Poland, not to mention the restoration of Germany's colonies. By contrast, their interest in moral questions, including the fate of the Jews, was strictly limited. Perhaps this had something to do with the fact that in the milieu where they lived and operated Jews were relatively few and far between. Some agreed with the Nazis that there *was* a Jewish problem, and that the world would not 'come to rest' until it was 'solved'; though their suggestion for doing so was less radical than Hitler's and was in fact quite similar to the Zionist one.[79]

Over time the situation changed. Tresckow's own strong revulsion against the regime dated to 1939–40, when he had witnessed Polish civilians being shot by the ss. He appealed to the chief of the Wehrmacht High Command, General Wilhelm Keitel, who shrugged off his protest. During the second half of 1941 Tresckow's commitment to the conspiracy became really serious. Serving on the Eastern Front at a time when the Wehrmacht seemed to be marching from one triumph to the next, he was appalled at the atrocities being committed in his army group's rear. From this point on he turned into the conspirators' leading spirit, working to recruit additional officers and concentrating all the manifold threads in his own hands.

Refusing to be misled by Hitler's early victories, quite some other key conspirators were also motivated, at least in part, by moral considerations, including the atrocities being committed in the occupied territories. Prominent among them were the above-mentioned Helmut von Moltke and Peter Yorck von Wartenburg.[80] Canaris too was involved, using his position to help some of the conspirators travel abroad and take up contact with Germany's enemies. The most important conspirator of all turned out to be Colonel Klaus Schenk von Stauffenberg, the man who in July 1944 planted the bomb that almost killed Hitler. Like Tresckow and many of the rest, Stauffenberg was descended from a noble family that had provided Germany's rulers with officers for generations past. His route into the conspiracy also resembled the one Tresckow had taken. Originally Stauffenberg had believed that getting rid of the 'brown pest', as he called it, would have to wait until after Germany had won the war. Later, as the tide began to turn and the *Endsieg* seemed further and further away, he changed his mind.

In the autumn of 1942 Stauffenberg reached the point where he told his fellows that he was ready not just to depose Hitler but to kill him.[81] In a country whose officers 'do not rebel', that represented a big step indeed. In August 1943 both Stauffenberg and Tresckow, who by this time were working closely together, told their secretaries, on whom they depended for typing messages and so on, that the regime had to be overthrown. That was not so much because things were going badly. After all, war was war and it was an officer's duty to obey the orders of the head of state and wage it as best he could. The real objective was to cleanse Germany's people and Germany's honour of the disgrace they had brought upon themselves by cruelly killing 'tens of thousands' of Jews.[82] Shortly after the Normandy Landings of 6 June 1944, Tresckow told Stauffenberg that they had to go ahead 'at any cost, and regardless of any practical objectives, if only as proof of the will to destroy Hitler and his regime'.[83]

Whatever their precise motives, there can be no doubt concerning the courage these men needed and did display. To that extent they succeeded even when they failed; not for nothing are their leaders honoured and commemorated in today's Germany. Yet when Hitler, addressing the nation on the evening of 20 July just hours after having survived the explosion that was supposed to kill him, told his listeners that they only formed a 'very small clique' within the Wehrmacht's officer corps, he was not far from the mark.[84]

Further down the social hierarchy things were quite different. The group of students who gathered around Hans and Sophie Scholl in Munich and distributed a few leaflets before they were caught certainly acted out of the purest of motives. Prominent among them were religion and deep revulsion at the anti-Jewish pogrom they had witnessed on 9 November 1939.[85] They concluded, quite rightly, that Germany had become an abomination and decided to do something about it.[86] Perhaps most admirable of all was the attempt made by Georg Elser on the night of 9 November.[87] His is a strange story that has often been retold – though without the mystery being solved.

Born in 1903, Elser was a highly skilled worker who had mastered both carpentry and watchmaking. He had some Communist sympathies, and as long as elections continued to be held he regularly gave his vote to the Party. He was also a member of the Rotfront, the Party's fighting organization. However, he seems to have taken the Pietist-Protestant faith in which he had been brought up much more seriously than he did politics. Having missed the First World War, he never served in the military, nor did he ever hold an official post. Unlike many of the rest, in other words, he did not bear even a tiny piece of responsibility. Apparently his resolve to kill Hitler, based on his belief that the latter was leading Germany towards war, grew in him from 1937 on. In November 1938, having listened to the Führer's speech on the anniversary of the Putsch of 1923, he decided to act. Some have claimed that he was also shocked by the events of Kristallnacht, when synagogues throughout Germany went up in flames, but this is uncertain.[88]

Variously described as either outgoing or a loner, Elser told nobody of his decision. Working entirely on his own, he was able to build a rather sophisticated bomb and plant it in the right place. Only bad luck – the fact that Hitler left the hall in which he was speaking much earlier than expected – prevented the attempt from succeeding and perhaps pushing history off-course. If ever there has been a hero whose activities were based on conscience and on conscience alone, then Elser was the man.

VI
Idols Old and New

Learning to Say No

Not everybody subscribed to Hegel's idea of the state as the lodestone that ought to govern the public conscience. There were always those who, while invoking some sort of higher morality – or, as in Nietzsche's case, amorality – raised their voices in protest. Often they were arrested, tried, convicted and punished. An important role in this respect has long been played by conscientious objection to military service. One reason for this is because such objection went straight to the heart of the state. The latter often saw waging war as its most important task. Another was that conscientious objectors put their money where their mouths were.

Resistance to military service can be traced as far back as the early days of Christianity. Whether at that time it was rooted in any moral objections to war as such or in religion – after all, the army was pagan and its commander in chief, the emperor, himself a God – has long been moot.[1] The fact that no sooner did the empire turn Christian in the fourth century AD than Christians started joining the army in large numbers points to the latter interpretation. Once God had told Emperor Constantine that in hoc signo vinces (in this sign you will conquer) most problems disappeared. From Charlemagne's campaigns in Spain and Saxony to those of Cromwell during the English Civil War, countless Christians went into battle under the sign of the Cross. As the Serb forces fighting Kosovan and Albanian terrorists in 1999 showed, on occasion they do so still.

Starting with the Reformation, some Protestant sects took the opposite tack. Citing Jesus's command to 'love your enemies' (Matthew

5:44), they refused to fight and asked to be exempted from military service on religious grounds. Among them were the Anabaptists, the Mennonites, the Hutterites and several others. In the Netherlands, in Switzerland and in parts of Germany they were often able to get their way, usually in return for agreeing to pay a special tax or 'contribution'. England too had some sects whose members refused to take part in the Civil War of 1642–51. However, the role they played should not be exaggerated. The numbers involved were never large, and during the second half of the seventeenth century one country after another started creating professional armed forces made up, in principle at any rate, entirely of volunteers. This made it easier to deal with objectors.

In America, where there was no 'standing army' and each colony had its own militia, the situation was different. As in England, the most important and best-organized sect was the Quakers. Like the rest, they were sometimes willing to contribute money for building fortifications and maintaining the various state militias. They also provided shelter to (white) refugees from war. Yet they adamantly refused to take up arms and fight.[2] On the eve of the War of the American Revolution, so strong were the sects that every one of the Thirteen Colonies recognized conscientious objection as a valid ground for exemption from service. This did not prevent a few objectors from being imprisoned for periods of up to two years.[3] Both in America and in Europe exemption was a question not of right but of privilege. It was always understood that the powers that granted that privilege also had the right to withdraw it if they wanted to.[4]

Nevertheless an important difference separated the two continents. At the time the U.S. was a remote country with fewer than 2.5 million white inhabitants. By contrast, France with 27 million was the greatest power of the age. The decision of the National Assembly in 1793 to adopt general conscription formed a critical turning point. In France itself the near complete absence of radical Protestant sects meant that the impact of conscientious objection, as opposed to draft-dodging and the like, was limited to non-existent. That handful who did object were often assigned to depots, lines of communication, hospitals and so on, a solution that subsequent armed forces also adopted on occasion.

As other countries followed the French example, objections to military service multiplied. As before, some of them were based on religion. During the American Civil War both sides followed the old practice of permitting objectors to hire substitutes. Those who could or would not do so were sent to prison; Lincoln at one point personally pardoned some Quakers and Mennonites who were serving time for this reason. It was, after all, hard to fight for freedom while at the same time holding prisoner those who demanded it in their own way. Seeing themselves as the underdogs, the Confederate authorities, though they did recognize conscientious objection in principle, were not as tolerant in practice. Many Southern objectors were mobbed, arrested, abused, starved and whipped. It has even been claimed that a few of them had muskets strapped to their bodies and were forcibly transported to the battlefield, to no avail.[5]

What set the period apart was the rise of secular pacifism. It condemned war and violence not on religious grounds but on purely moral ones. No longer as isolated as they had normally been in the past, pacifists could be found in many walks of life from the highest to the lowest. They set up countless organizations, systematically used modern communication techniques to conduct propaganda and held national and international congresses.[6] The most prominent pacifist of all was the Russian writer Leo Tolstoy (1828–1910). Having seen action during the Crimean War, during the 1880s he converted to non-violence. From then on he issued a whole series of treatises, denouncing war as 'the absolute evil'. His followers organized clubs in several countries. Another notable pacifist was an Austrian noblewoman, Bertha von Suttner (1843–1914) – agitator, lecturer and troublemaker. Her novel of 1889, *Die Waffen Nieder*, went through 37 German editions and was translated into sixteen languages. Her efforts earned her a Nobel Prize for Peace; much later her portrait was chosen to grace Austria's two-Euro coins.

As Tolstoy himself wrote, those who refused military service were sent first to priests, then to doctors, then to various penal battalions and finally to lunatic asylums.[7] Neither his followers nor those of von Suttner had a noticeable impact on the outbreak and course of the First World War. For example, as against some three million American men who were drafted in 1917–18, just some 2,000 objectors of all kinds were arrested and convicted.[8] Yet even while the conflict lasted, the British government, having introduced conscription for the first time in the country's history, decided to recognize conscientious objectors by granting them the right to perform alternative civil service. Later, taking their cue from Britain, several other countries, mostly Protestant ones in Western and Northern Europe, passed similar legislation. Denmark did so in 1917, Sweden in 1920, the Netherlands in 1922 and Finland in 1931.

In 1933 two Belgian citizens, Leo Campion and Hem Day (pseudonym for Marcel Dieu), were tried for refusing to be conscripted. The stir they caused was enormous. During the Second World War totalitarian countries such as Nazi Germany and the Soviet Union persecuted conscientious objectors with might and main, putting them into concentration camps or shooting them out of hand. By contrast, most democratic nations took a line similar to the British one of a generation earlier. Special commissions staffed by officers, psychologists and priests were set up to decide who was a genuine objector and who was not. American men who came before the commissions were likely to be asked whether they would refuse to fight if fighting would prevent their sister (if they had one) from being raped. Those who said yes to this and similar questions were sent to work in hospitals and the like. As a character in Joanne Greenberg's novel of 1964, *I Never Promised You a Rose Garden*, explains, the Government in its wisdom had decided to rub objectors' noses in it. And it was patients in a mental asylum who formed the 'it'.[9]

Compared with those who were drafted, the number of those who refused to be inducted on conscientious grounds and obtain a release was always very small. Still their ability, in many cases, to get what they wanted or at least rouse some public sympathy for their views signified the various states' tacit admission, previously all but inconceivable, that they themselves no longer necessarily held the moral high ground. Increasingly states reacted by surrendering their own absolute right to rule over conscience, if not in every respect, then at any rate in relation to the most important question of all: namely, that of citizens' right, and duty, to kill and die for their countries.

A landmark of sorts was reached in January 1967 when the Council of Europe adopted Resolution No. 337. The Resolution declared that persons liable to conscription for military service who, for reasons of conscience or profound conviction, arising from religious, ethical, moral, humanitarian, philosophical or similar motives, refuse to perform armed service shall enjoy a personal right to be released from the obligation to perform such service. This right shall be regarded as deriving logically from the fundamental rights of the individual in democratic Rule of Law states.[10]

It was based on 'Article 9 of the European Convention on Human Rights which binds member States to respect the individual's freedom of conscience and religion'. By issuing the declaration, the states in question to a large extent pulled the objectors' sting. Previously a principled refusal to serve had often had something heroic about it. Now it became just one of the numerous if rather tepid and uninteresting rights that citizens in liberal democracies enjoy, or are told they enjoy.

Concurrently, on the other side of the Atlantic, the Vietnam War led to a sharp rise in the number of U.S. citizens who made similar claims.[11] Almost 10,000 were put on trial and convicted; the number of those who refused to serve and found various ways to do so was much larger still. This time the objectors, merging as they did into a much broader protest movement that opposed U.S. policies in Southeast Asia, seriously interfered with the war effort. In so doing they were helped by several Supreme Court rulings that expanded the right to gain an exemption in such a way as to include not only those who based their objections on religious belief but those with 'deeply held moral and ethical' ones as well. Those rulings in turn contributed to the decision of the Nixon Administration to end conscription in favour of a professional all-volunteer force, the kind of force with which the U.S. has fought all its wars since.

Starting in the mid-1970s, one developed country after another followed suit. In 1996 even France, which two centuries earlier had introduced the modern levée en masse, decided to do away with it and rebuild professional armed forces instead.[12] Logically speaking the end of conscription should have caused conscientious objectors to become an extinct species. But this did not happen. Instead, the more rights they were granted, the greater their demands. Nowadays in the U.S. even uniformed military personnel – people who joined out of their own free will – are entitled to cite conscientious objection to war and ask for an exemption from deployment.[13] With this *reductio ad absurdum*, the state's surrender to conscience was complete.

Three factors made the surrender possible. The first was the fact that, in the wake of the Second World War and the defeat of Germany and Japan, 'militarism' became one of the worst of all terms of abuse. Niagaras of ink were spilled in an effort to expose it and denounce its evils. Resistance to militarism helped to spread the idea that refusing to wear uniform is a good and honourable thing to do. It also tied the hands of the authorities who tried to combat those who did so. The second was the waning of major war between major countries. Practically without exception, the wars the countries in question have waged from 1945 on have had nothing to do with national survival. Quite often they revolved around issues so picayune and geographically so far removed from the homeland as to be almost invisible.[14] Either way the outcome was a sharp drop in the percentage of the population that the armed forces required to meet their needs. Nowadays it is mainly beleaguered countries such as Israel, South Korea and Taiwan which continue to insist on denying their citizens the right to be exempted. And even they have made some concessions, or at least are contemplating the possibility of doing so.

The third and last factor was the lingering shadow of the Second World War and the Holocaust. To be sure, the latter was not identical with the former. Yet it was very much a part of it and witnessed many of the worst crimes associated with it. Starting with Thomas Hobbes in the middle of the seventeenth century, it had usually been taken for granted that states' most important quality was their sovereignty.[15] It gave them the right to do anything with and to the people who lived within their borders without interference from outside. It also worked the other way around. Anyone who, armed with the state's legal mandate, performed his duty towards it did not have to carry the responsibility for his or her deeds. By the middle of the eighteenth century that idea had come to be understood as a pillar, perhaps even the most important pillar, of civilized behaviour.

The Holocaust, and perhaps even more so the various trials by which it was followed, put the entire idea of duty in question. Great or small, one Nazi butcher after another tried to defend himself (occasionally, herself) by claiming that he or she was but a little cog and that 'orders are orders'. Among those who did so was Adolf Eichmann, the man who after Hitler, Himmler and Heydrich did more than anybody else to exterminate as many Jews as possible. Not once was the argument accepted. Each time an international or national court found an accused person guilty, it made clear that, under certain circumstances, not only could people not hide behind their 'duty' but that they were bound to say no and not obey their governments. As the London Charter of the International Military Tribunal, prepared in order to lay the juridical foundations of the Nuremberg Trials, put it as early as 1945, at best the need to follow orders could be used by the defence to mitigate the punishment the courts meted out.[16] Anything else was tantamount to an admission that conscience was powerless or that it did not exist.

Early on the problem was handled as if it were specific to the defeated powers of Germany and Japan (Italy did not count). Entire libraries were written to prove that 'authoritarian' fathers in those countries bred 'authoritarian' offspring who were more likely to blindly obey orders, hence allowing their consciences to be overridden, than others.[17] Some such works continue to be published even today. Regardless of whether the claims were true or false, it proved impossible to rebuild international society without granting equality to some of its potentially most important and most productive members. If only for that reason, in practice attitudes to the countries in question soon changed. At the time much of the world had had its fill of war and its accompanying horrors. This led to the rise of a vague feeling – analogous, at first, to the proverbial cloud no bigger than a man's hand – of the need to put some limits on what, starting around the middle of the seventeenth century, had been known as raison d'état.

As the above-mentioned Article 9 illustrates, much of this was done in the name of human rights. The English philosopher John Locke (1632–1704) was probably the first to suggest that human beings, simply by virtue of being such, have been endowed by nature with certain inalienable rights that apply from the moment of birth on and hence cannot be taken away. To him the rights in question included life, liberty and property.[18] No person should be deprived of them without cause, and then only after due process. During the eighteenth century the idea was incorporated in the American Declaration of Independence and the French Declaration of the Rights of Man.

However, the countries that adopted some form of rights could do so only within their own sovereign territories. As Thomas Paine in *The Rights of Man* (1791) pointed out, the authorities that granted the rights also had the power to take them away. That was just what happened in France itself following the return of the Bourbons in 1815. The Declaration only became a permanent part of the French Constitution under the Second Empire. Other countries took even longer to recognize the idea. It was only in 1948 that the Universal Declaration of Human Rights was signed.[19] From this point on, slowly but inexorably a vast body of legislation began to be built. Touching on a thousand different subjects and assuming a thousand different forms, its overarching purpose was to redefine and restrict state power both internally and externally. As part of the process, its relationship with morality and conscience was put on an entirely new footing.[20] For a period of about two centuries Kant, Hegel and their numerous followers had acclaimed duty as the greatest and most noble thing in life. Now it was pulled down from the throne it had occupied for so long. Its place was taken by what one political scientist has called, aptly enough, 'The Rights Revolution'.[21]

The most important pieces of international legislation were a Convention on the Prevention and Punishment of the Crime of Genocide and a Convention against Torture. To these were added some two dozen others. Still not content, the countries of some regions, notably Europe, the Americas and Africa, went ahead and created their own separate systems. In 1997, speaking in Tehran, of all places, the then Secretary General of the United Nations Kofi Annan told his audience that 'human rights are what reason demands and conscience commands.' 'They are', he said, 'what make us human . . . the principles by which we create the sacred home for human dignity'.[22] Admittedly some countries refused to sign. Others spiked their letters of acceptance with so many reservations as to make their signatures meaningless, and others still only signed by way of paying lip service to the concept.[23] Quite a few signed with no intention of changing their behaviour. By 1994 even Iraq, which at that time was governed by the unspeakable dictator Saddam Hussein, had joined five treaties protecting human rights.

Yet the treaties' very existence meant that, on paper at any rate, neither signatories nor non-signatories had the right any longer to mistreat their peoples in good conscience. Nor could those citizens use 'duty' to justify their own crimes. To that extent *raison d'état*, and indeed the state itself, were dealt a blow from which they have yet to recover and may never recover. Had Hobbes, and even more so Hegel, been able to witness these developments they would have rubbed their eyes. The former would have done so in disbelief, the latter in anger. Frederick the Great would no doubt have welcomed them, albeit while adding that, since Jesus had failed to prevent people from cutting each other's throats, conventions made without divine help were unlikely to do so either.

In many ways the process resembles the one we have observed several times in this volume. First the seed is sown in the form of a dramatic appeal to people's 'knowledge with themselves' to the effect that the moral status quo cannot and should not be maintained. Once enough of them have experienced the impact, conscience starts to be spelt out, codified and encapsulated. Gradually it is surrounded by all the paraphernalia that law and lawyers, ecclesiastical or lay, can muster. Those include elaborate written texts, prosecutors and courts – I am of course referring to the International Criminal Court in The Hague. Though stocks, stakes and scaffolds have fallen out of favour in most countries, their place has been taken by prisons as the main instrument for punishing serious transgressions.[24] Paradoxically, as the process unfolds the role of conscience, the very factor that produced the spark to begin with is progressively narrowed down. In the end all that is left to conscience is to decide whether or not the law in question should be obeyed even when nobody is looking or when it is powerless to intervene. The more powerful the law and its ability to reward and to punish, in other words, the less room is left for conscience.

Yet the long history of conscience suggests that people, certainly Western people since the time of Augustine and including even some of the worst criminals, consider living without it next to impossible.

Presumably that is one reason why so many of those criminals claim to have it and to have acted on it or have experienced its effects. That even applies in cases, such as that of Rudolf Höss, when the subject's actions and behaviour convince most of us that they do not and have not. They must justify themselves; if not in other people's eyes, then at least in their own. Conscience, like a chameleon, is always changing its colours. No sooner does the development of law narrow its scope in one respect than it starts looking for another one in which it can make its pangs felt. There seems to be no limit to the number of fields conscience can attach itself to.

Probably the vast majority of the attempts to find something people may feel guilty about, in other words to stir their conscience, fail to find many followers. Having occasioned a few pamphlets, a few TV shows and perhaps a couple of demonstrations, they soon disappear, leaving hardly a trace. However, here and there a few, often with no apparent reason, succeed in acquiring a mass following. Next they proceed to 'arm the prow and sail into the world' (the early twentieth-century poet Gabriele d'Annunzio). Among them are the anti-abortion crusade, the animal rights crusade and others. Here it is only possible to explore two such attempts: health conscience on the one hand and environmental conscience on the other.

Conscience and Health

At first sight the idea of linking people's quest for health to conscience – Shakespeare's mysterious 'it' which, anchored in the no less mysterious idea of morality, prevents us from doing things that are profitable for us or else makes us regret having done them – seems strange indeed. After all, health is nothing more than the sense of physical well-being we all enjoy when we have it and seek when we do not. Aside from the possibility that some people may interfere with the health of others, in which respect it does not differ from a great many other things they do or omit to do, nothing could be more personal than the quest for it or further removed from any idea of good versus evil. So how can the quest for it become mixed up with conscience?

This is how I saw the problem when my stepson, Jonathan Lewy, who at that time was studying the way the authorities in the Third

Reich treated drug addicts, first drew my attention to it. He soon convinced me I was wrong. If there was anything the Nazis tried to do it was to strengthen and beautify the German 'race'.[25] As the writer Hans Carossa (1876–1956) put it in a letter to a friend, 'we are being laundered, purified, scrubbed, disinfected, separated, Nordicized, toughened up.'[26] In this attempt they were by no means alone. With an eye to future wars, among other things, many other contemporary governments also did what they could to promote 'national fitness'. Among the methods used for the purpose were extensive, state-directed networks of clinics that looked after the welfare of mothers and small children; organized vacations for the children of the lower classes; organized sports; and, in quite a number of countries, the compulsory sterilization of those seen as being below par.[27]

Running a 'totalitarian' country, the Nazis were able to go much further than the rest. Here it is by no means unimportant to note that the German term *Heil*, as in Sieg Heil and Heil Hitler, means not only 'welcome' and 'long live' but also 'salvation', 'wholesomeness' and 'health'.[28] True to their word, the Nazis also instituted a large number of positive – in the sense that they were meant to help certain sectors of the population – measures. Among the most important was a massive programme known as Kraft durch Freude, Strength through Joy. It provided subsidized vacations to members of the working classes. Others were the Hitler Jugend and the BdM (Bund deutscher Maedel), the League of German Girls, both of which put a strong emphasis on physical education for the young. Then there was widespread screening for breast cancer, a programme personally supported by Hitler who had watched his mother die of the disease, as well as some of the earliest policies in any country aimed at discouraging cigarette smoking and tobacco usage in general. It worked: foreign observers watching German troops in France in 1940 commented on the striking physical difference between them and their English opponents in particular.[29] Health ceased to be something one sought simply for one's own sake. There appeared something known as *Pflicht zur Gesundheit*, the duty to stay healthy and produce healthy offspring. Health became something the individual owed his *Volk*, meaning nation or people. In the country of Luther and Kant, inevitably duty and conscience marched together.

Another factor that worked in the same direction was the spread of social medicine. To stay with Germany, such medicine had first been introduced during the Weimar Republic as a direct lesson derived from the First World War.[30] In many ways the Nazis did no more than take over the various programmes, adapt them to their racist ideas and expand them. Other countries, motivated by broadly similar considerations, developed their own programmes, first in Europe and then in the United States as well. To be sure, the process did not work in exactly the same way in all places. Not only was Europe ahead of the U.S. chronologically, but its governments put much greater emphasis on state-run insurance programmes as opposed to voluntary private ones. The former only reached the U.S. under President Obama from 2009 on.

However insurance was provided, the outcome was to take the quest for health out of the hands of the individual and his physician and entrust it to some kind of organization. Like most insurance companies those organizations did their best to economize. In doing so they soon ran head-on into two long-term trends. The first was the vast, largely technologically driven increase in the cost of healthcare that got under way from about 1970 on. The second, which to a large extent was the result of the first, was the rise in life expectancy. Taking the U.S. as our example, over four decades it went up by over 10 per cent. An end is not in sight.[31] Still remaining in the U.S., in 2010 healthcare accounted for 17.9 per cent of GDP. That is four times as much as defence – a field in which the U.S. spent almost as much as the rest of the world combined. Healthcare now represents by far the most important reason behind the growing budget deficit.[32] The situation in other 'advanced' countries, such as Britain, France and Germany, though less extreme, is broadly similar. In them, too, life expectancy has gone up. Though the proportion of GDP spent on healthcare is smaller, in these places it also exceeds that of national defence by about four to one.

One of the principal ways to achieve economies consisted of 'healthy living'. Both public and private healthcare organizations quickly realized this. They focused on hammering the need for it into people's heads. When I first started researching this chapter I thought that, aside from the kind of moral dilemmas that confront doctors who must decide whether to prolong the life of terminal patients, links between 'health' and 'conscience' would be rare. To my surprise, a Google search I did in February 2013 produced almost 39,000,000 hits. The combination of 'health' and 'morality' added another 27,000,000. Everybody and his neighbour seems to be involved: governments, insurance companies specializing in healthcare and corporations are all desperate to avoid bankruptcy by educating their citizens, clients and employees to lead healthier lives. This is to say nothing of a vast number of formal and informal consumer organizations hell-bent on achieving the same goal. In the past this kind of propaganda used to be conducted by priests. Now their place has been taken by health professionals. Many of them are, or are introduced as, physicians. Instead of black cassocks they wear white smocks; instead of crucifixes, stethoscopes which they wave about in a way meant to be either reassuring or threatening. Yet the method used, namely inculcating guilt until the latter is internalized and takes on the form of conscience, remains the same.

For example, the 'fact' that smoking is bad for you has now been 'known' for several decades. The list of evils allegedly associated with it has kept expanding. It has even been blamed for women's sagging breasts;[33] apparently the authors of this particular piece of nonsense have never heard either of breastfeeding, gravity or ageing. For those who like to smoke, doing so without experiencing feelings of guilt has been made all but impossible. They are hounded, persecuted and literally put into cages, all the while being milked for money through taxes and fines. Yet smoking only forms the tip of the proverbial iceberg. Fatty food is bad for you and should be avoided. The same applies to 'junk' food, fast food, processed food, genetically modified food (in Europe) and any kind of food that is not 'natural'. This, of course, begs the question as to whether there also exist such things as unnatural or supernatural foods and, if so, what they are like. Meat is bad. Both salt and sugar are bad. So are some of the things used as substitutes for the latter. Soft drinks are very bad (they have been called 'the devil's weapon against the body', no less).[34] But water too is bad. Unless, that is, it is fluoridated (or not, depending on whom you ask) and comes out of a plastic bottle; in which case, provided it has sufficient minerals added to it and consequently costs a hundred times as much as it should, it becomes good. Tea is bad, but gracious nature has also created coffee, which for many years used to be bad but has recently turned out to be good.[35]

For several centuries past potatoes were good – so much so that entire nations lived on them and starved if the crop failed. To this day grateful citizens continue to put them on the grave of Frederick the Great, who introduced them to Prussia two and a half centuries ago. However, of late the chair of the Nutrition Department at Harvard in its wisdom has ruled that they are actually bad.[36] The same applies to bread and other wheat products such as pasta (never mind that Italy is a Mediterranean country and that the so-called Mediterranean diet is supposed to be the best in the world).[37] Meat, which at many historical times and places used to be so expensive that many people could only eat it on rare occasions, has also become bad. Milk used to be very good – after all, we all lived on it when we were very young. Now it is only good, if at all, in case the cardboard or plastic container has the words non-, un-, de- or low- printed on it. Never mind, incidentally, that not one of these products is 'natural'.

Especially in the U.S., the outcome has been to make people see pleasurable and healthy eating as mutually exclusive.[38] If it tastes good it must be bad for you, and the other way around. But food, like smoking, only forms a very small part of the story. Measured in terms of happiness, not having enough money is bad for you, but so is having too much of it.[39] Not enough work is bad for you, but so is too much of it. A complete absence of stress is bad for you, but so is too much of it. The same goes for competition, rest, sleep, exercise, company, love, sex and a thousand other things and activities. As medical and psychological researchers compete with each other to find ways to promote themselves by frightening the public, the list keeps growing day by day.

Never mind that much of this amounts to reinventing the wheel or repeating Aristotle, the philosopher who 24 centuries ago told his son Nicomachos about the golden mean. Never mind, too, that nobody knows with any precision what that golden mean is. This is to say nothing of the fact that variations among different people often turn any attempt at generalization into nonsense; as the saying goes, what is one man's meat is another man's poison. Everywhere entire industries have been built to take advantage of the 'bad' things people like or do, causing the ripples to spread throughout society. Escaping the guilt-producing cant is all but impossible. One would have to learn to live without the Internet, television, radio, television, telephones, magazines and newspapers. To avoid meeting with advertisements of every kind, one would also have to close the shutters and stay at home.

Much of this has now been internalized to the point where one may speak of a true 'health conscience' (yes, such a term does exist). Backed by fear of divine punishment, health conscience prevents us from doing certain things. If we fall victim to temptation and do them nevertheless, it makes us feel guilty – even when there is no law against what we have done, and even when nobody but ourselves takes notice. This is to say nothing of the pleasure of looking down on, denouncing and sometimes threatening and ostracizing those who do not conform. The high priests of health conscience are the researchers, physicians, corporations, governments and consumer organizations that have invested so much work and money to maintain and improve our health. How can anyone in good conscience reject the advice all these wonderful people, with 'science' as their guide, keep proffering? Isn't doing so sinning against oneself and, indirectly, against society too? Won't the sins of the fathers be visited on the sons unto the third and fourth generation? Never mind that much of the advice is ill-founded, contradictory and plainly absurd. As the fact that it is constantly shifting shows, much if not most of the concern is not about health at all but about making people feel guilty. As long as one refrains from eating *some* kinds of food, conscience is assuaged.

Close on the heels of a 'healthy' lifestyle came preventive medicine. While ancient Greek physicians knew about healthy lifestyles, for millennia medicine was meant almost exclusively for the sick. The invention of inoculation against smallpox around the middle of the eighteenth century caused these things to change. Starting around 1870, vaccines were discovered for one disease after another. As the number of those afflicted by such dread ones as typhus, typhoid, diphtheria, tuberculosis and polio declined, the results have been extremely beneficial.[40] In this field too social medicine played a large and growing role. Spreading from the most developed countries outward, it enabled almost everybody to be inoculated at a young age. But that was just the beginning. As more and more tests became available, more and more people started being subjected to them not because they displayed symptoms of ill health but as a matter of bureaucratic routine. Depending on the nature of the tests, those who 'failed' to pass them were subjected to dietary regimes, exercise regimes, resting regimes, sleeping regimes and so many other kinds of regimes as to boggle the mind.

Marching side by side with the regimes was every kind of medicament. As an exhibit at the British Museum seeks to illustrate, the outcome was that most of us who are over 60 years old now swallow more of them in a year than we did during our entire previous lives.[41] Over two decades the total may easily reach 14,000 – and we are talking about people most of whom are not actually ill. Now that elderly people have surrendered to the onslaught, there is strong pressure to push down the age at which drugs start being taken; even as I was writing these lines, I learnt that one-third of Israel Defense Forces soldiers are using Ritalin, not because they are ill, but because the drug supposedly helps them cope with the stressful situations earlier armed forces used to handle by issuing their troops so and so many cigarettes a day.[42]

As with various kinds of foods, on occasion medicines that used to be good tuned out to be bad, and the other way around. For example, few people remember that, back in the 1970s, the supposedly dangerous drug known as ecstasy was considered beneficial. It was widely used to alleviate feelings of guilt (guilt!) and remorse as well as depression. With a little bit of luck some fancy version of it, manufactured by some pharmaceutical firm and labelled and sold in such a way as to drive its price into the sky, will serve similar purposes in the future.[43] That, after all, is just what happened to cocaine when it was metamorphosed into Ritalin.

The tests preventive medicine has invented and prescribed have also induced many millions of people to undergo serious surgical procedures ranging from mastectomy down to less serious procedures. As the ongoing debate about them shows, the real benefits of many measures and programmes remain in doubt. For example, are routine medical tests really effective in keeping those who undergo them healthy?[44] Does screening women for breast cancer really save lives? Isn't it true that, for every woman who does benefit from periodical check-ups by obtaining an early diagnosis, there are a great many others who are irradiated for no purpose? Are all mastectomies really needed, or are at least some of them superfluous and even harmful? Finally, isn't it true that not having to worry about one's health is itself an essential part of health? Yet anyone at all reluctant to embark on the hopeless task of ascending the descending escalator – hopeless, because we must all fall sick and die in the end – has been made to feel thoroughly guilty for neglecting him- or herself.[45] As is also the case with food, too often it is more a question of assuaging conscience, both one's own and that of society, than of anything else.

Again, what started as an appeal to the duty/guilt/conscience complex is rapidly being turned into something more formal. The two most active players in the field are schools and corporations. Neither has the authority to produce law in the strict sense of the term. But they certainly can and do produce rules of every sort. Schools regularly prohibit children, the segment of society least able to stand up for its rights, from eating this or drinking that. Just as I was writing these lines in January 2013, a six-year-old British schoolboy found himself at the centre of a major row. The headmistress of the school he attended had confiscated his biscuits, ordering him to bring a pear or a banana or else remain hungry, and the boy was suspended The more fond children are of any kind of food or drink, the greater the likelihood that they will be forbidden not only to consume it but to learn about it through advertisements. The issue is not whether junk food or bars of chocolate or sugary drinks are good or bad. As with anything else, it is probably a question of not consuming 'too much' of them. It is the way the victims are systematically denied access to information in order to instil them with a certain kind of 'conscience'.

Many modern corporations have developed so-called wellness programmes, whose primary purpose is to keep their employees' physical and mental health up and their own medical insurance expenses down.[46] Other objectives, such as increasing productivity, may also be involved. The measures taken vary enormously. They may include educational workshops, opportunities for exercise, cafeterias serving 'healthy' food, medical screening and much more. Often much attention is also given to psychological wellness. As in *Brave New World*, simply being healthy is not enough; one is obliged to be happy as well. Presumably it is only a matter of time before all of us will be chirping cheerfully. Most of the employees who take part probably do so out of their own free will. However, those who do not want to participate, or whose results are deemed unsatisfactory, such as failing to lose 'enough' weight, may very well find themselves subject to a variety of sanctions. For example, they may be charged more for medical insurance than their colleagues.

The introduction of sanctions marks the crossing of the border between conscience and law, whether that of the state or that issued by other bodies. In every modern country state legislation aimed at controlling medicine with the aim of improving public health is widespread. The outcome has been the emergence of a vast medico-bureaucratic complex that governs much of our lives and is constantly seeking to increase its power. Quite often, a refusal of the supposed benefits of the various programmes is treated as a violation of the law and an insult to the state that enacted it.

Already some governments have started taxing some types of popular food such as butter, potato crisps, sugar and ice cream. Those governments, we are told, are certain to draw the attention of the rest.[47] Other governments have wholly or partially banned ketchup, Kinder eggs, Marmite, ackee fruit, samosas and jelly beans. Another victim is raw milk. Never mind that raw (non-pasteurized) milk is the 'natural' form in which this particular product comes out of the udders of a cow, sheep or goat. Some governments take the opposite tack. For example, France does not permit vegetarianism in school canteens. Students will have meat served to them whether they like it or not, though whether they can also be forced to eat it seems to remain open.[48] Each ban comes complete with a plethora of experts, statistics and footnotes to explain why the food in question is bad. In a great many cases, as fashion changes, so do the statistics.

Admittedly much of this is simply a matter of filling the coffers. If there is one thing all 'health foods' have in common, it is that they cost much more than ordinary food. Another goal is to prevent those who are sick from harming others by infecting them. Yet lurking behind both of these is the need to spare the healthcare establishment, indeed society as a whole, from feelings of guilt by preventing people from 'harming' themselves – whatever that may mean. After all, if society is not becoming visibly healthier, why maintain an establishment that costs hundreds of billions each year? Starting at the earliest possible age, people must learn to use and practise what they dislike and not to use or practise what they do like. That is because, from Germany to India, 'health is the duty of every citizen.'[49]

In a world where duty has been all but suspended in favour of rights, paradoxically the culminating point of this sort of conscience consists of the refusal to recognize what may very well be the most important right of all: the right to put an end to one's life and die. Monotheistic religions have always denounced the idea of suicide,[50] seeing it as a challenge to God's ability to heal and therefore as a form of apostasy. Fortunately for humanity, neither governments nor doctors nor the assembled bleeding hearts of the world have yet been able to find a way to prevent free, healthy people from killing themselves if they want to. But they certainly have denied many of those who have the misfortune of being neither healthy nor free the right to be taken off life support. All too often that applies even when the persons in question are screaming in pain and beg to be left alone so as to be able to exercise it. To die, one must receive permission first. The ancient Stoics, who invoked *syneidēsis* and to whom the readiness of men and women to take their fate into their own hands and end their own lives was the supreme expression of what it meant to be human, would have been appalled.

Conscience and the Environment

Some kinds of Buddhism, especially Zen, have always seen humanity as an integral part of the environment and sought to protect the latter as much as possible.[51] This has led to images, often broadcast on TV, of Tibetan monks sweeping paths so as to avoid stepping on ants. The Judaic tradition, from which both Christianity and Islam are descended, saw things in a different light. All three religions considered man to be separate from and superior to the rest of nature. Of all living creatures, he alone had been created in God's image. Just a little later he was also granted the ability to distinguish evil from good. In the words of the book of Genesis: 'And God blessed them [Adam and Eve] and God said unto them, Be fruitful, and multiply, and replenish the earth, and subdue it; and have dominion over the fish of the sea, and over the fowl of the air, and over every living thing that moveth upon the earth.' Aristotle also thought that 'nature has made all things specifically for the sake of man.'[52] Given these two powerful influences, it is no wonder that, by and large, this is how things were understood during most of Western history until the Industrial Revolution.

As with 'health-conscience', among the first who took a different view of the matter and put in place practical measures to implement it were the Nazis. A central part of Nazi ideology was blood and soil (*Blut und Boden*, sometimes abbreviated to BLUBO). Simply put, it was the idea that the land nourished the people and the people fertilized the land with their labour. Each *Volk* owed much of its character to the soil from which it had sprung and on which it lived from one generation to the next.[53] Like the pure blood of the master race itself, the soil in question had to be preserved at all cost. This in turn led to numerous measures intended to preserve nature.

In overall charge was Hitler's second-in-command, Hermann Göring, who was an avid hunter. Assisted by his minions, he created nature reservations such as the Schorfheide, north of Berlin, where he built himself a house. The Nazis also set out to protect rivers, lakes and forests; regulated fishing and hunting; and much more. Particularly interesting in this respect were the famous *Autobahnen*, or motorways. They were built very much with environmental and aesthetic considerations in mind. Not just engineers but landscape architects, agricultural experts, botanists and zoologists were consulted.[54] At the time all this was known as *Heimatschutz*, protection of the homeland. As in other countries, occasions when environmental considerations had to give way to economic and military ones were not lacking. That was especially true during the period of accelerated rearmament from 1936 on. Still, so advanced were many of the regulations the Nazis put in place that many of them still remain in force.[55]

Running in parallel with health-conscience, and for much the same reasons, from the early 1960s on in all developed countries environmental protection started to be turned into a secular religion. The two movements, of course, were connected, indeed intertwined. A wholesome environment was and remains the first and most important prerequisite for the maintenance of health. Healthy people on their part would do what they could to maintain a wholesome environment. Other considerations were also involved. Some sought to anchor environmentalism in a reverence for God's handiwork. They combed the Bible for suitable passages to quote, fastening on the one in Genesis where 'the Lord God took the man and put him into the Garden of Eden to dress it and keep it.' Others saw a link between preserving the environment and the urgent need to do away with male wickedness and dominion. The former approach led to Christian environmentalism, the latter to something known as ecofeminism.[56]

That was not the end of the matter. While some feminists adopted environmentalism, others worried lest identifying women with nature would lead to more rather than less exploitation of women by 'the patriarchy'. And we have not even started to discuss liberal environmentalism, socialist environmentalism, conservative environmentalism, revolutionary environmentalism, 'realistic' environmentalism and 'deep' environmentalism. Realistic environmentalists want to take economic constraints into account; deep ones, to dethrone humanity from the high pedestal it has taken for itself for so long and make it re-merge into the nature which has given it birth. Since gay couples cannot be fruitful and multiply, some even saw an 'obvious connection' between homosexuality and the protection of the environment.[57]

Practically from the beginning, what all forms of environmentalism had in common was the fact that their proponents felt guilty. Guilty for mistreating living nature, both animal and vegetable; guilty for despoiling the earth; guilty for polluting the water as well as the air; guilty, one would almost say, for existing. They did their best to make other people feel guilty as well. Particularly effective in this respect were two bestsellers, Rachel Carson's *Silent Spring* (1962, later made into a movie) and Paul Ehrlich's *The Population Bomb* (1968). The former focused on the impact of pesticides such as DDT on wildlife. The latter explained that global population growth would soon lead to food shortages and war and demanded that measures be taken to limit it. A third influential work was the Club of Rome Report of 1973 called *Limits to Growth*. That report, incidentally, remains almost the only time anybody paid any attention to the club, a self-described 'Committee of 300 Subversive Body', at all.

As time went on, what started as an occasional feeling of discomfort concerning the damage humanity was inflicting on the environment was transformed into a deeply rooted and permanent environmental conscience. One step in that direction was made by the Stockholm Conference of 1971, which saddled 'man' with 'a solemn responsibility to protect and improve the environment for future generations'. As with other forms of conscience, the environmental one soon surrounded itself with an enormous literature. It also developed its own Church, its own priests (who are sometimes known as 'environs'), its own symbols, its own hallowed texts and its own martyrs. The last named are activists who were 'murdered and killed' while trying to do anything from saving the Brazilian jungle from loggers to stopping a lorry filled with veal. At the latest count there were about a dozen of them.[58] It also has its own heterodox dissenters. Some environmentalists went much further than the majority. Others, on the contrary, thought that the majority had gone too far and that it was time to inject a dose of realism so as not to alienate supporters. Ostensibly working for the same cause and seeking to attract the same audience, often adherents of the two schools fought each other even more viciously than they did society at large.

The 1970s saw the emergence of the first 'Green' parties. Currently almost 100 countries have them.[59] Environmentalists also influenced politics by joining existing parties, thus helping to change their agendas from within. The sense of guilt that started it all remained in existence. Increasingly it was reinforced by every kind of propaganda and, to a growing extent, the law. Over time the list of things to do and to avoid became longer and longer. They range from installing solar panels for the generation of electricity on the roof of one's home to avoiding certain kinds of detergents; and from computers with standby switches to 'light pollution'. As with health, to escape the hammering one would have to live – starve – alone in a wilderness. This has now been carried to the point where my grandson Orr ('Light'), then aged eight, asked me, in all seriousness, whether taking a bath – doing so is one of the greatest joys of his young life – would not deplete Israel's scarce water resources; also, what would happen to the Brazilian rainforests if he were to use some of my A4 paper to draw on.

Orr's innocent question echoes those asked by countless adults. To turn the above-mentioned Carossa on his head, we are being laundered, purified, scrubbed, disinfected and separated. In many cases we also have our heads softened. All so that we may be ready to receive the new gospel and spread it as far and as wide as we can. Under that gospel, 'right' is whatever 'tends to preserve the integrity, stability, and beauty of the biotic community'; 'wrong', whatever tends in the opposite direction.[60] Do we, as human beings, form part of that community? The old religious view, which insisted on our uniqueness, was that we do not and that consequently we could, or were even instructed to, do as we liked. The modern environmental one says that we do – and, having done so, insists that we sacrifice ourselves on behalf of frogs, plants or whatever.

Other people around the world now worry about heating their homes, driving their cars (especially large ones suitable for a family outing), doing their laundry, applying cosmetics, reading books and newspapers (since paper is made of wood pulp), using computers (since the materials they are made of are hard to dispose of) and, of course, growing and eating a very wide range of different foods. Meat-eaters in particular, beware of the holy rage that is being mustered and directed against you! Indeed there is hardly any activity, however essential or innocuous, that the environmental conscience has not targeted. That even includes having children. If future generations are to have a life it is imperative that a great many members of the present one expire first. Seen from an environmental point of view, no doubt, it would be best if we had never been born.[61]

The most remarkable thing about all of this is that the rationale on which much of it is based keeps changing. For the Club of Rome back in 1973 the cardinal consideration was the need to stop the growth of pollution. Other perceived dangers were overpopulation and a looming shortage of energy and raw materials, which had been brought about by several decades of very rapid economic growth. The date chosen to publish the Report was unfortunate; not long thereafter, the Arab-Israeli War of October 1973, the ensuing 'Energy Crisis' and the advent of a mysterious new phenomenon known as stagflation all but ended economic growth in most Western countries. The outcome was to make people scamper for something else to anchor their guilty consciences in. Responding to the challenge, scientists at the University of Wisconsin came up with 'global cooling'. In 1977 an organization calling itself 'The Impact Team' released its report. It claimed to have discovered a 'global weather conspiracy' and warned against 'a new ice age' whose coming was imminent.[62]

So serious was the issue considered that the Office of Research and Development of America's Central Intelligence Agency got involved. 'The western world's leading climatologists', its analysts intoned, 'have confirmed recent reports of a detrimental global climate change . . . The findings suggest that worldwide and synchronistic war–peace, population, and price cycles in recent centuries have been driven mainly by long-term climate change.'[63] America, prepare yourself for the wretched refuse of teeming faraway lands desperately trying to reach your blessed shores. In the event, the fallacy of global cooling was quickly recognized. However, the environmental high priests seldom allow people's consciences to remain quiescent for very long. Shortly thereafter global cooling was followed by its opposite, 'global warming'.

Depending on their supposed causes, both global cooling and global warming may or may not be capable of being corrected by humans. Assuming the former to be the case, both gave birth to some interesting solutions. One was to use gigantic pumps (one author specified that they had to be 'diesel pumps') to move masses of water around the globe, balancing the evil things that Mother Nature had done. Another was to set off a hydrogen bomb. Properly placed and timed, the explosion would send clouds of dust into the atmosphere, blocking the sun and bringing about a 'nuclear winter'.[64] If necessary, the process could be repeated. The trouble was that, ere these and other clever plans could be implemented, global warming started giving signs that it was linked to cooling, at least in certain places and for certain periods of time.[65] Some clever people even managed to get traction out of both phenomena. Switching from one to another, they sounded the alarm as their own mood, changing fashion and prospects for profitable business dictated. As time passed global warming gave way to climate change. That term in turn derives its usefulness from the fact that, like the Holy Trinity, it can contain both a thing *and* its opposite. From now on, whenever a storm occurred it was man who was at fault. Mental health workers, headed by the child psychologist Melanie Klein, have a name for this: they call it 'infantile omnipotence'.

Here our purpose is not to find out which of the claims are correct and which ones are wrong. Since the proponents of environmental ethics are as disposed towards hair-splitting as medieval scholars in their disputations about *synteresis* and *conscientia*, doing so would be impossible in any case. Instead we want to trace the process whereby the environmental conscience, once aroused, has acquired the rather sharp teeth it currently has. Propaganda apart, basically two methods were used. The first, which has been aptly compared to the indulgences of old, consisted of putting in place economic incentives. Governments sold corporations licences to produce so and so much pollution – for example, by spewing so and so much carbon into the air per megawatt of electricity generated. Next, supposing the corporations in question had succeeded in reducing the amount of carbon below the permissible limit, those who owned the licences were allowed to resell the difference to others. At every step in the chain of sellers and buyers the outcome was a strong incentive to reduce pollution. The greater the gap between what one is allowed to do and what one actually does, the larger one's profits. Similar methods could also be used to reduce consumption of allegedly scarce commodities, such as energy, clean water and certain raw materials.

Also as with the indulgences of old, much depends on the original price being correctly set. It should be neither so high as to occasion great losses to those who buy them nor so low as to be ignored. Once that is done, economically speaking the benefits of this approach can hardly be disputed. Nevertheless, when it was first proposed in the late 1980s it encountered ferocious opposition from the most unexpected corner – environmentalists themselves.[66] The riddle was soon solved. It turned out that the objectors' real purpose was not to help alleviate practical problems besetting humanity; if not to enable the latter to continue to exist and to prosper, then at least to prevent the disasters they are always predicting and warning against. Rather it was to make others feel as guilty as they themselves felt or claimed to feel. As used to be the case with Luther, Calvin, Kant and many present-day psychotherapists, the motto is: enjoy your sorrows. It is in them alone that salvation may be found.

The other method was legislation. One possibility is to use taxation – as is already often the case with every kind of liquid fuel. Being easy to collect, such taxes can be extremely profitable for the state and the authorities that run it. It has been claimed that, by simply taxing carbon, the U.S. budget deficit could be halved within ten years.[67] Another possibility is to enact laws that would cap or prohibit such and such 'polluting' or 'damaging' activities after such and such a point in time. That point having passed, those who do not comply would have heavy sanctions imposed on them. For example, it might be forbidden to burn leaves in one's garden; to throw away plastic bottles; to dispose of one's rubbish in any but officially sanctioned ways (in some places, only officially sanctioned plastic bags, sold at an exorbitant price, may be used); or to produce and drive cars that fail to travel so many miles on a gallon of fuel. The already endless list is being added to day by day, with no end in sight.

However it is done, the idea that there is a link between conscience and the environment has turned out to be enormously profitable for large numbers of people and organizations. To some, such as the former leader of Germany's Green Party Joschka Fischer, it brought power. He spent seven years as his country's foreign minister under Chancellor Gerhard Schroeder. He did some useful things, such as helping to prevent Germany from participating in the U.S. attack on Iraq of 2003. On the other hand, one doubts whether, holding this particular post, he was able to do much for German citizens eager for renewable energy, clean air and healthy forests in which to go hiking and rid themselves of their omnipresent 'circulatory diseases'. To others it brought riches as they manufactured any number of 'ecological' products and lobbied for (or against) environmental causes. Others still wrote about the environment, lectured about the environment and received grants to research the environment and find out, for example, how much carbon there used to be in the atmosphere so and so many eons ago. From former U.S. vice-president Al Gore down, some were even awarded Nobel Prizes for their efforts, misguided or not, in this direction.

As in any other kind of politics, different people, movements and interests jostled each other, fighting each other for attention as well as for pieces of the pie. As in any other kind of politics, too, often the outcome was to create strange bedfellows. Normally environmentalists of every kind detest and hate those who hunt for fun (while often admiring 'simple' tribesmen who do so for a living, but that is another matter). Conversely many hunters claim that the sport they practise is their particular way of identifying with nature. Meet interesting animals and kill them, seems to be the motto. Nutrition aside, the fact that even chimpanzees sometimes seem to hunt simply for fun shows that it is also one of the most ancient and most 'natural' of all human activities. Asking only to be left alone, hunters detest environmentalists who want to take away their licences.[68] Yet here and there the two groups have come together to protect forests, heaths, swamps and other habitats of wildlife against, say, loggers or those who would build motorways, oil pipes, electricity pylons or similar wicked things across them.

At other times environmentalists have joined forces with the military. On pain of being called 'the reason we may very soon witness a significant sea-level rise, accompanied by droughts, crop failures, and the mass migration of millions from the global south',[69] the armed forces have been trying to improve their environmental record. Among other things, doing so involved reducing their overall consumption of energy while increasing that of its renewable and non-polluting forms. They have also agreed to look after some kinds of spotted owl or desert turtle on their manoeuvre grounds, as at the U.S. Marine Corps' Camp Lejeune, North Carolina, and Twenty-nine Palms, California, respectively, where the Marines take special care to drive quietly and gingerly during exercises. Evidently some people consider preserving those and other forms of animal life more important than making sure that soldiers be properly trained so as to avoid being killed when their government sends them to fight for their country. In return, environmentalists agreed to help protect those grounds against the threat presented by developers.

So intense is the struggle, and so great the victors' spoils, as to induce some to claim that the entire environmental movement is a scam.[70] Others would argue that, in at least some cases, people's fear of 'pollution' may do more damage than the pollution itself.[71] The similarity with organized religion is unmistakable. After all, anyone can claim that God has spoken to him or her, preach the cause and try to gather believers. Once enough of them have been recruited, they can start using laws and cannon to force their views on the rest of us. Certainly if there is truth in the accusation, and perhaps even if there is not, so powerful and multifaceted has environmentalism become that it threatens to bury conscience under itself. Judging by the fact that, in quite a number of works about environmental ethics, the latter is not even mentioned, there is every reason to believe that this has already happened.

VII
The Man-machine

From Atomism to Behaviourism

The idea that man is a machine – that he has no soul and is governed solely by the interaction of natural factors such as matter and energy – goes back to classical antiquity, if not before. The most famous proponent of this belief was the Roman poet Titus Lucretius Carus (c. 99–c. 55 BC). Except for the fact that both Cicero and his brother Quintus read and admired his work, little is known about his life. He was a follower of Epicurus (341–270 BC), whom he revered as perhaps the best man who had ever lived. Along with the Cynic Diogenes and the above-mentioned Stoic Zeno, Epicurus was one of the most important Greek-Hellenistic philosophers of all. He taught that the gods, if they did in fact exist, neither rewarded people nor punished them. Human life ended with death and was devoid of any higher purpose such as serving God, the state, one's fellow humans or whatever. Hence the slogan should be: get the most out of it while you can. As he wrote in one of his few surviving letters, by that Epicurus meant neither power nor riches. Nor was it a question of engaging in debauchery of the kind associated with Casanova and his ilk. Instead he suggested staying out of other people's business and spending one's time on earth in some comfort, without pain and worry, in the company of family and friends.[1]

During the centuries after his death Epicurus attracted a substantial following.[2] Lucretius himself seems to have had access to many of Epicurus' writings that have since been lost. A productive writer, his masterpiece was a long poem (almost 7,500 lines) named De Rerum Natura (On the Nature of Things). Like so many other religious and philosophical works before and since, its real purpose was to offer liberation, in this case from the fear of death and the punishment that many feared would follow in the afterlife. True freedom could only be rooted in understanding. Apparently following his master rather closely, Lucretius did not explicitly deny the gods' existence. Instead he stripped them of the 'wicked and insane' myths ignorant and superstitious people had woven around them. That done, he revered them in their pure form as models of wisdom and imperturbability. Pursuing this logic, he insisted that no special act of creation underlay the world as we know it. Instead, taking up the ideas of the philosopher Democritus, he argued that the latter was made up of an inconceivably large number of tiny atoms (from a-tomos, indivisible).

The atoms themselves were indestructible. They had always existed and would always exist. Forever falling in a void, they kept combining and interacting with each other. Driven by heat, those interactions and combinations formed not just the body but the mind too. The only difference between the two was that the latter was made up of much smaller, more elusive particles. Death was no more than the dissolution of the particular combination that made up each individual into its constituent atoms. That explained why, when the body passed away, the mind went with it in much the same way as wine loses its bouquet and a perfume its scent: that is, without any measurable change in weight. Chance might cause atoms to meet atoms and come together and form some new combination, or it might not.

In this way Lucretius forged a direct link between the laws of physics and the attributes of the mind such as consciousness, the senses and the various drives. All were merely products, indeed manifestations, of atoms and the ways in which they move and interact. Imagine, he says, a dark room with a beam of light in which countless particles of dust dance about. What appears to us as free will is nothing but unaccountable swerves in the atoms' movements.[3] It is not free will and the conscience and morality that are rooted in it but the attraction of pleasure and the repulsion of pain that govern, and ought to govern, the world. Indeed in the entire long poem the term conscientia appears only once. On that occasion it is linked to other foolish inventions such as Tartarus, the Greek equivalent of hell, which people should forget about if they are ever to lead an enjoyable life.[4] Need one add that such a doctrine, which by reducing the soul to the materials (atoms) of which it was made denied its existence as a separate entity, was unacceptable to the Christian Church? Some Christian writers mention Lucretius only to refute him; St Jerome, whom we have met before, made short shrift of him. In his *Chronicle* he says the author had been driven insane by a love potion he had drunk. He ended by committing suicide at the age of 44.[5]

During the Middle Ages the poem, though its existence was known from other sources, was as good as lost. Only in 1417 did a humanist scholar, Poggio Bracciolini, stumble across a copy.[6] Even so the impact was limited. The amoral atheist Lucretius could not and did not appeal to turn-of-the-sixteenth-century humanist writers such as Erasmus. As the latter wrote in his dialogue *The Epicurean*, to follow him was to forfeit one's soul. Calvin, who when it came to using invective was almost as expert as Luther, at one point called Lucretius 'a filthy dog'.[7] Both in literature and in reality, men went to the stake for lesser offences than the one Lucretius had committed.

Bracciolini's discovery took place at the very time when the Council of Constance was burning heretics left and right. That may help explain, for example, why Machiavelli, who is known to have copied Lucretius' poem word for word and whose copy of it is preserved in the Vatican Library, never mentions it in any of his works. Only towards the end of the sixteenth century did things start changing. In England, a key figure who helped revive interest in Lucretius was Thomas Creech (1659–1700), an English scholar attached to the University of Oxford. Though he was not the first to translate the whole of *De Rerum Natura* into English, his work was the first to be printed.[8] Like his master Lucretius (if Jerome may be believed), Creech ended up by killing himself. Possibly he did so because of an abortive love affair, but the matter has never been cleared up. That, however, proved to be not the end of the matter but only the beginning. Creech's own translation proved unexpectedly popular. As time went on, numerous other editions and translations of Lucretius' works were published, and became the subject of a spirited debate.

In some ways the most important seventeenth-century follower of Lucretius was none other than Thomas Hobbes. By no coincidence, he was an excellent classical scholar in his own right. Both Epicurus and Lucretius had done their best to do away with superstitions of every kind and understand the universe in terms of tangible matter and visible motion. To this Hobbes, no doubt influenced by Galileo (with whom he was in touch and who at this time was engaged on his famous experiments with balls rolling down an inclined plane), added a third factor: force. Force could be neither seen nor felt (except indirectly, through the medium of the matter which it caused to move). Yet it linked the other two together. The way in which it did so was soon to find mathematical expression at the hands of Isaac Newton. Matter, motion and force together were the elements of which the world, man specifically included, were made.

The strongest urge felt by every living creature in the world was self-preservation and, as part of the latter, the 'mechanistic push' (Hobbes's own term) to avoid pain and enjoy pleasure. Pain, including psychological pain, obstructed the circulation of the blood, which had just been discovered by William Harvey (1576–1657). Pleasure, on the contrary, assisted it.[9] What distinguished man from other animals was not his possession of an immortal soul, as Christian writers, with Plato looking over their shoulder, had been claiming for 1,500 years. Instead it was his ability to think and to reason. By enabling him to link actions to consequences, reason acted as the psychological equivalent of self-preservation.[10] It made us understand the need for reciprocity – reinforced, when necessary, by the promise of reward and the threat of punishment – as the only possible basis of morality and, with it, an orderly social life. That in turn led directly to Hobbes's above-mentioned understanding of conscience. Far from being an expression of a divinely inspired 'inner truth', it was merely a name. It was what men 'vehemently in love with their own new opinions, however absurd, and obstinately bent to maintain them' called their opinions so as to increase their authority.[11]

Accused of atheism and a variety of other things besides, Hobbes had to flee for his life. So did other followers of Lucretius. Yet the idea that the world, again specifically including man, was mere matter and that such things as a soul and a conscience did not exist started spreading. Among those who advocated it were some of the Enlightenment's most important thinkers, such as Claude Helvetius (1715–1771) and Paul-Henri d'Holbach (1723–1789). The latter specifically referred to conscience, defining it as 'the internal testimony, which we bear to ourselves, of having acted so as to merit the esteem or blame of the beings, with whom we live'. It was a product not of some spark inspired by a (non-existent) God but of the hope for approval and fear of disapproval.[12] Not surprisingly, both men had their works put on the Index of prohibited books and both were lucky to escape more severe punishment at the hands of the Church.

More famous than either of them was Denis Diderot (1713–1784). A master littérateur, in the art of moving people to tears he was second only to Rousseau. The part of his work dealing with the subject at hand, especially the *Letter on the Blind for the Use of Those Who See*, was vigorously suppressed and he himself spent some months in prison.[13] As he explained, 'life' itself was nothing but a series of actions and reactions as well as shifting shapes. That was as true of the elephant as it was of the flea. Meanwhile the 'molecules' – the term, originating in the middle of the seventeenth century, means 'extremely small particles' – that formed the building blocks of the universe, living creatures specifically included, remained forever unchanged.[14]

Like the work of Epicurus from which it was ultimately derived, materialism entered the world as a bold new theory. Challenging the Church, it promised peace of mind by doing away with fear of divine punishment and similar metaphysical nonsense. However, by the last decades of the eighteenth century it had been turned into part of the furniture, as one present-day writer puts it. As the fact that he made his molecules 'sentient' shows, Diderot himself was not quite happy with the ability of materialism to explain the world.[15] In this he was representative of an entire generation of physiologists who did their best to find a link between dead matter – in this case, organic matter – and the thinking, feeling, moralizing creature known as man.[16] Proponents of the nascent Romantic Movement also refused to accept it. They claimed that by doing away with the soul, Hobbes and his successors had deprived man of his most important characteristic, turning him into a mere machine. Next they set out to show that the key to his actions, indeed his being, was not reason but sensibility.

The *Encyclopédie*, of which Diderot was the co-editor, defines sensibility as 'the faculty of sensing, the sensitive principle . . . the basis and conserving agent of life, animality par excellence, the most beautiful and most singular phenomenon of nature'.[17] To repeat some of what has been said in chapter III above, close on the heels of the *Encyclopédie* came *Emile*, the Savoyard vicar, and the 'divine instinct' known as conscience. Since the last was something a mere machine could never develop, its role in the debate was critical. Throughout the nineteenth century, now one prevailed, now the other. On one side were figures such as Jeremy Bentham, James and John Stuart Mill and other utilitarians. They did not go so far as to deny the existence of conscience but they did hope to anchor it in reason and cultivate it in order to increase human felicity and minimize suffering. On the other were found the Romantics and neo-Romantics. Among them pride of place was taken by English poets such as William Blake, William Wordsworth and Percy Bysshe Shelley. As one of them, Samuel Coleridge (1732–1834), wrote, doctors spent a lifetime applying their mind to gut and body; hence they could hardly imagine that man was anything more than body and gut.

In the present context, the most important poet of all was Alfred Tennyson (1809–1892). The son of a priest, in one of his early poems he wrote that 'I envy not the beast . . . whom a conscience never wakes.'[18] Conscience in turn implied the claim that, whatever Hobbes and the rest might say, such a thing as sin did in fact exist. Sin and our ability to commit it and regret it having been salvaged from the maw of materialism, it was allowed to reoccupy its place as a cardinal pillar of human life, indeed being identified as the very factor that makes us human. To drive home the point, Tennyson also wrote a long and, to modern sensitivities, rather flat-footed poem titled *Lucretius*. Using artistic licence and leaving the ancient sources far behind, he explained that the love potion had been administered by Lucilia, Lucretius' wife.[19] What motivated her was his failure to satisfy her in married life. However, she overshot her target in that the potion made him hallucinate about 'the breasts of Helen', among other interesting things. Seldom did a poet enjoy such success; so well did Tennyson capture the mood of his contemporary Victorians that he was created Poet Laureate, a title he held for 42 years. Queen Victoria, who was one of his most fervent admirers, made him a peer.

Insisting both that there was no God *and* that man should rid himself of his conscience and turn himself into the 'magnificent blond beast' nature had created, Nietzsche tried to end the debate once and for all. As Freud's ruminations on the subject (and, of course, the existence of the present book) inter alia prove, he did not succeed. The factors in which conscience was anchored – the things about which people felt or were made to feel guilty – kept changing. However, in one way or another it never ceased to make its effects felt. It haunted people about what they were about to do, had done and should have done. Subsequent philosophers on their part continued to speculate on its nature. Often rising to almost mystical heights of obfuscation, they spilled rivers of ink without getting any closer to real understanding.

That, however, was only part of the story and by no means the most interesting one. The annals of the twentieth century bristle with scientists and scholars who, knowingly or unknowingly following Hobbes, insisted that matter alone existed. Man, like all other animals, was merely a machine. Since machines do not know anything about morality they cannot distinguish good from evil. Conscience, in other words, was simply a name given a non-existent quality in order to boost our self-esteem. By this time the developing scientific method demanded that to establish a 'truth' it was not enough to philosophize or to observe. Instead, in the field of conscience as in any other, what was needed was experimental proof. One of the first to provide it, or at any rate to try to provide it, was Ivan Petrovich Pavlov (1849–1936). Like so many others who wrestled with the problem, Pavlov was the son of a priest. He started out with the intention of becoming one himself, but lost his faith after reading Darwin. He went to study medicine and became a superb surgeon instead.

Previously it had been thought that reflexes, such as the narrowing of the pupils when subjected to strong light, had been automatic. Pavlov's experiments with dogs seemed to show that they could be conditioned; the animals could be brought to the point where they would salivate upon being presented with a visual or auditory signal (contrary to legend, Pavlov never used bells). Once the conditioning has been completed, pressing such and such a button would lead to such and such a result. By implication a soul, let alone anything as complicated as a conscience, separate from the body did not exist. For his discovery he was awarded the Nobel Prize in medicine in 1904.

Later critics would say that Pavlov's experiments amounted to animal abuse, not to say torture, and that in performing them he simply showed that he had stowed his conscience away. The same applies to many of his successors, including several Nobel Prize-winners, who tried to find out how this or that behaviour was 'imprinted' on animals' minds.[20] Indeed there is a sense in which almost all psychological experiments involve some kind of abuse. Even better known than Pavlov was an American psychologist, Burrhus Frederic Skinner (1904–1990). The list of universities that made him a doctor *honoris causa* reads like a *Who's Who* of twentieth-century academia. Early on, reacting against his grandmother's all too vivid descriptions of hell, Skinner became an atheist. Much later he wrote a vivid account of the way in which institutionalized religion has always used promises and threats in order to induce what it saw as acceptable behaviour.[21] Drawing on this, he spent a lifetime trying to explain behaviour in terms of responses to the pressures, pleasant or otherwise, that are brought to bear on a person from the outside. As he wrote, 'what is felt or introspectively observed is not some nonphysical world of consciousness, mind or mental life but the observer's own body.'[22]

Skinner was no mere theoretician. His objective was not simply to understand behaviour but to devise more effective methods to influence it in this direction or that. As knowledge of the environment and the way it impacted on the body was perfected, for good or ill – Skinner believed, and tried to make others believe, for good – the day would come when humans would be reduced to puppets dancing, or perhaps one should say crawling, on strings. As he wrote, his objective was to 'abolish' the 'autonomous inner man', no less.[23] Hitler, who repeatedly said that the best soldiers were those who 'blindly obeyed' their orders, would have rejoiced.

During the late 1930s Skinner started taking an interest in pigeons as suitable subjects for his experiments in modifying behaviour. Employing his gift for devising gadgets of every kind, he used them to either provide his birds with food or deprive them of it. His greatest moment of public triumph came in 1952 when he used reinforcement and denial, systematically applied, to teach his pigeons to play ping-pong.[24] He also turned the experiment around. By feeding the birds at regular intervals with no reference to their own behaviour, he managed to make them associate food with whatever they had been doing the moment before: in other words, to act as if they were superstitious. Whether they really *were* superstitious, of course, remains not only unknown but unknowable.

From beginning to end, Skinner's intention was to show that what he liked to call 'mentalism', the idea that there existed in each living creature something like an autonomous, non-material mind, was false. As the mind went down the drain, so did the part of it known as conscience. In *About Behaviorism*, the book that sums up his life's work, it is only mentioned once and then only to counter Freud and deny that such a thing does in fact exist.[25] Elsewhere he says that 'guilt, shame, and a sense of sin' are all the result of previous behaviour that had led to severe punishment. So are its manifestations, 'the furtive look, the skulking manner, [and] the guilty way of speaking'.[26] Substitute 'whining' for 'speaking', and he might as well be describing my dogs. That, of course, was precisely the point Skinner wished to make.

As part of his programme, and much like Epicurus, Lucretius, Hobbes and others, Skinner hoped to liberate man from the pangs of conscience. However, he would not do so by providing him with a perfect education, as Rousseau had hoped to do. Nor would he have him take his courage in his hands, overcome conscience and lift himself above it, as Nietzsche had urged his readers and Richard III, his followers. Instead he planned to convince people that it was all an illusion and that in reality there was no such thing. His efforts – like those of his predecessors and, almost certainly, his future followers – were doomed to failure. Everything considered, it is probably better that way.

The Rise of the Robots

If man were indeed a machine made solely of material components and devoid of a soul, then – in principle at any rate – it should be possible to construct a mechanism capable of doing anything he could as well as he could. Stories about just such mechanisms, from the Greek *mēchanē*, machine, were already rife in antiquity. Most had supposedly been assembled by two figures, the smith-god Hephaestus and the equally mythological craftsman Daedalus. Some of the information we possess about automata (self-acting, in Greek) comes from Callistratus, a writer from the fourth or third century BC. Such an accomplished a craftsman was Daedalus, Callistratus says, that some credited him with having made 'statues endowed with motion and [able] to feel human sensations'.[27] But even Daedalus, though he was able to make his figures move and dance, found it impossible to endow them with the faculty of speech.[28] In this respect he was surpassed by the 'Ethiopians' who had made a statue (in fact there are two) of Memnon. In times long past, says Callistratus, whose name means Beautiful Sky, that statue had

> saluted the rising Day by its voice giving token of its joy and expressing delight at the arrival of its mother; and again, as day declined to night, it uttered piteous and mournful groans in grief at her departure . . . The statue of Memnon, as it seems to me, differed from a human being only in its body, but it had grief in its composition and again it was possessed by a feeling of pleasure according as it was affected by each emotion. Though nature had made all stones from the beginning voiceless and mute and both unwilling to be under the control of grief and also unaware of the meaning of joy . . . yet to that stone of Memnon art had imparted pleasure and had mingled the sense of pain in the rock; and this is the only work of art of which we know that has implanted in the stone perceptions and a voice.

Today we are surrounded by speaking machines capable of uttering any sound we want them to. Programming them to say or sing the appropriate words at any time we want, in response to practically every sign of condition we want, represents no problem. But does that fact mean the machines in question have emotions? Of course it does not.

Automata retained their popularity throughout the ages, and not just in Europe either. Depending on which story we want to believe, they walked, danced and sang. They rolled their eyes, shed tears and stood guard at the gates of palaces. Others played music or turned their faces towards the sun, following it in its daily movement.[29] One legendary Chinese automaton made such realistic advances to a king's ladies that he almost had its constructor, one Yan Shi, executed.[30] A famous eighteenth-century automaton in the shape of a bird, now at the Patek Philippe Museum in Geneva, could flap its wings, twitter, eat and defecate. Around 1800 a large chess-playing automaton in the shape of a turbaned Turk toured Europe playing exhibition games. One of those who tried to match his skills against it was Napoleon (he lost).[31] Later it turned out that the machine was a fraud and that a man was hidden inside.[32]

Most automata were powered either by weights or by clockwork. As in antiquity, some were made of materials such as gold, silver and every kind of precious stone. Others were crude devices made of painted tin or, in the case of dolls, porcelain, rubber and, later, plastic. Regardless of whether those who bought and played with them were adults or children, they were invariably understood as toys. Their purpose was to entertain, not to do work. At times they may also have been used to illustrate the idea that animals, man included, were in fact machines. Perhaps that is why Thomas Aquinas was said to have destroyed an automaton in the form of a mechanical man made of brass which could move and speak. Some eighteenth-century French religious authorities also considered automata proof of heresy and destroyed those they found.[33]

Automata designed to perform a useful function were entirely different. Among the earliest was the centrifugal governor. Apparently invented around the middle of the seventeenth century, it was used to regulate the distance between grinding stones in windmills.[34] In 1788 James Watt built a similar device to keep his steam engines working at fairly constant speed. He was aware that he was not the first in the field, and hence he did not try to take out a patent on it. Two metal balls were attached to movable arms linked to a central vertical axis. The faster the axis rotated the farther apart the balls spread, causing the machine to slow down again. Thus the governor regulated speed and speed, the governor. Much later, this ability to respond to the environment and change it in turn became known as a feedback loop. Yet the existence of the loop did not mean that the device 'sensed' the speed of the machine in the same way as living creatures 'sense' what is happening in the environment around them. It could never become dizzy or nauseated, or lose its balance and fall, let alone distinguish good from evil, experience guilt or develop a conscience.

By perfecting the steam engine, Watt did as much as anyone to unleash the Industrial Revolution, which in turn changed the technological balance between East and West, causing the former to lag behind the latter. However, this did not prevent the Japanese in particular from taking a very favourable view of automata. As in the West, originally they were seen as nice toys. Later they came to be perceived not just as labour-saving devices, servants or slaves, but as personal friends that were to some extent capable of meeting people's emotional needs. One example is AIBO the robotic dog, whose name means 'partner' or 'friend'. Later he was joined by Qrio, a bipedal humanoid robot.[35] In August 2013 yet another robot, equipped with speech and face recognition, was sent to join the crew of the International Space Station, reportedly to entertain astronauts and keep them company.[36] Some Japanese people are even said to dream of the day when they will adopt Qrio-like machines as their lovers.[37]

A less sympathetic reason behind the love affair between Japanese people and their robots might be the tightly knit nature of society. It caused some to quip that they themselves are robots. Overcome by a feeling of powerlessness, Japanese people seek to avenge themselves by exercising complete control over *something*. Or could the affair have something to do with the above-mentioned fact that, in Japanese culture, the compass that governs life is not guilt but respect? Be that as it may, to this day roboethics, a new field of study concerned with making sure that robots should not transgress certain ethical boundaries, is a subject that does not strike a chord in Japan.[38]

The situation in the West was entirely different. Dazzled by technological progress, nineteenth-century magazines took a light-hearted view of the matter. Writers delighted in inventing, and artists in drawing, imaginary creatures such as the steam man, the electric man, the boiler-plate man and the automatic man.[39] Much of this was meant to be good fun. The famous author Jules Verne (1828–1905) at one point wrote a story that figured a carriage pulled by an enormous steam-powered elephant. The British used it to re-establish their rule over India in the wake of the rebellion there.[40] After the First World War a more pessimistic mood set in and fear predominated. The person who did more than anybody else to bring that fear to the surface was a Czech writer, Karl Čapek (1880–1938), in his 1920 play R.U.R. *Rossum's Universal Robots*.[41] The original meaning of the word 'robot' is simply 'labourer' or 'hard worker'. However, Čapek used it to designate a class of artificial humans. Like the monster Mary Shelley wrote of in *Frankenstein* (1818/31), they were made not of metal but of organic materials that had somehow had 'life' infused into them. Unlike Shelley's monster, they were designed to do useful work and for a time did so successfully.

Known after the firm that made them, Rossum's robots were simpler than human beings. Having no 'souls', they were incapable of experiencing happiness, fear, appetite or curiosity. As one of the characters says, in this respect they are 'less than so much grass' (some modern environmentalists would regard this as an insult to grass). Their lack of feeling, and their consequent readiness to carry out massacres if ordered to do so, was precisely what made them useful as soldiers in the many wars that broke out after they were first invented. Next, strange things started happening. Following some unauthorized experiments by one of the designers, a number of robots developed irritability. No more content to do as they were told, they declared man to be their enemy and an outlaw. They organized and rose in revolt. Being stronger than humans, before long they did away with every man and woman in the world.

Towards the end of the play the robots laid siege to the factory where they had originally been invented. In the process the formula for building them was accidentally lost so that no more could be made. The robots stormed the factory and killed all the people inside except one, a builder named Alquist. Him they spared because, like them, he did not simply give instructions but worked with his hands. By that time the last human female capable of reproducing was dead. This left Primus Robot and his female companion, Helena, as the only creatures on earth capable of securing the future, if not of mankind then of some kind of copy of it. For good or ill, Primus and Helena have developed to the point where they express their love for one another. As Alquist, in the last line of the play, recognizes, they have turned into the latter-day equivalent of Adam and Eve – ready to take over from man and repopulate the earth.

Fear of what robots, having developed independent drives and wishes, might do were they to run out of control has been part and parcel of Western civilization ever since. A guru by the name of Ray Kurzweil is recorded as saying that humanity, confronted by its own creations, only stands a 50/50 chance of surviving. Not only was the above-mentioned field of roboethics brought into being, but learned conferences have been organized to define the problem and help find ways to prevent robots from doing all kinds of bad things. Do we feel guilty about what our hands have wrought? If so, then it should be no cause for surprise. After all, the guilt/conscience complex has been part and parcel of the Western soul at least since the early days of Christianity, if not before. At times it was anchored in one thing, at times in another.

Much more interesting is a different question: namely, whether robots themselves can be provided with, or develop, a conscience. Nobody took a greater interest in the problem than the most important twentieth-century writer of science fiction, Isaac Asimov (1920–1992). Asimov, the son of Russian Jews who had come to the U.S., had his interest in the subject triggered by pulp magazines he read during his youth. In 1942, in a short story titled 'Runaround', he came up with the so-called Three Laws of Robotics.[42] Taken together, they provided robots with a built-in conscience of sorts. The first law stated that 'a robot may not injure a human being or, through inaction, allow a human being to come to harm.' The second said that 'a robot must obey the orders given to it by human beings, except where such orders would conflict with the First Law.' The third was that 'a robot must protect its own existence as long as such protection does not conflict with the First or Second Laws.'[43] The laws have had a vast impact on all subsequent science fiction. However, they are not without difficulties, as Asimov himself was well aware: he kept tinkering with them for the rest of his life.

First, when Asimov through one of his characters talked about designing robots in such a way that they would be unable to 'harm' a human, what did he mean? In the case of killing or injuring, then the harm is clear enough and solutions to it are relatively easy to find. But how about inflicting emotional damage by means of behaviour that is or appears to be callous? How about violating privacy and spying, as is increasingly occurring even today? As the number of robots grows, how about their use of resources, such as energy, that humans also need? And how about robots that take the place of a human who may be thrown out of work and sent begging instead? Don't such things come under the rubric of inflicting harm? There are many questions but few answers. In this context it is worth noting that some attempts to provide answers are in fact being made; with what success remains to be seen.[44]

Another problem concerns identification. Robots need not necessarily resemble humans. From Watt's governor all the way to the Roomba vacuum cleaner familiar to many readers, many do not. However, the more the technology develops the easier it will become to make some of them do so if that is desired. Supposing work proceeds along these lines, will the robots always be able to tell members of the two races apart? Asimov's laws, in other words, can only work as long as human-like robots, also known as androids, are not made perfect; or else as long as some method is deliberately used to distinguish them from humans. As it is, the laws permit robots disguised as humans to do whatever they, or those who built them and programmed them, desire without having to worry about encountering opposition from other robots. Conversely robots that mistake (or claim to mistake!) humans for their own kind might very well violate the first law.

Next, how about using robots in order to oppose, and if necessary kill, people who are trying to kill other people? Even at present the military of all modern countries, hoping to increase effectiveness and avoid friendly casualties, are spending huge sums on robotic research.[45] Some of the machines now at various stages of development are fearsome indeed, to say nothing of the fact that in some fields, such as anti-aircraft and anti-missile defence, where speeds are enormous and decisions whether to open fire and at what must be made within fractions of a second, robots have long since taken over. Occasionally the results were disastrous, as happened in July 1988 when the USS *Vincennes* accidentally shot down an Iranian airliner over the Persian Gulf.[46] In South Africa in 2007, an experimental robotic anti-aircraft gun suddenly slewed around in the wrong direction while spitting out shells at a rate of hundreds per minute. By the time it was stopped it had killed nine soldiers and injured fourteen others.[47]

The problem is even more acute in the field of counter-terrorism. In any such campaign the first and most important requirement is the ability to distinguish between friend, bystander and foe. The second is to kill or otherwise 'neutralize' those forming part of the third category without, as far as possible, hurting the first two. As the title of one book on the subject put it, one must learn to eat soup with a knife. But Asimov's Laws do not apply to the situation – which is becoming increasingly common – in which robots may actually be designed to 'harm', incapacitate, wound or kill human beings in armed conflict. In such a conflict robots that obey the second law, precisely because they have a conscience of sorts built into them, would be entirely useless.

In situations other than war, things might be very different. For example, robots might be made to assist blind people who have difficulty in crossing a busy street. Imagine one of these machines using its legs or wheels to take the place of guide dogs. To be sure there may be some glitches, especially at the beginning. Yet dogs, and even flesh-and-blood people who perform similar functions, are not immune to errors. As experience is gained, it should be made possible to correct the initial bugs.

Other robots, kept at home, might provide first aid, automatically calling for help in case somebody is incapacitated. Others still, brought to a house that is going up in flames, might break into it in order to rescue the occupants. Robots could be provided with a shopping list and sent to the supermarket or else go from one house to another distributing food and other necessities to the people within. Some of these ideas are currently at various stages of development; in Japan engineers working for the Honda Corporation have built Asimo, a humanoid robot 1.40 m tall. It is capable, or will soon be capable, of carrying out similar tasks.[48] Switching back to military life, robots could be made to spare anybody less than 1.2 m tall (though people who crouch or take shelter might produce some difficulties). They might even be made to distinguish men from women, though how they would deal with people of both sexes who dress up as members of the opposite one, or with female fighters, is another question entirely. The number of possibilities appears endless. Except for a limited number of intransitive tasks only we can perform for ourselves, such as eating, drinking, studying, sleeping and exercising, robots could do practically anything.

At this point it is important to note that we are talking of truly autonomous robots. By that are meant those that have built-in sensors, make decisions and, on the basis of their programming, change their behaviour solely according to the information those sensors collect, store and process. That excludes machines such as remotely controlled cars, ships, aircraft and the like that do whatever they are designed to do by carrying out their operators' commands as transmitted to them by either wire or wireless. Such machines, used in war against enemies who may be thousands of miles away and who die before they even realize they are in danger, can face their operators with serious ethical dilemmas. Those ethical dilemmas have in turn been known to result in severe mental problems.[49] As has been said, though, those who walk on stilts are nevertheless using their legs. That is why the present chapter does not deal with them.

Suppose some of the machines described above, or others similar to them, are built and perform successfully. Does that mean they have been endowed with, or developed, a conscience? Will they have free will, the indispensable prerequisite for any kind of conscience? Will they be able to tell their owners, 'Sorry sir, this is something my conscience just does not allow me to do?' Will they be capable of feeling sorry for others of their kind, as chimpanzees are said to be? Will they understand the nature of shame, embarrassment or 'knowledge with themselves' of the kind the ancient Greeks used to speak of? Will they reproach themselves as Oedipus did? Will they maintain Stoic self-respect? Will they commit suicide when circumstances make doing so impossible? Will they understand the notion of God? Or that of truth, as St Paul and Luther hoped a conscience would?

Or of guilt, specifically including the kind of guilt arising out of sins not yet committed? Or of sin itself? Or of duty? Or of morality? Or of good? Or of evil? Or of rewards? Or of punishment? To recall Freud, will they be beset – one does not want to say, tormented – by conflicts between different elements in whatever kind of 'mind' they may have?

In respect to most of these questions the probable response is, who knows? Perhaps the day may come when robots will be able to do some or all of these things. However, they will still have to be programmed first; therefore whether this would really mean that they have a conscience is somewhat doubtful. The answer to the last question is definitely yes, but only because of inappropriate design. Presumably a machine with more than one soul built into it will soon cease to function. It may even self-destruct just as my computer occasionally does.

Robots might, however, be programmed to act *as if* they did, if not all, then at least some of these things. For example, they might be designed, in fact are already being designed, to 'choose' between several possible courses of action, thus in some sense obtaining a free will. Or they might shed tears or make noises when their comrades are hurt; or they might sacrifice themselves for some 'higher' goal. Asimov himself provides an example of a robot taking the initiative and saving the life of a little girl even though its sensors tell it that, by doing so, it puts its own existence at risk. Humans behaving in this way are lionized for having a conscience; so why not robots? As robots are taking a growing role in war, here and there attempts are being made to provide them with a sort of conscience that would prevent them from killing the wrong people in the wrong situation. In cases where they have done so they could perhaps be made to display signs of PTSD, including lack of appetite (by refusing to have their batteries recharged), dysfunctional movements, unaccountable aggressiveness and nightmares; though what purpose doing so might serve is hard to say.[50]

To put the question in a more abstract way, is conscience simply a mechanism, either innate, divinely inspired or planted in us by the education we have received, that will make whoever has it obey a certain category of rules we call ethical? That, for example, is how Jacques Pitrat, a French pioneer of artificial intelligence, sees it.[51] Or is it soething more, and if so, what? Theologians, philosophers and experts on ethics have wrestled with the problem for millennia past, but all they have come up with is words. Often the harder they tried to explain, the less intelligible they became. During the Middle Ages, and by no means during this period alone, some of them rose to mystical heights of obfuscation.

Thanks to the introduction of robots, even those that do not look anything like humans but capture at least some of the latter's abilities, our age may be the first in history where progressing beyond words may be possible, at least in principle. As far as may be determined from the literature, the attempts to date that have been made to build machines that act as if they had a conscience have only resulted in some very feeble imitations. One reason for this is that the problem, involving as it does many 'squishy' factors that interact with each other, is an extremely complex one. Another is that, partly because the problem is so complex, scientists and those who provide them with funding have not given it very high priority. That is not to say that such machines could not have their uses. On a practical level, autonomous robots with a built-in conscience could be entrusted with far more missions than robots that do not have one. On the theoretical one, such machines could be put side by side with humans and systematically compared with them. By highlighting both the similarities and the differences, they should enable us to present the riddle in a more vivid and starker form than ever before.

As Norbert Wiener, the father of cybernetics (the science that deals with automatic feedback loops), once wrote, the only things we can fully understand are those we are able to build. As my son Uri, who is both a first-class computer expert and a qualified psychotherapist, once told me, the chances are that we shall succeed in building something that seems to act somewhat like an artificial conscience before we ever understand what conscience really is.

The Electrical-chemical Machine

To try and construct artificial beings, whether organic or mechanical, that would behave as if they had a conscience is one thing. To study the living organism in order to discover in just which part of the body that conscience is located, how it works and how it can be influenced by means other than the traditional ones of education, reward and punishment is quite a different one. In one way or another, such attempts have been going on for a very long time. During most of the period in question the instruments and methods used for the purpose were extremely crude. The emergence over the last few decades of modern brain science has caused things to change – or has it?

Attempts to understand how the mind, and conscience as one of its most important parts, work go back millennia if not more. Ancient Greek and later Roman physicians and philosophers often considered the matter. At first, owing no doubt to the effect that different emotions have on the activity of our hearts, they believed that the mind was located in that organ. Homer's Odysseus often 'spoke to his heart',[52] as did many other heroes in the epics. As expressions such as 'take to heart', 'hearty', 'cordial', 'heartfelt' and 'heartiness' show, the same used to be the case in several other cultures. They include not only European ones but my own native Hebrew and, I am told, Japanese and Tibetan as well. However, even in antiquity some physicians and philosophers pointed to the brain as the organ responsible for both emotion and thought. As one modern work on the subject puts it, 'to understand what is going on when people engage in social interactions with one another, when they feel empathy of hostility . . . when they obey rules or violate laws, when they are affected by poverty or child abuse, when they do violence to others or themselves . . . we should turn to the brain.'[53]

During the Middle Ages the Church worried lest research would confirm the views of the atomists and show that man did not have a soul. Hence it prohibited any attempt to dissect the human body. Only after 1500 did interest in the subject revive. In 1654 an English doctor, Thomas Willis, invented the term 'neurology'. His work, the purpose of which was to discover a cure for epilepsy and other convulsive diseases, involved mapping the brain and cataloguing its various parts in much greater detail than before. He also tried to find out which of those parts were responsible for certain functions, such as walking.[54] Over the next 200 years this kind of study was pushed forward haltingly and at times erratically. On occasion it was assisted by accidents that destroyed parts of the brains of individual people. The most famous case in point was an American railway worker named Pinehas Gage (1823–1868). Gage accidentally had an iron rod driven straight through his head. He survived, but some of those who knew him thought that he had turned into a different person. The ways in which the accident affected his personality and behaviour, and what the changes meant in terms of our understanding of how the human brain functions, became the subject of a lively debate among doctors.[55]

Real progress only started being made during the very last years of the nineteenth century, when brain researchers came up with sophisticated techniques, such as staining, for the purpose. This led to the discovery that neurons, the exceedingly small and often all but transparent cells that make up the brain, are interconnected by means of knots known as synapses. Whereas the number of neurons in the brain of each human adult is around 100 billion, that of synapses has been estimated at 100 trillion. On average, therefore, each neuron forms a thousand links with its neighbours, both close and far. Some experts see this connectivity, which is far greater than that found in any other animal, as the real secret of whatever quality it is that separates us from those animals.[56] Information is transmitted through the synapses in the form of electrical signals. Medical texts of the 1920s often compared the brain to the headquarters of a large power station. The headquarters received information from the body's sensors, stored it, processed it and formulated commands in response to it. Next it made use of electrical links to send them throughout the system. This image remained substantially intact until the early 1930s, when it was realized that chemical signals play a dominant role; the implication being that the brain is an electrical-chemical machine.

The most important advances only started being made during the 1960s. The first was the development of ultra-thin electrodes that could be inserted into specific parts of the brain. That done, they could be used to modify the behaviour of animals, such a monkeys, for example by taking away their appetites or making them masturbate all the time. Next came ultrasound scanning. It worked in the same way as bats receive their information: by sending sound waves into selected parts of the body and registering the resulting echoes. This marked the first time when the body's internal organs, the brain included, could be observed in action without any need to operate. Hard on the heels of ultrasound came CT (computerized tomography) scanning. CT made it possible to take x-ray photographs not from one direction but from several at once. Next a computer was used to fuse the images, thus providing a three-dimensional image of internal organs in action. Subsequent machines also relied on computers. However, instead of x-rays they used gamma rays, radio-frequency waves, electrons and magnetic particles.[57] The most recent advances in the rapidly developing field appear to be Functional MRI (magnetic resonance imaging) and Tensor MRI. The former looks at blood flow in the brain to detect areas of activity, while the latter permits the measurement of the restricted diffusion of water in tissue in order to produce images of the neural tract in action.[58]

Between them the devices enabled researchers to do two things. First, continuing the work Willis had started 300-odd years before, they mapped the parts of the brain in an effort to find out the function of each. Second, they provided images of what happened in each part as its owner engaged in all sorts of activities. Among them were exercise, various kinds of intellectual work such as memorizing and problem solving, and – needless to say – 'the symphony of activity that leads to sexual climax'.[59] In doing all this many scientists were motivated by the desire to gain understanding. Others hoped to develop methods for curing and if possible even preventing all sorts of problems. That included dealing with certain kinds of emotion, such as depression; thought, such as the delusions schizophrenics often come up with; and behaviour, such as violence, considered harmful to the patient and to others. The fact that certain substances can affect human mood, emotion and behaviour had been known for thousands of years, if not more. One of them, alcohol, has always been used for the purpose and still is. Until the last years of the nineteenth century, when various factors caused the U.S. authorities in particular to place the first restrictions on psychoactive drugs such as opium, the same applied to them.[60]

The period between 1940 and 1970 saw frequent use of lobotomy, a procedure that mutilated people's brains by surgically severing some of the most important links among its various parts. Supposedly it had a beneficial effect on epileptics and schizophrenics. Other popular techniques were insulin-induced coma and electroshock. All three were sometimes used in ways that approached, if indeed they did not equal, torture. For this reason, but also because their effectiveness was hard if not impossible to measure, they remain quite controversial.[61] During the 1950s psycho-pharmaceutical drugs were introduced. Among the first was chlorpromazine, used to treat schizophrenics and bipolar people in the manic phase of their cycle. Many others followed, and the list keeps expanding almost day by day. Some consider these drugs the greatest advance since psychiatry first emerged as a separate discipline around 1860.[62] Others argue that they work mostly by suggestion; if true, that would explain why so many of them seem to lose their effectiveness after their novelty wears off.[63] Others still feel that their main effect, if any, is not to 'cure' mental diseases but to turn those who take them into zombies. Having done so decades ago, I personally tend to agree.

The importance attributed to neuroscience is evident from the fact that, starting with the Spaniard Santiago Ramón y Cayal in 1906, a list of Nobel Prize recipients in physiology and medicine reads like a *Who's Who* of workers in the field. Some studies were made on animals, others on humans. As of the beginning of the second decade of the twenty-first century refereed papers on the subject were being published at the rate of 600 a month, no less. The outcome has been the creation of an enormous scientific-medical-industrial complex. One estimate has it that in 2009 alone, the global value of the products and services generated by the neuro-industry amounted to $140 billion.

And what has all of this to do with conscience? From time immemorial, society's most important method for making people behave in ways it considered desirable, and avoid behaving in ways it considered undesirable, has been education. When necessary, education was reinforced by legislation that promised carrots and threatened the use of sticks, at which point conscience became mixed up with promises and rewards. Always the objective was to make people internalize prohibitions and to inculcate guilt feelings. That way the prohibitions would cause them to avoid doing certain things even when they were useful to themselves. The guilt feelings would make them avoid doing them even when nobody was looking and to feel contrition (and, very often, seek relief) for having done them nevertheless.

Put together, the internalized prohibitions and the guilt feelings were known as conscience. Mountains of books were written in an effort to find out whether conscience was innate or acquired; just how it was linked with religious faith as well as other factors such as truth and duty; what, if anything, it was good for; which parts of the mind were involved in awakening and maintaining it; and so on and so on right down to the present day. Some authors, including Lucretius, Hobbes and Skinner, claimed that it did not exist at all. But the objections they raised did not prevent the majority from trying to understand it, instil it and follow its dictates. In one sense that majority must have included the doubters themselves, or else they would have found themselves in trouble even more often than they did, albeit for entirely different reasons.

Modern brain researchers have taken a different approach. On the one hand they rejected the idea that the mind, and of course the part of it known as conscience, is some disembodied spirit. What else could they do, given that the existence of such spirits was not subject to experimental proof? On the other, they insisted that, along with other mental functions, it 'is what the brain does'. Some went further still, claiming that 'even the capacity to think ethically, to make moral judgments, is a brain kind of thing'.[64] Thus the emphasis has shifted from matter to the processes that go on inside it. True, to this day nobody knows exactly how the brain, seen as an enormously complex and, what is more, adaptive machine inside which however many electronic and chemical signals are passed from one neuron to another every second, creates the mysterious thing known as conscience (and a great many others besides) and interacts with it. As a result neuroscientists, who study the way the brain functions, and all kinds of psychotherapists, much of whose work consists of coping with symptoms as the patient experiences and expresses them, are as far apart as they have ever been. The former accuse the latter of lacking any scientific basis and have gone so far as to discontinue using their work in their own research projects. The latter respond by saying that, when it comes to helping mentally diseased people, the former's work is useless. The publication of DSM-V has provided the debate with a new impetus.[65]

When scientists say that mind is cerebral activity, what they really mean is that, considering everything they know and ignoring everything they do not, it *must* be so.[66] Either that, or they will have to reintroduce some of the obscure concepts with which Hobbes in *Leviathan* had so much fun, such as '*hypostatical, transubstantiate, consubtantiate, eternal-now*, and the like canting of schoolmen'.[67] To hide the fact that they do not really know they often resort to terms such as 'probably', 'may' and 'likely', which no engineer building a machine would use.[68] Another way to disguise ignorance is to say that this or that function is 'diffused' among various parts of the brain. Meanwhile, by some estimates, one in five Americans, both young and old, suffer from some mental disorder *each year*. Others claim that 40 per cent of European Union citizens have them.[69] If that is true, then clearly neither neuroscience nor psychiatry nor any of their numerous affiliated disciplines have done much to make our world a healthier, saner place. If it is not, then one hardly knows what to think of those disciplines at all.

Some neuroscientists claim that they have identified the brain's frontal lobe as the part most involved in 'moral cognition'.[70] Should it be destroyed, that cognition will be lost. However, the same lobe is also responsible for logical thinking, including the ability to foresee the consequences of our actions. Hence it is hard to say whether what is lost is hope for reward and fear of consequences or conscience proper, the kind that supposedly operates regardless of those considerations. That, and more: just how an electrical dysfunction or chemical reaction in or physical damage to soft grey matter translates into what scientists, on the basis of the social norms to which they are used, consider an impaired conscience, they have not the slightest clue. Finally it has long been known that different parts of the brain are sometimes capable of taking over from each other, thus facilitating recovery from any injury that may have occurred. That is why, instead of saying that part X is responsible for function Y, researches often say that it is 'involved'.

Instead the ongoing scientific assault on the brain appears to have done two things. First, it has all but knocked conscience, especially the kind of conscience that focuses on calling attention to evil and changing the world, out of the discussion. It has been relegated to such 'soft' disciplines as theology, philosophy and ethics. Those disciplines in turn proceed almost as if neuroscience did not exist. On google.com, 'neuroscience' brought over 25,000,000 hits. However, the combination of 'neuroscience' and 'conscience' brought just 5,140,000, 20 per cent of the former figure. Even that number is misleading. Closer examination will show that the vast majority of hits refer not to conscience but to consciousness – a related but far from identical thing. Unless he or she is a robot, anybody who has a conscience must have a consciousness. However, not everyone who has a consciousness has a conscience too. Many of the hits that do refer to conscience are in French. That is because, in that language, the word *conscience* can refer either to conscience or to consciousness.

By this criterion, the number of neuroscientists who have even tried to understand conscience is close to zero. Instead, the concept has been pushed aside in favour of empathy, identification, emotional contagion, caring, altruism, cooperation, 'prosociality' and so on. All these, we are told, are under the control not of the conscious self but of something known as 'mirror neurons', which fire both when a person performs some action and when he or she observes someone else doing the same.[71] Even more important than any of these are inhibitions (31,000,000 hits). In medieval Latin an inhibition meant simply a formal prohibition. It got its present meaning shortly before 1900 when psychology for the first time came to be regarded as an important discipline. An inhibition, *Webster's Thesaurus* explains, is 'prevention, restraint, hindrance, barrier, impediment, interference'. Reader, note: there is no reference here either to any conscious, conscience-induced, choice, much less to the critical distinction between good and evil. Regardless of whether we see inhibitions as something that have been built into us by nature or that have been implanted into us by society until they become an integral part of the self, the critical point about them is that the restraints they place on behaviour are unconscious.

Conscience is usually understood as a single entity that applies to many different fields. By contrast, inhibitions are to conscience what small change is to a $100 bill. One kind of inhibition may prevent us, say, from killing our neighbour, raping his wife and burning down his house. Another, such as the one autistic persons are said to suffer from, may prevent us from loving or even communicating with our fellow human beings. Just how the various kinds of inhibitions are related, and what causes them, is very much in doubt. A person who lacks the former kind will be handled by the justice system and, if all goes as it should, end up in prison or else on the electric chair. A person who suffers from the latter will be treated by a suitably quali-fied psychotherapist. Inhibitions, if they are put aside and violated, do not result in guilt feelings, regret and/or a wish for atonement. Clearly inhibitions, which are supposed to act as automatic governors of behaviour, and conscience, which often makes its impact in the form of long and agonizing deliberations both before and after a social rule has been violated, are two very different things. Returning to our discussion of robots, one might even question whether an 'automatic' conscience – one that is not under the conscious control of its owner's brain – deserves to be called a conscience at all.

Second, traditionally the emphasis used to be on immoral or amoral behaviour as the product of the will. By contrast modern neuroscience looks at conscience in terms of the functioning of the brain. A well-ordered brain secretes oxytocin and vasopressin and any number of other hormones and enzymes. If the amounts of all those chemicals and the ways they are distributed are as they should be, we are told, the outcome will be the kind of behaviour the individual can live with and the society in which he lives finds acceptable. If they are not – if, in other words, the brain is disturbed – the outcome will be behaviour that is the opposite from this. But assuming it is all a reflection of cerebral activity, one that is itself purely electrical-chemical by nature, how can people be held responsible for their actions? Suppose Hitler, Himmler, Goebbels, Heydrich, Bach-Zelewski and the rest suffered from deficiencies, or surpluses as the case may be, of the above-mentioned hormones and others like them, which for all we know may have been the case. Surely that does not mean that we must stop denouncing them for the crimes they committed and start sympathizing with them for the mental problems that were the outcome of those problems. Or does it?

The question, which might equally well be applied to smaller fry such as Globocnik, Höss and Stangl, Kaduk, Boger and Klehr, is not meant to be facetious. The origins of the insanity defence, the method whereby people accused of having committed a crime can escape punishment by reason of being insane either at the time or all the time, can be traced back all the way to ancient Greece and Rome. Underlying the strategy in question is the assumption that there exists a difference between 'bad' and 'mad'. For centuries, perhaps millennia, jurists have done their best to draw clear lines between the two things. Starting in 1860 or so they have been assisted by members of the merging psychiatric profession, all with no more than mediocre success. Now that we know, or believe we know, that the mind is simply a process or activity that takes place within the brain, the problem has become more acute still.

Take the notorious case of Charles Whitman. Born in 1941, Whitman was a former U.S. Marine who at one point received a good conduct medal. Having enrolled as an engineering student at the University of Texas, on 1 August 1966 he went on a rampage. He killed seventeen people and injured another 32 before he himself was killed by a police officer. Later an autopsy brought to light the fact that he had been suffering from a highly aggressive and invariably fatal brain tumour known as an astrocytoma (star-shaped growth). At the time Whitman did what he did, he had only a few months left to live. Initially doctors who were asked for an opinion concluded, or claimed to have concluded, that the tumour had nothing to do with his behaviour.[72] Later, though, a medical commission appointed to look into the case concluded that it 'conceivably could have contributed to his inability to control his emotions and actions'.[73]

Such cases are not as rare as one might think. By one estimate, 30–40 per cent of America's prison population consists of 'psychopaths': people whose brains differ significantly from that of 'health controls' in terms of electric activity.[74] Nor is it only a question of tumours. In 1979 a British physician named Katharina Dalton published a bestseller with the title *Once a Month*. She argued that changes in the secretion of hormones, subsequently identified as tryptophan and serotonin, during menstruation regularly turns women into raging maniacs. It predisposes them to suicide, homicide, child abuse and many similar bad things. The book's success led to Dalton being invited to act as a star witness at several sensational murder trials. If it is true that we are prisoners of our tumours and/or hormones, then one wonders why many criminals are in jail rather than in hospital. Conversely, whatever neuroscientists may say concerning the future promise of their rapidly developing science, clearly a world in which they are taken at their word and in which nobody can be justly either rewarded or punished for anything he or she did is not yet at hand. A survey taken of American judges in 2012 revealed that most would refuse to accept the 'it was not me, it was my brain that did it' defence. Neurologists agree with them, saying that it would be very risky to link judicial issues to any given image of a person's brain responses.[75]

On the one hand courts appear more inclined to ask for the testimony of experts, especially psychologists, psychiatrists and neurologists, than ever before. On the other, the more those experts claim to approach a complete understanding of the way the brain functions, thus obviating the very ideas of 'innocence' and 'guilt', the less inclined judges are to take them and their advice seriously. With rare exceptions, the most a person who is diagnosed as suffering from a brain tumour or a surplus of certain hormones that are known to cause aggression, such as testosterone, can expect in court is to have his or her sentence reduced.[76] That even applies to a serious genetic fault, such as the XYY syndrome that many violent male criminals are said to harbour.[77]

Even more paradoxically, the fact that certain substances can affect the functioning of the brain, weaken the barriers traditionally known as conscience and allow, if not cause, behaviour that would otherwise be repressed has been known for millennia. Most of the time, in most civilizations, it was taken for granted that persons who engaged in anti-social behaviour while 'under the influence', as the current terminology goes, were not completely responsible for their actions. Here and there they were given sacred status and seen as capable of providing insights unavailable to the rest of us.[78] In case their violations of social norms were brought to court, the altered consciousness brought about by alcohol or drugs was often used to justify the imposition of a lesser penalty, if not acquit. Ancient Greek law, Roman law, Celtic (ancient Irish), Germanic law, eleventh-century Russian Law, Dutch law and English law (but not Chinese law) all recognized this principle.[79]

Over the last few decades, in most 'advanced' countries, things have been turned upside down. To quote a statute of the State of California, the rule is that 'no act committed by a person while in a state of voluntary intoxication is less criminal by reason of his having been in such a condition.'[80] On the contrary: often a person who, while 'under the influence', commits a crime such as negligent driving resulting in a serious traffic accident, or assault, is held to be *more* culpable than one who does so while sober. If he is lucky, such a person will be given a more severe sentence than would otherwise have been the case. If he is not he may very well find himself charged with two offences instead of one and made to bear two different punishments, either separately or together.

Three and a half centuries ago Hobbes attributed the functions of the brain to the impressions made by particles striking matter and leaving some kind of dent in it.[81] Since then our understanding of it has greatly improved. One after the other, old images of it have been left behind. We have long realized it is not some kind of plasticine. Neither is it an assembly of gears, nor some sort of electrical machine. It is not even a super-sophisticated computer with its constituent parts, linked by countless billions of connections, working in parallel. Probably not a day passes that does not witness some new discoveries about the way it is constructed and functions. Some researchers, by apparently showing that certain physiological changes involving motion start inside the brain seconds before the owner of that brain consciously decides to carry out the movement in question, have challenged the existence of free will itself.[82]

Meanwhile, according to one of the foremost experts in the field, in respect to identifying the biological roots of conscience, let alone manipulating and controlling them, we seem not to have made any progress at all, though he does believe that such discoveries will be made in coming decades.[83] Instead most neuroscientists, in their effort to demystify the problem by limiting themselves to what they can see, measure, model and experiment with, seem to have all but abandoned the concept. In the hundred-page booklet that outlines the Human Brain Project, a gigantic research effort aimed at building a computer model of the brain that European donors are funding to the tune of a billion Euros over ten years, it is not even mentioned.[84] There is much there about saving money – and thus justifying the investment – by understanding, preventing and curing all kinds of brain diseases, such as Alzheimer's. There also is a sentence or two about the ethical problems that might arise if any of the new technologies are put at the disposal of the military and the police. But there is not a word about what is surely the most important question of all: namely, the choice between good and evil and the ways to make people prefer the former over the latter.

Conclusion:
At Journey's End

To return to the introduction, is conscience rooted in our biology, as evolutionists from Darwin on have argued? Or is it something our human ancestors invented? Observation and experiments suggests that primates do indeed have some of the rudiments of conscience. However, whether they also have anything like the full-blown thing, including the critical ability to distinguish between good and evil and the occasional will to do the former regardless of consequences, will likely remain forever unknown.

Furthermore, throughout evolutionists' discussions runs the belief that conscience originated in such things as caring, altruism, empathy and 'prosociality'. At best, they are only speaking of common or garden-variety conscience. However, that is just part of the story and probably not the most important one. From the moment Antigone first gave it voice, often conscience did not simply serve to enforce the law when the latter happened to be looking away. Instead, as with Socrates, the self-styled gadfly who gave the Athenians no rest and was executed for his pains; Paul, who relied on *syneidēsis* to distinguish truth from falsehood and ended up martyred; Luther, who in respect to conscience followed Paul and who, had pope and emperor had the last word, would have shared his fate; Rousseau, until everybody became as perfect as his Emile; and various conscientious objectors from Georg Elser to Edward Snowden of PRISM fame,[1] conscience did just the opposite. Far from being 'pro-social', initially at least these people were seen very much as anti-social. Relying on their *syneidēsis, conscientia, Gewissen, conscience,* conscience, they set out, deliberately and sometimes literally, to blow the law sky-high in the name of some higher ideal; one which, at first, only they could see. With all respect to evolutionists, I very much doubt whether any animal, however clever and however close to us, has ever developed anything of the kind.

In the West it has long been assumed that conscience originated in Christianity's parent religion, Judaism. If Rauschning's account may be trusted, that was just why the Führer wanted to rid the world of it. Certainly as long as the Third Reich lasted, and to some extent afterwards too, he seems to have succeeded all too well. The later the date and the closer defeat looked Germany in the face, the greater the emphasis on 'hardness', 'ruthlessness' and 'fanaticism' and the greater also his willingness, and that of his subordinates, to engage in indiscriminate, often counter-productive killing.[2]

Though the Old Testament presents the ability to distinguish between good and bad as the essence of what it is to be human, it does not have a word for conscience. The same applies to the Talmud and subsequent rabbinical literature. The fundamental idea seems to be that human nature cannot be trusted; hence an exceptionally dense network of laws, constantly supervised by an all-seeing God, is needed.

The situation in Greece was very different. As many ancient authors complained, and as many modern ones have noted, Greek religion had little to do with morality. Only in the great tragedies of the fifth century BC do we meet with something at all similar to conscience as we understand that term. To the Greek and Roman Stoics, *syneidēsis*, and its Latin equivalent *conscientia*, was a sort of inner voice, janitor or perhaps one should say monitor. It enabled those who adopted it and cultivated it to lead an honourable life without fear and without reproach.

As a Jew addressing other Jews, Jesus had little to say about conscience. Not so the real founder of Christianity, Paul the Apostle, in whose letters *syneidēsis* is recommended as the compass Christ's followers could and should use to distinguish the truth of their creed from the falsehood of all the rest. Conscience became the guarantor of religion, so to speak, a substitute for Jewish Law which Paulus, trying to address the Gentile world, had discarded. This principle having been firmly established, a lengthy debate ensued. For centuries on end scholars argued whether people who did not know Jesus had a soul and, therefore, the conscience that was an important, perhaps the most important, part of it. Since the treatment meted out to non-Christians depended on the answer, the debate carried enormous practical consequences.

The Church, as the most important organization responsible for men's souls, tried to cope with the problem in two ways. First, it went to great lengths in trying to define and codify proper behaviour. Second, it established ways and means by which people who had not behaved as conscience dictated could be relieved of their feelings of guilt. In the process what had started as conscience – an outgrowth, let me repeat, of the free will, uninfluenced by either reward or punishment – gradually turned into a highly formalized system of law. One is reminded of something Franz Kafka said long ago: 'every revolution evaporates, leaving the slime of bureaucracy behind.'[3]

In the end it fell to Luther to tear down the edifice the Church had built and rescue conscience from under the ruins. Going back to Paul, he restored it to its position as the ultimate arbiter of truth. Going back to Augustine, he emphasized that the one thing that could redeem sinful man was faith. In Protestantism, which he founded, guilt was turned from a state or feeling into nothing less than a duty. To this day, he or she who does not feel guilty is considered barely human. The implications, both for the religious life and for the secular one, were and remain immense.

In 1532 there appeared in Florence a slim volume with the title The Prince. By the 1560s its full implications had begun to sink in. From antiquity to Machiavelli's contemporary Erasmus, it had always been assumed that there only existed one kind of morality and that conscience, whatever that meant, should guide all human affairs, the great as well as the small. Machiavelli's contribution was to tear away this mask, which he presented as both hypocritical and useless. Instead he pointed out that, however indispensable conscience might be in private life, to follow it in politics was tantamount to suicide. This caused an uproar that has lost none of its force since.

During the Christian centuries it was taken for granted that conscience originated in God. As secularism started gaining ground from about 1650 on, though, people looked for a different rock to chain their consciences to. To Rousseau, the most eloquent of them all, the rock in question consisted of man's nature, which civilization had corrupted and with which he was to be reunited by means of education. To Hegel it was the state, which he lifted into the supreme moral entity; and to Kant it was duty, which he sometimes confused with whatever the authorities had decreed.

Half a century later it was Nietzsche who questioned whether a rock was in fact needed at all. Claiming to return to pre-classical antiquity, he saw conscience not as the cardinal element of human life but as an obstacle, indeed the most important obstacle, to the latter's free development. It prevented him from reconciling himself with himself, standing straight and turning himself into the Übermensch, more-than-man. 'What is good?' Zarathustra's disciples asked. Like a cannon shot, back came the answer: 'To be brave is good.'[4]

Whereas Nietzsche wanted to rid man of his conscience so as to enable him, force him, to reach his full potential, Freud hoped to assuage it and teach his patients how to live with the pain it caused them. Late in his life, he doubted whether the enterprise had succeeded. After his death psychotherapy became increasingly institutionalized, taking the same road as the Church. It piled rule upon rule, often turning itself into a form of dressage similar to the methods used to make horses follow their orders. The fact that, more and more, it was paid for not by the patients but by insurance helped. The objective was to make people meet society's requirements and enable them to 'function'. Here and there a later-day Luther raised his voice against it. However, so far none has succeeded in seriously denting the system as he did, let alone overthrowing it.

The publication in 1900 of Freud's most important work, The Interpretation of Dreams, happened to coincide with the height of European imperialism. With it came attempts to export his doctrines. Success, however, was limited since other civilizations had long since developed their own methods for dealing with wayward souls. In Japan shame rules supreme, and in China, reverence. In both, confessing to the police and to the courts may result in lenient treatment. But neither is much interested in either guilt or conscience as an inner emotion.

This brings us to the question I myself started with: conscience in the Third Reich. In one way Hitler, by turning the state, or rather the racial community that the state claimed to represent, into the measure of all things, did no more than follow in Hegel's footsteps.[5] This being the case, perhaps it is not surprising that, in his rather crude way, he repeatedly ruminated on the relationship between personal ethics and the morality, or lack of it, that he believed his role in history forced him to adopt. Considering himself a good person – Nietzsche's Zarathustra apart, is anybody strong enough not to entertain that illusion? – he forced himself to order the crimes committed in his name. Doing so, he saw himself obliged to turn his back on some of the people he liked best, particularly women. As the case of Himmler – and to some extent that of several of the latter's subordinates – shows, in this he was not alone. To repeat, none of this is to justify Hitler – as if such a justification were even conceivable. On the contrary, it emphasizes the peculiarly horrible, twisted character of his crimes and tries to explain them.

Certainly conscience, some of it inspired by religion and some of it rooted in other factors, did make itself felt here and there in the Third Reich. Equally certain is the fact that it was not nearly strong enough to prevent those who killed from carrying out their grizzly work. Discipline, unit cohesion and a growing dose of what Hitler liked to call 'ruthlessness' and 'fanaticism' prevailed. Throughout the murderous machine, a key role was played by the sense of duty. No doubt that sense was often understood in a much bowdlerized form. Perhaps even more often it was no more than a kind of defensive shield, adopted both at the time – if Höss may be believed – and later in order to cover one's misdeeds. Nevertheless at bottom it was the very same duty the great Kant had made into the basis of conscience. To that extent conscience, far from obstructing mass murder, assisted it and made it possible.

In those who resisted, the role played by conscience, here understood in the most basic sense of choosing between good and evil, was much greater. That was particularly true of ordinary people who saved Jews and others, as well as anti-regime activists such as Hans and Sophie Scholl and Georg Elser. Often they put their own lives at risk; in the face of such heroism, to point out that conscience was

not always the only motive is churlish. Getting rid of National Socialism, contacting the Allies and laying the foundations of a new Germany
was a political question above all. One does not set out to kill the
leader and change the regime of a nation of 70 million in the midst
of a world war without considering what the future may bring. That
is why, among the handful of relatively high-ranking soldiers and
civilians who actively plotted against Hitler, conscience was always
mixed up with all kinds of other considerations. The most important
manifestations of 'pure' conscience are found in the early years of
the regime, when Georg Elser made his decision, and towards the
end, when Henning von Tresckow decided to carry out the attempt
on the Führer's life regardless of consequences. To these men, as
well as the women who sometimes joined them and acted on similar
principles, hats off.

In the aftermath of the Second World War and the Holocaust,
and starting in the West, the Hegelian idea of the state as the solid
rock on which to build morality and conscience was largely discredited.[6]
However, everything said so far seems to show that man, at any rate
Western man, simply cannot live without guilt feelings for very long.
Perhaps the reason for this is because, compared with Japan and
China, for example, society is seen as made up of individuals above
all. It is not sufficiently tight to keep people in their proper places.
Especially in China, good and evil were seen as the creations of society
and therefore as relative. Not so in the West: there people were always
looking for some Archimedean point to hang their guilt on. New
idols had to be found, and new idols were found.

Three of the most important idols were 'human rights', 'health'
and 'the environment'. In tune with the ongoing decline of religion,
all were resolutely secular in outlook. All had small beginnings in
the attempts of certain individuals to call attention to specific evils
that they had witnessed and which shocked them into action. As
those individuals found an audience and the audience grew and
became organized, all three became very big indeed. In the process
they grew teeth, and in quite some cases they even sprouted cannon.
Just as the present volume has not attempted to question the 'truth'
of Judaism, Catholicism or Protestantism, or psychoanalysis and its
numerous offshoots, so far be it from me to question that of human

is conformity to whatever norms society has dreamt up at that particular moment. Most of them never tried to study history. Hence they are unaware that the norms in question keep changing and that quite a few of them, when compared with those in force even as recently as a few decades ago, appear very foolish indeed. Shall we, then, come to live in a world so tightly controlled as to snuff out our conscience and/or make our minds so transparent as to render it unnecessary? Some horrible combination of *Brave New World* and *1984*, perhaps? Shall we be transformed into organic robots similar to those Čapek described almost a century ago? If so, what, if anything, will be left of our humanity? If not, what is the alternative?

However that may turn out, this is where our journey must end. If the goal has been to arrive at a clear-cut 'scientific' definition of conscience and provide a full explanation of its origins and nature, then the present volume is a failure. Since definitions only apply to unchanging things which have no history, that failure was foreseeable and foreseen. But if it aimed to trace conscience as far back as the available evidence allows and to show how people at times and places as different as those of the Old Testament and the modern world understood whatever passed for it; the ways it interacted with all kinds of other factors from religion to health and from politics to the environment; how it can be, and has been, perverted and abused; the attempts to imitate or influence it by means other than the traditional rewards and punishments; its repeated tendency to develop from something small, spontaneous and liberating into something big, obligatory, monstrous and even totalitarian; and the manner in which its very existence is being challenged by a combination of robots, advancing neuroscience and computerized surveillance methods – in that case, perhaps, it may be called a qualified success. Looking back, I can only hope that readers, having accompanied me on the journey, enjoyed what they saw on the way.

rights, the health industry or environmentalism. All I wanted to do was to draw attention to the remarkable similarities between the ways each of the eight, first growing out of conscience and then outgrowing it, turned into law, religious or secular. As they did so, each in its own way they ended up by all but burying the former under the weight of the latter.

That much having been said, I cannot resist treating the reader to the following passage:

> Surely it is obvious enough, if one looks at the whole world, that it is becoming daily better cultivated and more fully peopled than anciently . . . What most frequently meets our view and occasions complaint is our teeming population: our numbers are burdensome to the world, which can hardly supply us from its natural elements; our wants grow more and more keen, and our complaints more bitter in all mouths, whilst Nature fails in affording us her usual sustenance.[7]

Is this Al Gore? Is this some other present-day 'environ' trying to make us feel guilty for existing? Wrong guess. It is our friend Tertullian; he who wrote that one had to believe in Jesus's resurrection *because* it was impossible. The time was the reign of Marcus Aurelius, when the number of humans on earth probably stood at about 4 per cent of today's figure and per capita consumption of energy was 15–20 per cent of what it is now.[8]

To resume, throughout the 3,000 years or so covered by this study, there have always been those who believed, in Hobbes's words, that conscience was merely a term men had invented to make themselves feel better about themselves. In reality, they claimed, behaviour is determined by the laws of physics or whatever field of science was considered to have the greatest explanatory powers at the time. True or false, this view led to two different developments. First, attempts were made to build machines, known first as automata and later as robots, which would imitate human behaviour. Ever since Asimov and others made it clear that there were certain things robots could not be permitted to do, providing them with something like conscience became one element, perhaps the most important, of the exercise.

In a way the goal of the engineers and computer programmers involved was the opposite from the one Nietzsche had set himself. He called on men to rid themselves of the hump of conscience so as to clear their gaze, straighten their backs and realize their full potential. They tried to endow robots with an artificial conscience so as to make them innocuous.

Working parallel to and increasingly hand in hand with the engineers were the neuroscientists. Focusing on the brain, their objective was to understand it and, when considered necessary and appropriate, influence it by means other, and hopefully more effective, than the traditional education, reward and punishment. Over the last few decades billions have been sunk into the enterprise. There have been some spectacular successes, such as devices that connect nerve-ends to artificial limbs, making it possible to move the latter with the aid of thought alone, and others that can partially restore the sight of some kinds of blind people. These advances in turn were made possible by new methods and instruments that laid bare many mechanisms inside the brain. Yet whether we have come an inch closer to understanding the biological roots of conscience, assuming they do exist, is doubtful. At times the neuroscientists and those who interpreted their findings, by distinguishing between different kinds of conscience, have come close to hair-splitting remarkably similar to that which Thomas Aquinas engaged in almost eight centuries ago.[9] That in turn explains, among other things, why the courts have only taken the experts' analysis reluctantly, if at all.

Attempts to understand the brain have also caused the term 'conscience' to be replaced by 'inhibition', a very different and much narrower thing. Ignorance has not prevented many experts from trying to interfere with their patients' brains. Indeed there is reason to think that, as nanotechnology in particular continues to advance, we have only just embarked on the process. Starting with so-called sociopaths, and spreading to 'normal' members of society, there is a good chance that, in the not-so-remote future, each of us will be implanted with some kind of chip or capsule. At first wearing it will be 'voluntary', as in some ways and for some people, such as certain classes of criminals and the mentally ill, it already is. Later the pretence of voluntarism will be dropped and doing so will be made mandatory for all of us.

The chip will steadily monitor the amount of oxytocin, vasopre testosterone, progesterone and any other -cins and -rones in our br as well as the electric activity, blood flow, water diffusion and knows what else in them. The results will be transmitted back central computer. The latter will respond automatically. It will rel more of this or less of that chemical from the capsule it controls stimulate or depress electrical activity, or increase or decrease bl flow and water diffusion as appropriate, all in real time, and all while leaving a record for the purpose of study and further experim tation with even better methods of control. The outcome will be mimic conscience while at the same time rendering it superfluous; this, most probably, before we ever learn just what conscience really

To make mind control tighter still, we will be surrounded by a ever-growing network of video cameras, aka telescreens. Along wit any number of other gadgets now on the market, they can and d track and record our every move. As more and more everyday gadget – not just telephones but cars, microwave ovens, refrigerators and the like – are linked to the Net, each of them has the potential to sp on their owners. If it is true, as has been claimed, that neuroscientist have built devices that can read people's dreams,[10] then why not the waking thoughts as well? Even now, several companies are trying develop thought-reading machines of the kind, say, that will enab soldiers at a roadblock to determine whether the person approachii them does or does not have hostile intent.[11] There is no reason w all these methods for taming rebellious mankind, those relying neuroscience and those involving electronics and computer scien may not be fused together. Reinforcing each other, so fine will the resulting mesh, and so tight the control, as to make conscie no more necessary than it was in the days when the God of the (Testament kept close watch over the 'hidden' things inside us March 2013 the FBI asked for greater powers to monitor electro communications of every kind. So, four months later, did its Geri counterpart, the BND.[12] But why bother? The disclosures of Edv Snowden shook the world. They amply confirmed everything Nietz had ever said about the state, and more besides.

In truth, on the rare occasions when neuroscientists and puter experts speak of conscience, too often what they really

References

Introduction

1 David Hume, *A Treatise of Human Nature* [1739–40], book 3, § 1.
The text is available at www.gutenberg.org.
2 Charles Darwin, *The Descent of Man* [1871], n.p., Digireads (2009), p. 85.
3 Richard Dawkins, *The Selfish Gene* [1976] (New York, 1999).
4 Frans de Waal, *Our Inner Ape: The Best and Worst of Human Nature*
(New York, 2005) pp. 201–19; also, more recently, Frans de Waal,
The Bonobo and the Atheist: In Search of Humanism among the Primates
(New York, 2013).
5 De Waal, *The Bonobo and the Atheist*, locs 2246 and 2649.
6 Paul Mellars, 'Why Did Modern Human Populations Disperse from
Africa 60,000 Years Ago?', *Proceedings of the National Academy of Science*
(PNAS), CIII/25 (2006), pp. 9381–6.

1. At the Beginning

1 Hermann Rauschning, *Gespräche mit Hitler* [1938] (Vienna, 1988), p. 189.
2 J. Milgrom, *Cult and Conscience: The Asham and the Priestly Doctrine of
Repentance* (Leiden, 1976), pp. 3, 84, 117–20, 123–4.
3 See A. Olman, 'Did King David Have a Conscience?' (Jerusalem,
2012), at http://levinsky.academia.edu/AryeOlman/Papers/117518.
4 See John Barton, *Understanding Old Testament Ethics: Approaches and
Explorations* (Louisville, KY, 2003), pp. 66–7.
5 For this aspect of Judaism, see O. Hempel, *Das Ethos des Alten
Testaments* (Berlin, 1938), pp. 189–92.
6 Maimonides, *Royal Ways* [Hebrew], 8:11. The English translation is by

Marvin Fox, *Interpreting Maimonides: Studies in Methodology, Metaphysics and Moral Philosophy* (Chicago, IL, 1990), p. 132.

7 A. Schopenhauer, 'Preisschrift über die Grundlage der Moral', in J. Frauenstaedt, ed., *Saemtliche Werke* (Leipzig, 1922), vol. IV, p. 192.

8 See L. R. Saslow et al., 'My Brother's Keeper? Compassion Predicts Generosity More among Less Religious Individuals', *Social Psychology and Personality Science*, IV (2013), pp. 31–8.

9 See, for what follows, F. Nietzsche, *On the Genealogy of Morals* [1887] (New York, 1966), pp. 12, 13, 15, 22, 25, 44.

10 The most succinct account is F. Nietzsche, *The Anti-christ* [1895] (Harmondsworth, 1969), p. 116.

11 Homer, *The Iliad* (I, 40–100).

12 Ibid. (XIX, 287–300); Homer, *The Odyssey* (VI, 196–210, XIII, 4–15).

13 See, on feminine *aidos* in general, Gloria Ferrari, 'Figures of Speech: The Picture of *Aidos*', *Metis*, V (1990), pp. 185–204 (pp. 186–7); for *pudicitia*, see R. Langlands, *Sexual Morality in Ancient Rome* (Cambridge, 2006), pp. 37–77, 186, 346.

14 *Odyssey*, VI, lines 127–37.

15 See, for the history of the concept, D. L. Cairns, *Aidos* (Oxford, 1993).

16 Suetonius, *The Life of Caligula*, chap. 29.

17 *Iliad* (X, 237).

18 Ibid. (XII, 93 and XVII, 95).

19 Ibid. (XIX, 243–314).

20 Ibid. (V, 787 and VIII, 228).

21 Ibid. (VI, 493).

22 Hesiod, *Works and Days*, 317–19.

23 Plutarch, *Parallel Lives*, 'The Life of Solon', vol. II/I.

24 Solon, fragment no. 32, in *Elegy and Iambus*, vol. II, p. 146.

25 Cairns, *Aidos*, p. 167.

26 Aeschylus, *The Persians*, lines 699–704; Book of Esther, 4:5–5:3.

27 Sophocles, *Antigone*, 511.

28 See, for women's timidity, C. R. Post, 'The Dramatic Art of Sophocles', *Harvard Studies in Classical Philology*, XXIII (1912), p. 79. Antigone putting her own judgement first: Ursula Stebler, *Entstehung und Entwicklung des Gewissens im Spiegel des Griechischen Tragödie* (Berne, 1971), vol. V, p. 69.

29 Euripides, *Electra*, 43–6.

30 Euripides, *Orestes*, 396–7.

31 Euripides, *The Suppliants*, 909–17.

32 Euripides, *Iphigenia at Aulis*, 563–68; see also Cairns, *Aidos*, pp. 342–3.

33 Democritus, in *The Atomists: Leucippus and Democritus, Fragments*, ed. and trans. C.C.W. Taylor (Toronto, 2010), fragment B 181.

34 Ibid., fragment B 262.

35 Ibid., fragment B 215.

36 Plato, *Apology*, 30a.

37 Plato, *Seventh Letter*, §328d.

38 Plato, *The Republic*, Book 4, §439e–440a, and 548c.

39 See John M. Cooper, 'Plato's Theory of Human Motivation', *History of Philosophy Quarterly*, I/1 (1989), pp. 3–21 (pp. 14–15).

40 Aristotle, *Nicomachean Ethics* (IX, ch. 1).

41 Ibid., *Rhetoric*, b12–14.

42 Antiphon, quoted in Stobaeus, *Florilegium*, 2.d.11–2 and 3.24.7.

43 J. M. Rist, *Stoic Philosophy* (Cambridge, 1969), p. 92.

44 Isocrates, *Orationes* (I, 16 and II, 59).

45 See Martin Revermann, 'The Competence of Theatre Audiences in Fifth- and Fourth-century Athens', *Journal of Hellenic Studies*, CXXVI (2006), pp. 99–124.

46 Plutarch, 'Nicias', in *Parallel Lives*, 29:3.

47 This is the way Philo of Alexandria puts it; *On the Decalogue* (Cambridge, MA, 1908), 64.

48 See K. Algra, 'Stoic Theology', in *The Cambridge Companion to the Stoics*, ed. B. Inwood (New York, 2003), pp. 153–78.

49 See E. W. Leach, 'The Implied Reader and the Political Argument in Seneca's Apolocyntosis and De Clementia', in *Seneca*, ed. J. G. Fitch (Oxford, 2008), pp. 293–4.

50 See, on the history of the idea, H. Cotton, 'The Concept of *Indulgentia* under Trajan', *Chiron*, XIV (1984), pp. 245–66.

51 See I. G. Kidd, 'Moral Actions and Rules in Stoic Ethics', in *The Stoics*, ed. J. M. Rist (Berkeley, CA, 1978), pp. 248–50.

52 Philo, *The Unchangeableness of God*, 135.

53 Philo, *The Confusion of Tongues*, 121; *On Drunkenness*, 125.

54 Philo, *On the Decalogue*, 87.

55 Philo, *The Special Laws*, I, xliii, 235–38.

56 See, for anti-Jewish views of Philo's rough contemporaries, Cicero,

Pro Flacco (XXVIII, 69); Seneca, quoted by Augustine, *The City of God* (XIV, 96); Juvenal, *Satires* (XIV, 96).

57 Epictetus, *Discourses*, fragment 109.

58 See Cleanthes' famous Hymn to Zeus, printed in J. L. Saunders, *Greek and Roman Philosophy after Aristotle* (New York, 1966), pp. 149–50; also Rist, *Stoic Philosophy*, pp. 10–20.

59 Epictetus, *Discourses* (I, 14.16).

60 See D. E. Marietta Jr, 'Conscience in Greek Stoicism', *Numen*, XVII/3 (1970), pp. 178–90.

61 Philo, *On Joseph*, X, 47–8; Philo, *On Flight and Finding*, 159.

62 Epictetus, *Enchiridion*, 24.2.

63 Cicero, *Ad Atticum* (XIII, 20), and *de Finibus* (II, 71); Seneca, *Epistles* (XII, 9, XIII, 5 and XXIII, 12).

64 Cicero, *Ad Atticum* (X, 4.5 and XIII, 20.4); Seneca, *Epistles* (XLIII, 4). See also G. Molenaar, 'Seneca's Use of the Term "Conscientia"', *Mnemosyne*, XXII/2 (1969), pp. 170–80.

65 *Historia Augusta* (II, 6).

66 Marcus Aurelius, *Meditations* (VI, 97).

67 Ibid. (VII, 13).

68 Seneca, *Epistles* (LXXXVII, 4–5); Tacitus, *Annales* (LXVI).

69 C. A. Pierce, *Conscience in the New Testament* (London, 1955), p. 16.

70 Stobaeus, *Florilegium* (II, 198); Seneca, *Epistle* (LXVI, 1); see also C. Stough, 'Stoic Determinism and Moral Responsibility', *The Stoics*, ed. Rist, especially pp. 261–4.

71 Philo, *On Dreams* (I, 16–17).

72 Philo, *On Instruction* (XIII).

73 Epictetus, *Handbook* (XXII).

74 Quintilian, *The Orator's Education* (X, 1.19 and II, 18.22).

75 See, for a description of life in one such club, Cicero, *On Divine Nature*, I, 6.

76 Epictetus, *Handbook* (XXXIII, 1).

77 Epictetus, *Discourses* (IV, 7.24).

78 See D. M. Engel, 'Women's Role in the Home and the State: Stoic Theory Reconsidered', *Harvard Studies in Classical Philology*, CI (2003), pp. 267–88.

11. The Christian Centuries

1 See, for a passage-by-passage analysis, H.-J. Eckstein, *Der Begriff Syneidēsis bei Paulus* (Tübingen, 1983), pp. 137–311.

2 C. A. Pierce, *Conscience in the New Testament* (London, 1955), pp. 13–20.

3 See, above all, M. E. Andrews, 'Paul, Philo, and the Intellectuals', *Journal of Biblical Literature*, LIII/2 (1934), pp. 155–60.

4 See, on these efforts, J. W. Drane, *Paul: Libertine or Legalist?* (London, 1975), pp. 12–23.

5 For Paul's diatribes against the Law, see Romans (II, 17–III, 20); I. Corinthians, 7:17–24; and *Galatians* (III, 10–12).

6 Translation by Thomas P. Scheck, *Commentary on the Epistle to the Romans (The Fathers of the Church)* (Washington, DC, 2001), p. 94, n. 294.

7 *Sola conscientia* (by conscience alone); Marcus Minucius Felix, *Octavius* (XXXV, 6).

8 Aelius Aristides, *Apology* (XV, 3–7).

9 Lactantius, *The Divine Institutes* (III, 29.12–14).

10 Epistola CXXV ad Rusticum Monachum, in *Patrologiae Cursus Completus*, ed. J. P. Migne, Series Latina (Leiden, 1864–6), vol. XXII, col. 1079.

11 See Douglas Kries, 'Origen, Plato, and Conscience (Synederesis) in Jerome's Ezekiel Commentary', *Traditio*, VII (2002), pp. 76–8.

12 Augustine, *Confessions* (VIII, 7.17).

13 Augustine, *De Nuptiis et Concupiscentia* (I, 23); Augustine, *De gratia Christi et de peccato originali* (II, 34).

14 See, however, D. Capps and J. E. Dittes, eds, *The Hunger of the Heart: Reflections on the Confessions of Augustine* (West Lafayette, IN, 1990).

15 Augustine, *Confessions* (VII, 7.29).

16 R. K. Rittgers, 'Private Confession in the German Reformation', in *Repentance in Christian Theology*, ed. M. J. Boda and T. T. Smith (Collegeville, MI, 2006), pp. 189–20.

17 Ibid., p. 61.

18 Johannes Stelzenberger, *Conscientia bei Augustinus* (Paderborn, 1959).

19 Augustine, *Confessions* (I, 18.29). The text is available at www.ling.upenn.edu.

20 F. van Fleteren and J. S. Schnaubelt, eds, *Collectanea Augustinia* (New York, 2001), Sermon 154.12.

21 Augustine, *Psalms* (XLV, 3 and LXVI, 7); Sermon (XLVII, 12–14);

and *Psalms* (XLV, 9).

22 Augustine, *Confessions* (V, 6.11).

23 Augustine, *Against Faustus* (XX, 23).

24 See M. T. Clark, 'Augustine on Conscience', in *Augustine and His Opponents*, ed. E. A. Livingstone (Louvain, 1997), pp. 63–8.

25 Augustine, *Confessions* (XI, 18.27).

26 *La Chanson de Roland* (86, 1); *Book of Huon*, 204.16.

27 The quotes are from Dorotheus of Gaza, in *Discourses and Sayings*, trans. E. P. Wheeler (Kalamazoo, MI, 1978), pp. 104 and 107. See also S. Thomas, 'Conscience in Orthodox Thought', in *Conscience in World Religions*, ed. Jayne Hoose (South Bend, OH, 1999), pp. 112–13.

28 D. E. Luscombe, *Peter Abelard's Ethics* (Oxford, 1971), p. XVII.

29 The relevant part of the English text is printed ibid., pp. 55–7.

30 The Gospel of Luke, 23:24.

31 Luscombe, *Peter Abelard's Ethics*, p. 97.

32 Ibid., p. 67.

33 Ibid., p. 63.

34 Bernard of Clairvaux, *Epistola* no. 189, to Pope Innocent II, in *Sancti Bernardi Opera*, ed. J. Leclercq et al. (Rome, 1957–77), vol. VIII, pp. 13–14.

35 Summary based on Philip the Chancellor, *Summa de Bono*, English translation in *Conscience in Medieval Philosophy*, ed. Timothy C. Potts (Cambridge, 1980), pp. 94–109.

36 For what follows see Potts, *Conscience*, pp. 60.

37 M. G. Baylor, *Action and Person: Conscience in Late Scholasticism and the Young Luther* (Leiden, 1977), p. 90.

38 On the ludic element in scholasticism, see Johan Huizinga, *Homo Ludens* [1938] (Boston, MA, 1955), pp. 112 and 114; and in greater detail, M. A. Bossy, 'Medieval Debates of Body and Soul', *Comparative Literature*, XXVIII/2 (1976), pp. 150–51.

39 See William V. Harris, *Ancient Literacy* (Cambridge, MA, 1989), pp. 25–42.

40 See M. Innes, 'Memory, Orality and Literacy in an Early Medieval Society', *Past and Present*, 158 (1988), pp. 303–6.

41 See Carlos Steel et al., eds, *Paganism in the Middle Ages: Threat and Fascination* (Louvain, 2013).

42 On the emergence of Christian ritual, see Meeks, *The Origins of Christian Morality*, pp. 91–110.

rights, the health industry or environmentalism. All I wanted to do was to draw attention to the remarkable similarities between the ways each of the eight, first growing out of conscience and then outgrowing it, turned into law, religious or secular. As they did so, each in its own way they ended up by all but burying the former under the weight of the latter.

That much having been said, I cannot resist treating the reader to the following passage:

> Surely it is obvious enough, if one looks at the whole world, that it is becoming daily better cultivated and more fully peopled than anciently . . . What most frequently meets our view and occasions complaint is our teeming population: our numbers are burdensome to the world, which can hardly supply us from its natural elements; our wants grow more and more keen, and our complaints more bitter in all mouths, whilst Nature fails in affording us her usual sustenance.[7]

Is this Al Gore? Is this some other present-day 'environ' trying to make us feel guilty for existing? Wrong guess. It is our friend Tertullian; he who wrote that one had to believe in Jesus's resurrection *because* it was impossible. The time was the reign of Marcus Aurelius, when the number of humans on earth probably stood at about 4 per cent of today's figure and per capita consumption of energy was 15–20 per cent of what it is now.[8]

To resume, throughout the 3,000 years or so covered by this study, there have always been those who believed, in Hobbes's words, that conscience was merely a term men had invented to make themselves feel better about themselves. In reality, they claimed, behaviour is determined by the laws of physics or whatever field of science was considered to have the greatest explanatory powers at the time. True or false, this view led to two different developments. First, attempts were made to build machines, known first as automata and later as robots, which would imitate human behaviour. Ever since Asimov and others made it clear that there were certain things robots could not be permitted to do, providing them with something like conscience became one element, perhaps the most important, of the exercise.

In a way the goal of the engineers and computer programmers involved was the opposite from the one Nietzsche had set himself. He called on men to rid themselves of the hump of conscience so as to clear their gaze, straighten their backs and realize their full potential. They tried to endow robots with an artificial conscience so as to make them innocuous.

Working parallel to and increasingly hand in hand with the engineers were the neuroscientists. Focusing on the brain, their objective was to understand it and, when considered necessary and appropriate, influence it by means other, and hopefully more effective, than the traditional education, reward and punishment. Over the last few decades billions have been sunk into the enterprise. There have been some spectacular successes, such as devices that connect nerve-ends to artificial limbs, making it possible to move the latter with the aid of thought alone, and others that can partially restore the sight of some kinds of blind people. These advances in turn were made possible by new methods and instruments that laid bare many mechanisms inside the brain. Yet whether we have come an inch closer to understanding the biological roots of conscience, assuming they do exist, is doubtful. At times the neuroscientists and those who interpreted their findings, by distinguishing between different kinds of conscience, have come close to hair-splitting remarkably similar to that which Thomas Aquinas engaged in almost eight centuries ago.[9] That in turn explains, among other things, why the courts have only taken the experts' analysis reluctantly, if at all.

Attempts to understand the brain have also caused the term 'conscience' to be replaced by 'inhibition', a very different and much narrower thing. Ignorance has not prevented many experts from trying to interfere with their patients' brains. Indeed there is reason to think that, as nanotechnology in particular continues to advance, we have only just embarked on the process. Starting with so-called sociopaths, and spreading to 'normal' members of society, there is a good chance that, in the not-so-remote future, each of us will be implanted with some kind of chip or capsule. At first wearing it will be 'voluntary', as in some ways and for some people, such as certain classes of criminals and the mentally ill, it already is. Later the pretence of voluntarism will be dropped and doing so will be made mandatory for all of us.

The chip will steadily monitor the amount of oxytocin, vasopressin, testosterone, progesterone and any other -cins and -rones in our brains, as well as the electric activity, blood flow, water diffusion and God knows what else in them. The results will be transmitted back to a central computer. The latter will respond automatically. It will release more of this or less of that chemical from the capsule it controls, or stimulate or depress electrical activity, or increase or decrease blood flow and water diffusion as appropriate, all in real time, and all the while leaving a record for the purpose of study and further experimentation with even better methods of control. The outcome will be to mimic conscience while at the same time rendering it superfluous; all this, most probably, before we ever learn just what conscience really is.

To make mind control tighter still, we will be surrounded by an ever-growing network of video cameras, aka telescreens. Along with any number of other gadgets now on the market, they can and do track and record our every move. As more and more everyday gadgets – not just telephones but cars, microwave ovens, refrigerators and the like – are linked to the Net, each of them has the potential to spy on their owners. If it is true, as has been claimed, that neuroscientists have built devices that can read people's dreams,[10] then why not their waking thoughts as well? Even now, several companies are trying to develop thought-reading machines of the kind, say, that will enable soldiers at a roadblock to determine whether the person approaching them does or does not have hostile intent.[11] There is no reason why all these methods for taming rebellious mankind, those relying on neuroscience and those involving electronics and computer science, may not be fused together. Reinforcing each other, so fine will be the resulting mesh, and so tight the control, as to make conscience no more necessary than it was in the days when the God of the Old Testament kept close watch over the 'hidden' things inside us. In March 2013 the FBI asked for greater powers to monitor electronic communications of every kind. So, four months later, did its German counterpart, the BND.[12] But why bother? The disclosures of Edward Snowden shook the world. They amply confirmed everything Nietzsche had ever said about the state, and more besides.

In truth, on the rare occasions when neuroscientists and computer experts speak of conscience, too often what they really mean is conformity to whatever norms society has dreamt up at that particular moment. Most of them never tried to study history. Hence they are unaware that the norms in question keep changing and that quite a few of them, when compared with those in force even as recently as a few decades ago, appear very foolish indeed. Shall we, then, come to live in a world so tightly controlled as to snuff out our conscience and/or make our minds so transparent as to render it unnecessary? Some horrible combination of *Brave New World* and 1984, perhaps? Shall we be transformed into organic robots similar to those Čapek described almost a century ago? If so, what, if anything, will be left of our humanity? If not, what is the alternative?

However that may turn out, this is where our journey must end. If the goal has been to arrive at a clear-cut 'scientific' definition of conscience and provide a full explanation of its origins and nature, then the present volume is a failure. Since definitions only apply to unchanging things which have no history, that failure was foreseeable and foreseen. But if it aimed to trace conscience as far back as the available evidence allows and to show how people at times and places as different as those of the Old Testament and the modern world understood whatever passed for it; the ways it interacted with all kinds of other factors from religion to health and from politics to the environment; how it can be, and has been, perverted and abused; the attempts to imitate or influence it by means other than the traditional rewards and punishments; its repeated tendency to develop from something small, spontaneous and liberating into something big, obligatory, monstrous and even totalitarian; and the manner in which its very existence is being challenged by a combination of robots, advancing neuroscience and computerized surveillance methods – in that case, perhaps, it may be called a qualified success. Looking back, I can only hope that readers, having accompanied me on the journey, enjoyed what they saw on the way.

References

Introduction

1 David Hume, *A Treatise of Human Nature* [1739–40], book 3, § 1. The text is available at www.gutenberg.org.
2 Charles Darwin, *The Descent of Man* [1871], n.p., Digireads (2009), p. 85.
3 Richard Dawkins, *The Selfish Gene* [1976] (New York, 1999).
4 Frans de Waal, *Our Inner Ape: The Best and Worst of Human Nature* (New York, 2005) pp. 201–19; also, more recently, Frans de Waal, *The Bonobo and the Atheist: In Search of Humanism among the Primates* (New York, 2013).
5 De Waal, *The Bonobo and the Atheist*, locs 2246 and 2649.
6 Paul Mellars, 'Why Did Modern Human Populations Disperse from Africa 60,000 Years Ago?', *Proceedings of the National Academy of Science* (PNAS), CIII/25 (2006), pp. 9381–6.

1. At the Beginning

1 Hermann Rauschning, *Gespräche mit Hitler* [1938] (Vienna, 1988), p. 189.
2 J. Milgrom, *Cult and Conscience: The Asham and the Priestly Doctrine of Repentance* (Leiden, 1976), pp. 3, 84, 117–20, 123–4.
3 See A. Olman, 'Did King David Have a Conscience?' (Jerusalem, 2012), at http://levinsky.academia.edu/AryeOlman/Papers/117518.
4 See John Barton, *Understanding Old Testament Ethics: Approaches and Explorations* (Louisville, KY, 2003), pp. 66–7.
5 For this aspect of Judaism, see O. Hempel, *Das Ethos des Alten Testaments* (Berlin, 1938), pp. 189–92.
6 Maimonides, *Royal Ways* [Hebrew], 8:11. The English translation is by

Marvin Fox, *Interpreting Maimonides: Studies in Methodology, Metaphysics and Moral Philosophy* (Chicago, IL, 1990), p. 132.

7 A. Schopenhauer, 'Preisschrift über die Grundlage der Moral', in J. Frauenstaedt, ed., *Saemtliche Werke* (Leipzig, 1922), vol. IV, p. 192.

8 See L. R. Saslow et al., 'My Brother's Keeper? Compassion Predicts Generosity More among Less Religious Individuals', *Social Psychology and Personality Science*, IV (2013), pp. 31–8.

9 See, for what follows, F. Nietzsche, *On the Genealogy of Morals* [1887] (New York, 1966), pp. 12, 13, 15, 22, 25, 44.

10 The most succinct account is F. Nietzsche, *The Anti-christ* [1895] (Harmondsworth, 1969), p. 116.

11 Homer, *The Iliad* (I, 40–100).

12 Ibid. (XIX, 287–300); Homer, *The Odyssey* (VI, 196–210, XIII, 4–15).

13 See, on feminine *aidos* in general, Gloria Ferrari, 'Figures of Speech: The Picture of *Aidos*', *Metis*, V (1990), pp. 185–204 (pp. 186–7); for *pudicitia*, see R. Langlands, *Sexual Morality in Ancient Rome* (Cambridge, 2006), pp. 37–77, 186, 346.

14 *Odyssey*, VI, lines 127–37.

15 See, for the history of the concept, D. L. Cairns, *Aidos* (Oxford, 1993).

16 Suetonius, *The Life of Caligula*, chap. 29.

17 *Iliad* (X, 237).

18 Ibid. (XII, 93 and XVII, 95).

19 Ibid. (XIX, 243–314).

20 Ibid. (V, 787 and VIII, 228).

21 Ibid. (VI, 493).

22 Hesiod, *Works and Days*, 317–19.

23 Plutarch, *Parallel Lives*, 'The Life of Solon', vol. II/I.

24 Solon, fragment no. 32, in *Elegy and Iambus*, vol. II, p. 146.

25 Cairns, *Aidos*, p. 167.

26 Aeschylus, *The Persians*, lines 699–704; Book of Esther, 4:5–5:3.

27 Sophocles, *Antigone*, 511.

28 See, for women's timidity, C. R. Post, 'The Dramatic Art of Sophocles', *Harvard Studies in Classical Philology*, XXIII (1912), p. 79. Antigone putting her own judgement first: Ursula Stebler, *Entstehung und Entwicklung des Gewissens im Spiegel des Griechischen Tragödie* (Berne, 1971), vol. V, p. 69.

29 Euripides, *Electra*, 43–6.

30 Euripides, *Orestes*, 396–7.

31 Euripides, *The Suppliants*, 909–17.

32 Euripides, *Iphigenia at Aulis*, 563–68; see also Cairns, *Aidos*, pp. 342–3.

33 Democritus, in *The Atomists: Leucippus and Democritus, Fragments*, ed. and trans. C.C.W. Taylor (Toronto, 2010), fragment B 181.

34 Ibid., fragment B 262.

35 Ibid., fragment B 215.

36 Plato, *Apology*, 30a.

37 Plato, *Seventh Letter*, §328d.

38 Plato, *The Republic*, Book 4, §439e–440a, and 548c.

39 See John M. Cooper, 'Plato's Theory of Human Motivation', *History of Philosophy Quarterly*, I/1 (1989), pp. 3–21 (pp. 14–15).

40 Aristotle, *Nicomachean Ethics* (IX, ch. 1).

41 Ibid., *Rhetoric*, b12–14.

42 Antiphon, quoted in Stobaeus, *Florilegium*, 2.d.11–2 and 3.24.7.

43 J. M. Rist, *Stoic Philosophy* (Cambridge, 1969), p. 92.

44 Isocrates, *Orationes* (I, 16 and II, 59).

45 See Martin Revermann, 'The Competence of Theatre Audiences in Fifth- and Fourth-century Athens', *Journal of Hellenic Studies*, CXXVI (2006), pp. 99–124.

46 Plutarch, 'Nicias', in *Parallel Lives*, 29:3.

47 This is the way Philo of Alexandria puts it; *On the Decalogue* (Cambridge, MA, 1908), 64.

48 See K. Algra, 'Stoic Theology', in *The Cambridge Companion to the Stoics*, ed. B. Inwood (New York, 2003), pp. 153–78.

49 See E. W. Leach, 'The Implied Reader and the Political Argument in Seneca's Apolocyntosis and De Clementia', in *Seneca*, ed. J. G. Fitch (Oxford, 2008), pp. 293–4.

50 See, on the history of the idea, H. Cotton, 'The Concept of *Indulgentia* under Trajan', *Chiron*, XIV (1984), pp. 245–66.

51 See I. G. Kidd, 'Moral Actions and Rules in Stoic Ethics', in *The Stoics*, ed. J. M. Rist (Berkeley, CA, 1978), pp. 248–50.

52 Philo, *The Unchangeableness of God*, 135.

53 Philo, *The Confusion of Tongues*, 121; *On Drunkenness*, 125.

54 Philo, *On the Decalogue*, 87.

55 Philo, *The Special Laws*, I, xliii, 235–38.

56 See, for anti-Jewish views of Philo's rough contemporaries, Cicero,

Pro Flacco (XXVIII, 69); Seneca, quoted by Augustine, *The City of God* (XIV, 96); Juvenal, *Satires* (XIV, 96).

57 Epictetus, *Discourses*, fragment 109.

58 See Cleanthes' famous Hymn to Zeus, printed in J. L. Saunders, *Greek and Roman Philosophy after Aristotle* (New York, 1966), pp. 149–50; also Rist, *Stoic Philosophy*, pp. 10–20.

59 Epictetus, *Discourses* (I, 14.16).

60 See D. E. Marietta Jr, 'Conscience in Greek Stoicism', *Numen*, XVII/3 (1970), pp. 178–90.

61 Philo, *On Joseph*, X, 47–8; Philo, *On Flight and Finding*, 159.

62 Epictetus, *Enchiridion*, 24.2.

63 Cicero, *Ad Atticum* (XIII, 20), and *de Finibus* (II, 71); Seneca, *Epistles* (XII, 9, XIII, 5 and XXIII, 12).

64 Cicero, *Ad Atticum* (X, 4.5 and XIII, 20.4); Seneca, *Epistles* (XLIII, 4). See also G. Molenaar, 'Seneca's Use of the Term "Conscientia"', *Mnemosyne*, XXII/2 (1969), pp. 170–80.

65 *Historia Augusta* (II, 6).

66 Marcus Aurelius, *Meditations* (VI, 97).

67 Ibid. (VII, 13).

68 Seneca, *Epistles* (LXXXVII, 4–5); Tacitus, *Annales* (LXVI).

69 C. A. Pierce, *Conscience in the New Testament* (London, 1955), p. 16.

70 Stobaeus, *Florilegium* (II, 198); Seneca, *Epistle* (LXVI, 1); see also C. Stough, 'Stoic Determinism and Moral Responsibility', *The Stoics*, ed. Rist, especially pp. 261–4.

71 Philo, *On Dreams* (I, 16–17).

72 Philo, *On Instruction* (XIII).

73 Epictetus, *Handbook* (XXII).

74 Quintilian, *The Orator's Education* (X, 1.19 and II, 18.22).

75 See, for a description of life in one such club, Cicero, *On Divine Nature*, I, 6.

76 Epictetus, *Handbook* (XXXIII, 1).

77 Epictetus, *Discourses* (IV, 7.24).

78 See D. M. Engel, 'Women's Role in the Home and the State: Stoic Theory Reconsidered', *Harvard Studies in Classical Philology*, CI (2003), pp. 267–88.

11. The Christian Centuries

1 See, for a passage-by-passage analysis, H.-J. Eckstein, *Der Begriff Syneidēsis bei Paulus* (Tübingen, 1983), pp. 137–311.

2 C. A. Pierce, *Conscience in the New Testament* (London, 1955), pp. 13–20.

3 See, above all, M. E. Andrews, 'Paul, Philo, and the Intellectuals', *Journal of Biblical Literature*, LIII/2 (1934), pp. 155–60.

4 See, on these efforts, J. W. Drane, *Paul: Libertine or Legalist?* (London, 1975), pp. 12–23.

5 For Paul's diatribes against the Law, see Romans (II, 17–III, 20); I. Corinthians, 7:17–24; and *Galatians* (III, 10–12).

6 Translation by Thomas P. Scheck, *Commentary on the Epistle to the Romans (The Fathers of the Church)* (Washington, DC, 2001), p. 94, n. 294.

7 *Sola conscientia* (by conscience alone); Marcus Minucius Felix, *Octavius* (XXXV, 6).

8 Aelius Aristides, *Apology* (XV, 3–7).

9 Lactantius, *The Divine Institutes* (III, 29.12–14).

10 Epistola CXXV ad Rusticum Monachum, in *Patrologiae Cursus Completus*, ed. J. P. Migne, Series Latina (Leiden, 1864–6), vol. XXII, col. 1079.

11 See Douglas Kries, 'Origen, Plato, and Conscience (*Synederesis*) in Jerome's Ezekiel Commentary', *Traditio*, VII (2002), pp. 76–8.

12 Augustine, *Confessions* (VIII, 7.17).

13 Augustine, *De Nuptiis et Concupiscentia* (I, 23); Augustine, *De gratia Christi et de peccato originali* (II, 34).

14 See, however, D. Capps and J. E. Dittes, eds, *The Hunger of the Heart: Reflections on the Confessions of Augustine* (West Lafayette, IN, 1990).

15 Augustine, *Confessions* (VII, 7.29).

16 R. K. Rittgers, 'Private Confession in the German Reformation', in *Repentance in Christian Theology*, ed. M. J. Boda and T. T. Smith (Collegeville, MI, 2006), pp. 189–20.

17 Ibid., p. 61.

18 Johannes Stelzenberger, *Conscientia bei Augustinus* (Paderborn, 1959).

19 Augustine, *Confessions* (I, 18.29). The text is available at www.ling.upenn.edu.

20 F. van Fleteren and J. S. Schnaubelt, eds, *Collectanea Augustinia* (New York, 2001), Sermon 154.12.

21 Augustine, *Psalms* (XLV, 3 and LXVI, 7); Sermon (XLVII, 12–14);

and Psalms (XLV, 9).

22 Augustine, *Confessions* (V, 6.11).

23 Augustine, *Against Faustus* (XX, 23).

24 See M. T. Clark, 'Augustine on Conscience', in *Augustine and His Opponents*, ed. E. A. Livingstone (Louvain, 1997), pp. 63–8.

25 Augustine, *Confessions* (XI, 18.27).

26 *La Chanson de Roland* (86, 1); *Book of Huon*, 204.16.

27 The quotes are from Dorotheus of Gaza, in *Discourses and Sayings*, trans. E. P. Wheeler (Kalamazoo, MI, 1978), pp. 104 and 107. See also S. Thomas, 'Conscience in Orthodox Thought', in *Conscience in World Religions*, ed. Jayne Hoose (South Bend, OH, 1999), pp. 112–13.

28 D. E. Luscombe, *Peter Abelard's Ethics* (Oxford, 1971), p. XVII.

29 The relevant part of the English text is printed ibid., pp. 55–7.

30 The Gospel of Luke, 23:24.

31 Luscombe, *Peter Abelard's Ethics*, p. 97.

32 Ibid., p. 67.

33 Ibid., p. 63.

34 Bernard of Clairvaux, *Epistola* no. 189, to Pope Innocent II, in *Sancti Bernardi Opera*, ed. J. Leclercq et al. (Rome, 1957–77), vol. VIII, pp. 13–14.

35 Summary based on Philip the Chancellor, *Summa de Bono*, English translation in *Conscience in Medieval Philosophy*, ed. Timothy C. Potts (Cambridge, 1980), pp. 94–109.

36 For what follows see Potts, *Conscience*, pp. 60.

37 M. G. Baylor, *Action and Person: Conscience in Late Scholasticism and the Young Luther* (Leiden, 1977), p. 90.

38 On the ludic element in scholasticism, see Johan Huizinga, *Homo Ludens* [1938] (Boston, MA, 1955), pp. 112 and 114; and in greater detail, M. A. Bossy, 'Medieval Debates of Body and Soul', *Comparative Literature*, XXVIII/2 (1976), pp. 150–51.

39 See William V. Harris, *Ancient Literacy* (Cambridge, MA, 1989), pp. 25–42.

40 See M. Innes, 'Memory, Orality and Literacy in an Early Medieval Society', *Past and Present*, 158 (1988), pp. 303–6.

41 See Carlos Steel et al., eds, *Paganism in the Middle Ages: Threat and Fascination* (Louvain, 2013).

42 On the emergence of Christian ritual, see Meeks, *The Origins of Christian Morality*, pp. 91–110.

43 For a short account, see Richard Newhauser, 'Alle Sunde hant Unterschidunge', in Sin: Essays on the Moral Tradition in the Middle Ages, ed. Richard Newhauser (Aldershot, 2007), pp. 287–303.

44 J. McNeill and H. M. Gamer, Medieval Handbooks of Penance (New York, 1990), p. 254.

45 In general, see N. Swanson, Indulgences in Late Medieval England: Passports to Paradise (Cambridge, 2011).

46 Thomas Aquinas, Summa Theologica (II, I), question 109. The text is available at www.basilica.org.

47 See Ronald K. Rittgers, The Reformation of the Keys: Confession, Conscience and Authority in Sixteenth-century Germany (Cambridge, MA, 2004), p. 24.

48 Martin Luther, 'Concerning the Sacrament of Penance', in The Babylonian Captivity of the Church. The text is available at http://amazingdiscoveries.org.

49 See Berndt Hamm, 'Froemmigkeitstheologie am Anfang des 16. Jahrhunderts', Beitrage zur Historische Theologie, LXV (1982), pp. 250–52.

50 See B. Moeller, 'Piety in Germany around 1500', in The Reformation in Medieval Perspective, ed. Steven E. Ozment (Chicago, IL, 1971), p. 52; also, at much greater length, Jean Delumeau, Le Péché et le Peur (Paris, 1990).

51 Johann Wolfgang von Goethe to Karl Ludwig von Knebel, 22 August 1817, no. 7,847 in Goethes Werke (Weimar, 1887), vol. IV, chapter 27, § 227, p. 23.

52 Martin Luther, Tischreden (Table Talk) [1912–3] (Weimar, 2010).

53 Quoted in E. Gordon Rupp, The Righteousness of God: Luther Studies (London, 1993), p. 104, and I. D. Kingston Siggins, Luther (New York, 1973), p. 34.

54 Constance M. Furey, 'Invective and Discernment in Martin Luther, D. Erasmus, and Thomas More', Harvard Theological Review, XCVIII (2005), pp. 469–88.

55 L. W. Spitz, The Renaissance and Reformation Movements (St Louis, MO, 1987), p. 354.

56 See, above all, Erik Erikson, Young Man Luther (New York, 1958).

57 For background, see Y.J.E. Alanen, Das Gewissen bei Luther (Helsinki, 1934), pp. 17–32.

58 Martin Luther, Martin Luthers Werke (Weimar, 1883–9), part 56, 237, chaps 5–9.

59 Quoted by Martin Brecht, in *Martin Luther: His Road to Reformation,*
    1483–1521 (Philadelphia, PA, 1985–93), vol. I, p. 460.

60 See Baylor, *Action and Person*, pp. 264–8.

61 Martin Luther, 'Lectures on the Epistle to the Hebrews', in *Luther: Early*
    Theological Works, ed. James Atkinson (Philadelphia, PA, 1962), p. 172.

62 Luther, *Tischreden*, XLVI/2.

63 On the sixteenth-century Protestant idea of conscience, see Jonathan
    Wright, 'The World's Worst Worm: Conscience and Conformity
    during the English Reformation', *Sixteenth Century Journal*, XXX/I
    (1999), pp. 113–33.

64 Martin Luther, 'Discussion of Confession' [1520], in *Works of Martin*
    Luther (Philadelphia, PA, 1943), vol. I, pp. 87, 89, 92, 95. On the
    institution of the private confession see also Rittgers, *The Reformation*
    of the Keys, pp. 203–6.

65 Luther, 'Discussion of Confession', p. 90.

66 John Woolton, *Of the Conscience* (London, 1576), A1v–A2; Heinrich
    Bullinger, in *The Decades of Heinrich Bullinger*, ed. T. Hardy (Cambridge,
    1849), I, p. 194.

67 W. Tyndale, *The Obedience of a Christian* (Antwerp, 1528), p. xii.

68 John Calvin, *Institutes of the Christian Religion* [1536], ed. John T.
    McNeill (Philadelphia, PA, 1960), I, 15.2.

69 Calvin, *Institutes*, IV, 10.5; also R. C. Zachman, *The Assurance of Faith*
    (Minneapolis, MI, 1993), p. 117. For a discussion of Calvin's own use
    of the term see G. Bosco, 'Conscience as Court and Worm: Calvin and
    the Three Elements of Conscience', *Journal of Religious Ethics*, XIV/2
    (1986), pp. 333–55.

70 See N. S. Davidson, 'Fuggir la libertà della conscienza: Conscience
    and the Inquisition in Sixteenth-century Italy', in *Contexts of Conscience*
    in Early Modern Europe, 1500–1700, ed. H. Braun and E. Vallance
    (Basingstoke, 2004), pp. 49 and 54.

71 See Rittgers, *The Reformation of the Keys*, pp. 218–19.

72 *Martin Luthers Werke*, 7, 317, 1–8.

73 *Luthers Tischreden*, No. 6,008.

74 See R. Gawthrop and G. Strauss, 'Protestantism and Literacy in Early
    Modern Germany', *Past and Present*, CIV/I (1984), pp. 35–8.

75 D. B. Barrett et al., *World Christian Encyclopedia* (New York, 1982), vol. I,
    p. 16.

76 A summary of the articles is available at http://en.wikipedia.org.

77 For a brief account of the processes whereby the early modern state imposed itself on religion, see M. van Creveld, *The Rise and Decline of the State* (Cambridge, 1999), pp. 62–74.

78 Quoted in G. R. Elton, *Reformation Europe, 1517–1559* (London, 1963), p. 62.

79 S. Schmitt, *Territorialstaat und Gemeinde im kurpfälzischen Oberamt Alzey vom 14. bis zum Anfang des 17. Jahrhunderts* (Stuttgart, 1964), p. 70.

80 See O. Friedrich, *The Deluge: A Portrait of Berlin in the 1920s* (New York, 1972), pp. 27, 34, 51, 69, 377.

81 See H. Mommsen, 'Van der Lubbes Weg in den Reichstgag: der Ablauf der Erreignisse' in *Reichstagsbrand: Aufklaerung einer Historischen Legende*, ed. U. Backes (Munich, 1986), pp. 42–7.

82 M. Domarus, ed., *Hitler: Speeches and Proclamations* (Mundelein, IL, 2004), vol. IV, p. 2860.

83 Corruption Perceptions Index, at www.transparency.org/research/cpi.

III. From Machiavelli to Nietzsche

1 Aurelius, *Meditations*, 4.22 and 7.54.

2 See, for what follows, Lester K. Born, ed., *The Education of a Christian Prince*, by Desiderius Erasmus (New York, 1963), pp. 99–132; also Born, 'The Specula Principis of the Carolingian Renaissance', *Revue belge de philologie et d'histoire*, XII (1933), pp. 583–612.

3 A good list of 'mirrors' written at various times and places may be found at 'Mirrors for Princes', http://en.wikipedia.org.

4 Born, *The Education of a Christian Prince*, p. 187.

5 Ibid., p. 203.

6 See, for the text, H. Bettenson, ed., *Documents of the Christian Church* (Oxford, 1967), pp. 115–16.

7 Born, 'The Specula Principis', p. 610.

8 N. Rubinstein, 'Notes on the Word Stato in Florence before Machiavelli', in *Florilegium Historiale: Essays Presented to Wallace K. Ferguson*, ed. J. G. Rowe et al. (Toronto, 1971), pp. 313–26.

9 S. de Grazia, *Machavelli in Hell* (New York, 1989), pp. 145–50.

10 Niccolò Machiavelli, *The Prince* (Harmondsworth, 1968), p. 92.

11 A. Gilbert, ed., *The Letters of Machiavelli* (New York, 1961), no. 137, p. 144.

12 See on this de Grazia, *Machiavelli in Hell*, pp. 293–317.

13 Machiavelli, *The Prince*, pp. 102–3.

14 See Felix Gilbert, 'On Machiavelli's Idea of Virtù', *Renaissance News*, IV/4 (1951), pp. 53–4.

15 F. Meinecke, *Machiavellism* (London, 1957), p. 47.

16 F. Bonaventura, *Della ragione di stato et della prudenza politica*, quoted in Meinecke, *Machiavellism*, p. 78, fn. 1.

17 The quote is from G. M. Trevelyan, *Garibaldi and the Making of Modern Italy* [1911] (London, 1948), p. 23.

18 Antonio Salandra, *Neutralita Italiana 1914: Ricordi e Pensieri* (Milan, 1938), pp. 377–78.

19 *Il Popolo d'Italia*, 24 (14 January 1915).

20 Meinecke, *Machiavellism*, p. 51.

21 Edward Meyer, *Machiavelli and the Elizabethan Drama* (Weimar, 1897).

22 Thomas Hobbes, *Leviathan* [1652] (London, 1961), p. 287; B. Spinoza, *Tractatus Theologico-Politicus* [1677] (Leiden, 1989), 19.22.

23 Frederick the Great, 'Réfutation de Machiavel', in *Oeuvres* (Berlin, 1857), 8, pp. 169 and 298; much of what follows is based on Meinecke, *Machiavellism*, pp. 272–390.

24 Frederick the Great, 'Dissertation sur les raisons d'établir ou d'abroger les lois' [1750], in *Oeuvres*, 9, p. 33.

25 Frederick the Great, *Avant-propos au Histoire de mon temps* [1743], in *Oeuvres*, 2, p. xxvi.

26 *Oeuvres*, 15, 138, p. 59.

27 *Oeuvres*, 2, p. xxv.

28 R. B. Haldane, 'Hegel', *Contemporary Review*, LXVII (1895), p. 232.

29 G.W.F. Hegel, *The Philosophy of Right* [1820] (Oxford, 1952), §132.

30 Ibid., p. 279.

31 G.W.F. Hegel, *Hegel Heute: Eine Auswahl aus Hegels Politischer Gedankenwelt* (Leipzig, 1934), pp. 11–12.

32 Quoted in Stephen A. Garrett, *Conscience and Power: An Examination of Dirty Hands and Political Leadership* (New York, 1996), p. 5.

33 Niccolò Machiavelli, *Discourses*, in *Machiavelli: The Chief Works*, ed. A. Gilbert (Durham, NC, 1965), vol. 1, pp. 228–9.

34 Machiavelli, *The Prince*, p. 50.

35 See, for some examples, H. D. Kittsteiner, *Gewissen und Geschichte* (Heidelberg, 1993), pp. 30–34, 37.

36 See E. J. Dijksterhuis, *The Mechanization of the World Picture* (Oxford, 1969).

37 Suetonius, *The Life of Caligula*, chapter 51.

38 See, for Franklin's deism, Merton A. Christensen, 'Franklin on the Hemphill Trial: Deism versus Presbyterian Orthodoxy', *The William and Mary Quarterly*, x/3 (1953), pp. 422–40.

39 Adam Smith, *The Theory of Moral Sentiments* [1759] (Beckenham, 1985), p. 105.

40 Leo Damrosch, *Jean-Jacques Rousseau: Restless Genius* (New York, 2005), p. 121.

41 See A. Levene, 'The Estimation of Mortality at the London Foundling Hospital, 1741–99', *Population Studies*, LIX/1 (2005), p. 88, table 1.

42 See J. Darling, *Child-centered Education and Its Critics* (Beverly Hills, CA, 1964).

43 See, for changing educational beliefs, J. H. Plumb, 'The New World of Children in Eighteenth-century England', *Past and Present*, LXVII/1 (1975), pp. 64–95; and, for a brief account of the different ways boys and girls were educated, M. van Creveld, *The Privileged Sex* (London, 2013), pp. 50–62.

44 Jean-Jacques Rousseau, *Emile; or, on Education* [1762] (New York, 1990), p. 50.

45 Ibid., p. 289.

46 Ibid., p. 267.

47 Ibid., p. 67; See J. Marks, 'The Divine Instinct? Rousseau and Conscience', *The Review of Politics*, LXVIII (2006), pp. 564–85.

48 Rousseau, *Emile, or on Education*, p. 290.

49 See Z. Elmarsafy, *The Histrionic Sensibility: Theatricality and Identity from Corneille to Rousseau* (Tuebingen, 2001), pp. 193–202.

50 Quoted in C. A. Spirn, *Prayer in the Writings of Jean-Jacques Rousseau* (New York, 2008), p. 25.

51 See, for a short account of what Rousseau had in mind, J. L. Talmon, *The Origins of Totalitarian Democracy* (London, 1961), pp. 38–49.

52 Immanuel Kant, *The Critique of Pure Reason* [1781], trans. J.M.D. Meiklejohn. The text is available at www.hn.psu.edu.

53 Immanuel Kant, *The Metaphysics of Morals* [1797] (Cambridge, 1996), p. 189.

54 Ibid., p. 346

55 Ibid., p. 189.

56 Immanuel Kant, *The Critique of Practical Reason* [1788], 1.3.30. The text is available at www.gutenberg.org.

57 Immanuel Kant, *Ueber der Gemeinspruch: Das mag in der Theorie richtig sein, taught aber nicht für die Praxis* [1793] (Berlin, 1870), 7, p. 286. The emphasis is mine.

58 Immanuel Kant, *Religion within the Limits of Reason Alone* [1793] (New York, 1934), p. 16.

59 Ibid., p. 50; M. J. Seidler, 'Kant and the Stoics on Suicide', *Journal of the History of Ideas*, XLIV/3 (1983), pp. 429–523.

60 P. Menzer, ed., *Eine Vorlesung Kants uber Ethik* (Berlin, 1925), pp. 307–8.

61 G.W.F. Hegel, 'Ueber die wissenschaftlichen Behandlungsarten des Naturrechts', in *Werke*, ed. E. Moldenhauer and K. M. Michel (Frankfurt, 1969), vol. II, p. 464.

62 See Michel Foucault, *Discipline and Punish* (London, 1979), pp. 195–228.

63 G. Himmelfarb, *Marriage and Morals among the Victorians* (New York, 1975), p. 4.

64 Editorial blurb of Christie Davis, *The Strange Death of Moral Britain* (London, 2006), available at www.books.google.co.uk.

65 See Adam Kuper, *Incest and Influence: The Private Life of Bourgeois England* (Cambridge, MA, 2010).

66 William Acton, quoted in N.J.D. Nagelkerke, *Courtesans and Consumption* (Delft, 2012), n.d., p. 13.

67 Walter, *My Secret Life* [1888], available at www.horntip.com.

68 J. Adams, *Wounds of Returning: Race, Memory and Property on the Postslavery Plantation* (Chapel Hill, NC, 2007), p. 45.

69 See, for a survey of the evidence, S. Pinker, *The Better Angels of Our Nature: Why Violence Has Declined* (New York, 2011), pp. 85–128.

70 Friedrich Nietzsche, *Ecce Homo* [1889] (Harmondsworth, 1979), p. 75.

71 By far the best analysis of Nietzsche's use of *ressentiment* is Esam Abou El Magd, *Nietzsche: Ressentiment und Schlechtem Gewissen auf den Spur* (Wuerzburg, 1996).

72 See, for Nietzsche's account of Christianity, *Beyond Good and Evil* [1886] (Harmondsworth, 1974), pp. 57–71.

73 Ibid., p. 130.

74 Tertullian, *On the Flesh of Christ*, p. 19. The text is available at www.tertullian.org.

75 Friedrich Nietzsche, *The Genealogy of Morals* [1887] (Oxford, 1996), pp. 42–3, 65, 73.

76 Nietzsche, *Beyond Good and Evil*, p. 78.

77 See, for a discussion of what he meant by the phrase, K. J. Winninger, *Nietzsche's Reclamation of Philosophy* (Amsterdam, 1997), pp. 17–46.

78 G.W.F. Hegel, *Philosophische Abhandlungen* (Berlin, 1845), p. 153; see also E. von der Luft, 'Sources of Nietzsche's "God Is Dead" and Its Meaning for Heidegger', *Journal of the History of Ideas*, XLV/2 (1984), pp. 263–76.

79 F. Galton, *The Language of God: A Scientist Presents Evidence for Belief* (New York, 2007), p. 218.

80 Friedrich Nietzsche, *The Gay Science* [1882] §125. The text is available at www.holybooks.com.

81 Friedrich Nietzsche, *Thus Spoke Zarathustra* [1884–5] (Harmondsworth, 1969), p. 75; Nietzsche, *The Genealogy of Morals*, p. 62.

82 Friedrich Nietzsche, *The Twilight of the Idols* [1884] (Harmondsworth, 1969), p. 101.

83 Nietzsche, *Thus Spoke Zarathustra*, p. 42.

84 See J. Richardson, 'Nietzsche Contra Darwin', *Philosophy and Phenomenological Research*, LXV/3 (2002), pp. 537–75.

85 Friedrich Nietzsche, *On the Future of Our Educational Institutions* [1872], Kindle edition, locs. 349, 366, 388, 405, 427 (on journalism), 1139. See also *The Genealogy of Morals*, pp. 110–27.

86 Friedrich Nietzsche, Preface to *Daybreak* (Cambridge, 1997).

87 Friedrich Nietzsche, *The Anti-Christ* [1895] (Harmondsworth, 1969), p. 121.

88 Nietzsche, *Beyond Good and Evil*, p. 92.

89 Nietzsche, *The Genealogy of Morals*, p. 47.

90 Nietzsche, *Twilight of the Idols*, p. 99.

91 On Nietzsche's debt to Dostoyevsky, see M. Stoeber, 'Dostoyevsky's Devil: The Will to Power', *The Journal of Religion*, LXXIV/1 (1994), pp. 26–44.

92 Nietzsche, *Beyond Good and Evil*, p. 107.

93 Nietzsche, *Ecce Homo*, p. 48.

94 Nietzsche, *Ecce Homo*, p. 134.

IV. Life without God

1 On Nietzsche's view of Shakespeare see Friedrich Nietzsche, *The Birth of Tragedy* [1872], p. 59. The text is available at http://records.viu.ca.

2 Friedrich Nietzsche, *The Wanderer and His Shadow* [1880] (Cambridge, 1965), p. 139.

3 See, for what follows, L. Anderson, 'Freud, Nietzsche', *Salmagundi*, no. 47/48 (1980), pp. 3–29.

4 See, for Salome's relations with Freud, L. Appignanesi and J. Forrester, *Die Frauen Sigmund Freuds* (Munich, 2000), pp. 350–71.

5 Friedrich Nietzsche, *Thus Spoke Zarathustra* [1884–5] (Harmondsworth, 1969), p. 110.

6 Sigmund Freud, *The Ego and the Id* [1923], in *The Freud Reader*, ed. P. Gay (London, 1995), pp. 643 and 655.

7 This and all the following quotes from Sigmund Freud, *Civilization and Its Discontents* [1929] are from the Internet edition, available at www2.winchester.ac.uk/edstudies.

8 Gay, *The Freud Reader*, p. 240.

9 Freud, *The Ego and the Id*, p. 637.

10 Gay, *The Freud Reader*, pp. 9–11.

11 A. Kolnai, *Psychoanalysis and Sociology* (London, 1921), p. 77.

12 John 8:32.

13 See on this J. Scharfenberg, 'Die Rezeption der Psychoanalyse in der Theologie', in *Die Rezeption der Psychoanalyse*, ed. J. Cremerius (Frankfurt, 1981), pp. 256–8.

14 *The Ego and the Id*, p. 642.

15 See, for a short account of the way it was done, Ingrid Lund, 'The Professionalization of Psychology in Europe', *European Psychologist*, IV/4 (1999), pp. 240–47; also, in respect to psychoanalysis, E. Kurzweil, *The Freudians: A Comparative Perspective* (New Brunswick, NJ, 1998), pp. 201–27.

16 W. R. Scott and J. C. Lammers, 'Trends in Occupations and Organizations in the Medical Care and Mental Health Sectors', *Medical Care Review*, XLII/1 (1985), p. 43, table 2 and p. 47, table 5.

17 See on Ferenczi's methods, 'Freud to Ferenczi' (18 September 1931), in Freud-Ferenczi correspondence, quoted in *Freud: A Life for Our Time*, ed. P. Gay (New York, 1998), p. 578; also S. Ginger, 'Sándor Ferenczi',

paper read at the 13th Congress of EA (2005), pp. 4–6, at
www.sergeginger.net.

18 Gay, Freud, pp. 438–42.

19 See, for a brief account of the process, P. E. Mullen, 'Psychoanalysis:
A Creed in Decline', *Australian and New Zealand Journal of Psychiatry*,
XXIII/1 (1989), pp. 17–20; and, at greater length, H. J. Eysenck, *The
Decline and Fall of the Freudian Empire* (New York, 1985).

20 See R. D. Laing, *The Divided Self* (Harmondsworth, 1960); and Thomas
Szazs, *The Myth of Mental Illness* (New York, 1961). A useful list of
works attacking psychoanalysis may be found at Library Thing,
www.librarything.com.

21 See R. D. Miller and R. Weinstock, 'Conflict of Interest between
Therapist-patient Confidentiality and the Duty to Report Sexual
Abuse of Children', *Behavioral Sciences and the Law*, V/2 (1987),
pp. 161–74.

22 Sigmund Freud, *New Introductory Lectures on Psychoanalysis:
A Comparative Perspective* (New Brunswick, NJ, 1998), pp. 59–61.

23 Sigmund Freud, 'Analysis Terminable and Interminable', in *The
Standard Edition of the Complete Psychological Works of Sigmund Freud*
[1937] (London, 1964), vol. XXIII, p. 250.

24 Alexis de Tocqueville, *Democracy in America* [1835–40] (Stilwell, KS,
2007), I, p. 191.

25 Kurzweil, *The Freudians*, p. 204.

26 See ibid., pp. 49–56.

27 P. C. Cohen, *A Calculating People: The Spread of Numeracy in Early America*
(London, 1999).

28 Gay, Freud, p. 570.

29 See, on the expansion of the DSM, R. J. McNally, *What Is Mental Illness?*
(Cambridge, MA, 2011), pp. 16–27.

30 Gay, Freud, p. 566.

31 See I. D. Yalom, *The Gift of Therapy* (New York, 2009), especially pp. xx,
4–5, 9–11.

32 J. A. Weis and C. A. Weiss, 'Social Scientists and Decision Makers
Look at the Usefulness of Social Research', *American Psychologist*,
XXXVI/8 (1981), p. 838, table 1.

33 Inoue Nobutaka, 'Perspectives toward Understanding the Concept of
Kami', in *Kami*, ed. Inoue Nobutaka (Tokyo, 1998), p. 2.

34 Sasaki Kiyoshi, 'Amenominakanushi no Kami in Late Tokugawa Period Kokogagu', in *Kami*, ed. Inoue Nobutaka, p. 169.

35 According to D. K. Reynolds, *Morita Psychotherapy* (Berkeley, CA, 1976), p.120.

36 G. H. Blowers and S. Yang Hsueh Chi, 'Freud's Deshi: The Coming of Psychoanalysis to Japan', *Journal of the History of the Behavioral Sciences*, XXXIII/2 (1997), pp. 119–21.

37 Keigo Okigani, 'Psychoanalysis in Japan', in *Freud and the Far East*, ed. S. Akhtar (Boston, MA, 2009), p. 10.

38 See on him Taketomo Yashuhiko, 'Cultural Adaptation to Psychoanalysis in Japan, 1912–1955', *Social Research*, LVII/4 (1990), p. 963.

39 J. C. Moloney, 'Understanding the Paradox of Japanese Psychoanalysis', *International Journal of Psychoanalysis*, XXXIV/4 (1953), pp. 291–303.

40 See on this Kazushige Shingu, 'Freud and Lacan and Japan', paper presented at the 2nd International Conference of the Japanese-Korean Lacanian Psychoanalytic Groups (2005), available at www.discourseunit.com/manchester-psychoanalytic-matrix.

41 P. Dahan, 'La Loi et les lois du significant', n.p., n.d., at www. champlacanienfrance.net/IMG/pdf/Mensuel6_PDahan.pdf; Fuhido Endo, 'Review: Kojin Karatani and the Return of the Thirties: Psychoanalysis in/of Japan', *The Semiotic Review of Books*, XIII/I (2002), pp. 3–4.

42 Takie Sugiyama Lebra, *The Japanese Self in Cultural Logic* (Honolulu, HI, 2004), pp. 31–2.

43 M. Mead, ed., *Cooperation and Competition among Primitive Peoples* [1937] (New Brunswick, NJ, 2003), pp. 307 and 493–4.

44 Ruth Benedict, *The Chrysanthemum and the Sword* (Boston, MA, 1946), p. 223; also pp. 22–4, 195, 273, 287–8, 293.

45 There is a good discussion of the differences in D. L. Cairns, *Aidos* (Oxford, 1993), pp. 14–19, 21–2, 27, 29; see also G. Taylor, *Pride, Shame and Guilt* (Oxford, 1985), pp. 34–43, 64.

46 See, for the reception of the book in Japan, S. Ryang, 'Chrysanthemum's Strange Life: Ruth Benedict in Postwar Japan', Japan Policy Research Institute (2004), at www.jpri.org.

47 This and the following quotes from Benedict, *The Chrysanthemum and*

the Sword, pp. 106–7, 224, 293.

48 D. W. Plath and R. J. Smith, 'How "American" Are Studies of Modern Japan Done in the United States?', in *Otherness of Japan: Historical and Cultural Influences on Japanese Studies in Ten Countries*, ed. H. Befu and J. Kreiner (Munich, 1992), p. 206.

49 J. Robertson, 'When and Where Japan Enters: American Anthropology since 1945', in *The Postwar Development of Japanese Studies in the United States*, ed. H. Hardacre (Leiden, 1998), p. 311.

50 P. N. Dale, *The Myth of Japanese Uniqueness* (New York, 1986), pp. 44 and 51.

51 B. A. Shilonny, 'Victors without Vanquished: A Japanese Model of Conflict Resolution', in *Japanese Models of Conflict Resolution*, ed. S. N. Eisenstadt and E. Ben Ari (London, 1990), p. 127.

52 V. L. Hamilton and J. S. Sanders, *Everyday Justice* (New Haven, CT, 1994), p. 37.

53 J. Braithwaite, *Crime, Shame and Reintegration* (Cambridge, 1989), p. 61.

54 Lebra, *The Japanese Self*, p. 11.

55 'Japan Whistleblower at Highest Court', International Whistleblowers, n.d., at www.internationalwhistleblowers.com.

56 A convenient summary is provided by S. M. Lipset, *American Exceptionalism* (New York, 1996), pp. 211–66.

57 L. H. Long, 'On Measuring Geographic Mobility', *Journal of the American Statistical Association*, LXV/331 (1970), table 2, p. 1197, and table 3, p. 1199.

58 Lebra, *The Japanese Self*, pp. 166–7.

59 Hiroshi Ono, 'Lifetime Employment in Japan', *Journal of the Japanese and International Economies*, XXIV/1 (2010), pp. 1–27.

60 Lebra, 'Compensative Justice and Moral Investment among Japanese, Chinese and Koreans', in *Japanese Culture and Behavior*, ed. T. S. Lebra and W. P. Lebra (Honolulu, HI, 1986), pp. 278–91.

61 Lebra, *The Japanese Self*, pp. 118–26, 210–15.

62 Greenhouse Japan, 'Are Japanese Tourists Easy Targets for Robbers Abroad?', 7 June 2012, at http://greenhousejapan.blogspot.co.il.

63 I. Morris, *The Nobility of Failure* (Boston, MA, 1974), pp. 93, 98–9, 102.

64 Ibid., pp. 107, 126.

65 Ibid., pp. 103–5.

66 Quote from The Heiko Monogatari, in P. Valery, *Warriors of Japan*

(Honolulu, HI, 1994), p. 113.

67 See Taku Tamaki, 'Confusing Confucius in Asian Values? A Constructivist Critique', *International Relations*, XXI/3 (2007), pp. 284–304.

68 See H. Creel, *The Origins of Statecraft in China* (Chicago, IL, 1970), pp. 493–506.

69 Confucius, *The Analects* (VIII, 21) (London, 1979).

70 See, on such families, Shu-Ching Lee, 'China's Traditional Family: Its Characteristics and Disintegration', *American Sociological Review*, XVIII/3 (1953), pp. 272–80.

71 See, for one person's account of the problem, Fan Shen, 'The Classroom and the Wider Culture: Identity as a Key to Learning English Composition', *College Composition and Communication*, XL/4 (1989), pp. 459–66.

72 Here it is only fair to add that some attempts have been made to adapt the system to symmetrical relations too; Anon, 'Confucian Ethics and the Limits of Rights Theory', n.d., chapter from book retrieved from www.bates.edu, accessed 19 September 2012.

73 Confucius, *The Analects* (XII, 2 and XV, 24).

74 Ibid. (XIII, 18.1–2).

75 Ibid. (IV, 18).

76 Ibid. (X, 1–5).

77 See S. T. Ames and H. Rosemont, 'Were the Early Confucians Virtuous?', in *Ethics in Early China*, ed. C. Fraser et al. (Hong Kong, 2011), pp. 17–35.

78 See B. Hook, 'The Campaign against Lin Piao and Confucius', *Asian Affairs*, V/3 (1974), pp. 311–16.

79 See S. J. Marshall, *The Mandate of Heaven* (Richmond, VA, 2001), pp. 18–19, for an example of this.

80 See on this O. Bedford and Kwang-Kuo Hwang, 'Guilt and Shame in Chinese Culture', *Journal of the Theory of Social Behavior*, XXXIII/2 (2003), p. 139.

81 Kwong-Loi Shun, 'Ren and Li in the Analects', in B. W. van Norden, *Confucius and the Analects* (Oxford, 2002), p. 53.

82 See ibid., especially pp. 62–7, for the relationship between ren and li.

83 *Analects* (III, 3).

84 *Analects* (V, 20).

85 Chang Wing-tsit, *Instructions for Practical Living and Other Neo-Confucian Writings by Wang Yang-Ming* (New York, 1963), pp. 272–80.

86 *Analects* (XV, 9); *Mencius*, p. 166.

87 See M. Ricci, *Entrata nella China de' padri della Compagnia del Gesu* [1622] (Rome, 1983).

88 Philip J. Ivanhoe, *Ethics in the Confucian Tradition* (Atlanta, GA, 1990), pp. 40–41.

89 *Analects* (XII, 13), 1–6.

v. Conscience in the Third Reich

1 Adolf Hitler, *Mein Kampf* [1924] (Mumbai, 1988), p. 19; H. R. Trevor-Roper, ed., *Hitler's Secret Conversations* (New York, 1953), pp. 155–7, 566–7, entries for 8–9 January 1942 and 7 September 1942.

2 The letter is printed in W. Maser, *Hitler's Letters and Notes* (New York, 1974), p. 30.

3 H. Mend, *Adolf Hitler im Felde, 1914–1918* (Diessen, 1931); F. Wiedemann, *Der Mann der Feldherr Werden Wollte* (Dortmund, 1964).

4 Quoted in B. Hamann, *Winifred Wagner oder Hitlers Bayreuth* (Munich, 2005), p. 343.

5 Trevor-Roper, *Hitler's Secret Conversations*, pp. 127, 128–9, 200, 221, 517, entries for 28–9 January 1941, 1 February 1941, 24–5 January 1942 and 2 February 1942.

6 D. Irving, ed., *Die geheime Tagebücher des Dr Morell* (Munich, 1983), p. 17.

7 Trevor-Roper, *Hitler's Secret Conversations*, pp. 24, 209–10, 214, entries for 19–20 August 1941, 27 January 1942 and 28–9 January 1942.

8 E. von Manstein, *Lost Victories* [1958] (Chicago, IL, 1982), p. 281, fn 1.

9 Albert Speer, *Inside the Third Reich* (New York, 1971), p. 259, note 1.

10 P. Longerich, *The Unwritten Order: Hitler's Role in the Final Solution* (Stroud, 2005).

11 Trevor-Roper, *Hitler's Secret Conversations*, p. 21.

12 See on this C. R. Browning, *Collected Memories* (Madison, WI, 2003), pp. 29–33.

13 Trevor-Roper, *Hitler's Secret Conversations*, p. 193.

14 Ibid., pp. 212–13.

15 Ibid., p. 37, entry for 25–6 September 1941.

16 Hamann, *Winifred Wagner*, p. 457.

17 R. Gerwarth, *Hitler's Hangman: The Life of Heydrich* (New Haven, CT, 2011), pp. 214 and 223.

18 W. Schellenberg, *The Schellenberg Memoirs* (London, Deutsch, 1956), p. 337.

19 The Testament is printed in W. Maser, *Hitler's Letters and Notes* (New York, 1974), p. 358.

20 Quoted in D. Irving, *Göring: A Biography* (New York, 1989), p. 159.

21 The quote is from A. Read, *The Devil's Disciples: Hitler's Inner Circle* (New York, 2003), pp. 379–80.

22 The memorandum is available at www.ns-archiv.de/krieg/ untermenschen/himmler-fremdvolk.php.

23 See Irving, *Göring*, pp. 343–9.

24 See, for a detailed analysis of this episode, R. Breitman, 'Himmler and "The Terrible Secret" among the Executioners', *Journal of Contemporary History*, XXVI/3–4 (1991), pp. 442–4.

25 International Military Tribunal, *Trials of the Major War Criminals* (Nuremberg, 1947), 42, page 546.

26 The parts quoted are available online at http://holocaust-history.org/himmler-poznan/speech-text.shtml.

27 See, for some references, M. Wolfson, 'Constraint and Choice in the ss Leadership', *The Western Political Quarterly*, XVIII/3 (1965), pp. 551–3.

28 See Gerwarth, *Hitler's Hangman*, pp. 73–5 and 144–5.

29 Quoted in I. Kershaw, *The End: Germany, 1944–45* (London, 2012), pp. 37–8.

30 On his use of the term see P. Longerich, *Heinrich Himmler* (Oxford, 2012), p. 198.

31 Ibid., pp. 301–2, 308–10.

32 F. Kersten, *The Kersten Memoirs* (New York, 1947), pp. 60, 209.

33 G. Sereny, *Into That Darkness: An Examination of Conscience* (London, 1974), p. 20.

34 Goebbels's diary, entry for 18 December 1941.

35 Himmler to Kersten, 21 March 1945, printed in Kersten, *Memoirs*, p. 227. The English translation is mine.

36 See J. M. Steiner, 'The ss Yesterday and Today: A Sociopsychological View', in *Survivors, Victims, and Perpetrators; Essays on the Nazi Holocaust*, ed. J. E. Dimsdale (Washington, DC, 1980), pp. 431–4 and 443.

37 H. J. von Moltke, *Letters to Freya* (New York, 1990), p. 183 and 183 n. 2.

38 See M. Messerschmidt, *Die Wehrmachtjustiz* (Munich, 2005), p. 79.

39 See Sereny, *Into That Darkness*, p. 83.

40 See on this R. Wittmann, *Beyond Justice: The Auschwitz Trials* (Cambridge, MA, 2005), p. 99.

41 See Longerich, *Heinrich Himmler*, pp. 315–51.

42 Christopher Browning, *Ordinary Men: Reserve Police Battalion 101 and the Final Solution in Poland* (Harmondsworth, 2001), pp. 13–14.

43 See, for a recent evaluation of the Milgram and Zimbardo experiments, as well as a critique, S. Reicher and S. A. Haslam, 'Rethinking the Psychology of Tyranny', *British Journal of Social Psychology*, XLV (2006), pp. 1–40.

44 See B. Naumann, *Auschwitz* (New York, 1966), pp. 67–8.

45 The volume is available in several English editions. I used A. Pollinger, ed., *The Commandant* (London, 2011).

46 Quoted in Kersten, *Memoirs* (London, 1956), p. 154.

47 For Dirlewanger and Globocnick, see Longerich, *Heinrich Himmler*, pp. 345–58; for Stangl, see Sereny, *Into That Darkness*, pp. 51, 55, 78, and 134.

48 Sereny, *Into That Darkness*, p. 119.

49 *Trials of the Major War Criminals*, I, p. 251.

50 G. M. Gilbert, *Nuremberg Diary* (New York, 1947), entry for 12 April 1946.

51 Quoted in J. J. Hughes, 'A Mass Murderer Repents: The Case of Rudolf Hoess, Commandant of Auschwitz', Archbishop Gerety Lecture at Seton Hall University, 25 March 1998. Available at www.shu.edu.

52 See on this R. Sczuchta, 'Teaching about the Holocaust in Poland' (1997), at www.iearn.org.

53 E. Demant, ed., *Auschwitz: 'Direkt von der Rampe Weg'* (Reinbek, 1979), pp. 60, 61, 63, 67, 83, 85, 86, 87.

54 Ibid., pp. 102 and 116.

55 Claudia Koonz, *Mothers in the Fatherland: Women, the Family and Nazi Politics* (New York, 1987), pp. 404–5.

56 Longerich, *Heinrich Himmler*, p. 12.

57 Grawitz to Himmler, 4 March 1942, quoted in Browning, *Ordinary Men*, p. 231.

58 Tomasz Żuroch-Piechowski, 'Innocent Man at the Nuremberg Trials' (Polish), *Tygodnik Powszechny*, XXXIX (2006), 24 September 2006.

59 Browning, *Ordinary Men*, p. 154; Benjamin Ferencz, 'Mass Murderers Seek to Justify Genocide', http://archive.today/jxfl; Sereny, *Into That Darkness*, p. 349.

60 G. Aly et al., *Cleansing the Fatherland: Nazi Medicine and Racial Hygiene* (Baltimore, MD, 1994), p. 156.

61 Programme introduction available at http://db.yadvashem.org/righteous/search.html?language=en.

62 S. P. Oliner, *The Altruistic Personality* (New York, 1988), p. 1.

63 See on this M. Hoffman, 'Does Higher Income Make You More Altruistic? Evidence from the Holocaust', *Review of Economics and Statistics*, XCIII/3 (2011), pp. 876–87; also Oliner, *The Altruistic Personality*, p. 260.

64 L. Wijler, *Herinneringen* (Herzliya, 1975), p. 142.

65 Oliner, *The Altruistic Personality*, pp. 50, 81 and 114.

66 Ibid., p. 260.

67 Ibid., p. 237.

68 According to Schellenberg, *The Schellenberg Memoirs*, p. 338.

69 See W. Meyer, *Unternehmen Sieben: Eine Rettungsaktion* (Berlin, 1976), pp. 212 and 214.

70 See J. H. Waller, 'The Double Life of Admiral Canaris', *International Journal of Intelligence and Counter-intelligence*, IX/3 (1996), pp. 271–89; also P. Hoffman, *Behind Valkyrie: German Resistance to Hitler* (Cambridge, MA, 1988), pp. 93, 235, 246.

71 H. Camlot, 'Did Wallenberg's Family Aid the Nazis while He Saved Jews?', *JWeekly.com*, 14 June 1996, www.jweekly.com.

72 Oliner, *The Altruistic Personality*, pp. 168 and 260.

73 Ibid., p. 260.

74 Ibid., pp. 154–5 and 260.

75 Ibid., p. 159.

76 See on these plots, T. Parssinen, *The Unknown Story of the Military Plot to Kill Hitler* (London, 2004).

77 N. Reynolds, *Treason Was No Crime: Ludwig Beck, Chief of the German General Staff* (London, 1976), p. 207.

78 Quoted in M. Balfour, *Withstanding Hitler* (London, 1988), p. 126.

79 Goerdler memorandum, 1941–2, in Hoffmann, *Behind Valkyrie*, p. 200.

80 Hoffmann, *Behind Valkyrie*, pp. 131–5.

81 J. Kramarz, *Stauffenberg* (Frankfurt, 1965), p. 122.

82 See P. Hoffmann, 'Oberst i. G. Henning von Tresckow und die Staatsstreichpläne im Jahr 1943', *Vierteljahrshefte für Zeitgeschichte*, LV (2007), p. 344.

83 Quoted in F. von Schlabrendorff, *Revolt against Hitler* (London, 1948), p. 131.

84 An English version of the speech is available at http://comicism.tripod.com/440720.html.

85 See on Hans and Sophie Scholl, I. Jens, ed., *Hans Scholl, Sophie Scholl: Briefe und Aufzeichnungen* (Frankfurt, 1983), pp. 157–8, 171, 179, 223–7.

86 Theodor Haecker, *Tag-und-Nachtbücher, 1939–1945* (Munich, 1947), p. 30.

87 See, for Elser's life and his attempt to kill Hitler, H. G. Haasis, *Den Hitler jag' ich in die Luft: Der Attentäter Georg Elser* [1999] (Hamburg, 2009).

88 See U. Renz, 'Elser und die Juden', *Tribüne: Zeitschrift zum Verständnis des Judentums*, CLV (2000), pp. 47–55.

VI. Idols Old and New

1 See, for the debate, J. Hegeland, 'Christians and the Roman Army AD 173–337', *Church History*, XLIII/2 (1974), pp. 149–63.

2 M. B. Weddle, *Walking in the Way of Peace: Quaker Pacifism in the Seventeenth Century* (Oxford, 2001), pp. 180, 228–9.

3 S. M. Kohn, *Jailed for Peace: The History of American Draft Law Violators, 1658–1985* (Westport, CT, 1986), pp. 9–11.

4 On the way these things worked before and during the War of the American Revolution, see E. M. West, 'The Right to Religion-based Exemptions in Early America: The Case of Conscientious Objectors to Conscription', *Journal of Law and Religion*, X/2 (1993–4), pp. 367–401.

5 Kohn, *Jailed for Peace*, pp. 20–21; For Marx's own view on this see *The Communist Manifesto* [1848], p. 2, www.marxists.org.

6 See C. C. Moskos and J. Whiteclay Chambers, *The New Conscientious Objection: From Religious to Secular Resistance* (New York, 1993), pp. 3–21.

7 See P. Brock, *Pacifism in Europe to 1972* (Princeton, NJ, 1972), I, p. 467.

8 C. H. Smith, *Smith's Story of the Mennonites* (Kansas City, KS, 1957), p. 545.

9 J. Greenberg, *I Never Promised You a Rose Garden* (New York, 1964).

10 The Resolution is available at http://assembly.coe.int.

11 See, for a short overview of the legal aspects of the problem, David
    Malament, 'Selective Conscientious Objection and Gillette Decision',
    Philosophy and Public Affairs, I/4 (1972), pp. 363–86.

12 C. Jehn and Z. Selden, 'The End of Conscription in Europe?',
    Contemporary Economic Policy, XX/2 (2002), pp. 93–100.

13 See Conscientious Objection Fact Sheet, at http://girightshotline.org.

14 See J. Muller, *The Remnants of War* (Ithaca, NY, 2004); also M. van
    Creveld, *Nuclear Proliferation and the Future of Conflict* (New York, 1993).

15 Thomas Hobbes, *Leviathan* [1652] (London, 1961), pp. 203, 284–95.

16 See H. T. King, 'The Legacy of Nuremberg', *Case Western Journal of
    International Law*, XXXIV (2002), p. 335e.

17 For a good example of the genre, see B. Schaffner, *Father-land: A Study
    of Authoritarianism in the German Family* (New York, 1948).

18 John Locke, *Second Treatise on Government* [1689] (Cambridge, 1967),
    p. 289.

19 The text is available at www.un.org/en.

20 For a short account of the process, see L. Henkin, 'Human Rights
    and State "Sovereignty"', *Georgia Journal of International and Comparative
    Law*, XXV/31 (1995), pp. 31–46; also R. Dworkin, *Taking Rights Seriously*
    (London, 1977).

21 M. Ignatieff, *The Rights Revolution* (Toronto, 2000).

22 Speech of 10 December 1997, available at www.un.org/en.

23 See on this E. M. Hafner-Burton et al., 'Human Rights in a Globalizing
    World: The Paradox of Empty Promises', *American Journal of Sociology*,
    X/5 (2005), pp. 1373–411.

24 On the origins and development of the International Criminal Court,
    see B. Broomhall, *International Justice and the International Court: Between
    Sovereignty and Law* (New York, 2004).

25 See F. Spott, *Hitler and the Power of Aesthetics* (New York, 2009),
    especially pp. 112–36.

26 Quoted in C. Koonz, *The Nazi Conscience* (Cambridge, MA, 2003), p. 138.

27 See, for example, M. Spivak, 'Un Concept Mythologique de la Troisième
    Republique: Le Reinforcement du Capital Humain de la France',
    Information Historique, IV/2 (1987), pp. 155–76; and L. W. Burgener,
    'Sport et Politique dans un Etat Neutre: L'instruction Préliminaire en
    Suisse, 1918–1947', *Information Historique*, XLVIII/1 (1986), pp. 23–9.

28 See on the significance of this D. Schaefer, *Heil bei Hitler: Geschichte und Missbrauch einer Medizinischer Metaphor* (Basel, 2005).

29 W. L. Shirer, *Berlin Diary* (New York, 1941) p. 327, entry for 27 June 1940.

30 E. Wu, 'Public Health Service in the Weimar Republic and in the Early History of West Germany' [German], *Öffentliches Gesundheitswesen*, LI/5 (1989), pp. 215–21.

31 'Life Expectancy at Birth by Race and Sex, 1930–2010', at www.infoplease.com.

32 See A. B. Artin et al., 'Growth in U.S. Health Spending Remained Slow in 2010', *Health Affairs*, XXXI/1 (2012), pp. 208–19; R. Shinkman, 'Health Costs Drive Entire U.S. Deficit', 10 April 2012, at www.fiercehealthfinance.com.

33 Anon, 'Saggy Boobs from Smoking, Not Suckling', *Aphrodite*, 8 November 2007, at www.aphroditewomenshealth.com.

34 Anon, 'Health Conscience', n.d., at http://corporatewelfare.org/health.

35 M. Woodward and H. Tunstall-Pedoe, 'Coffee and Tea Consumption in the Scottish Heart Health Study Follow Up', *Community Health*, LIII (1999), pp. 481–7.

36 W. Willett, *Eat, Drink, and Be Healthy* (New York, 2001), p. 54.

37 See W. C. Willett, 'The Mediterranean Diet: Science and Practice', *Public Health Nutrition*, 9 February 2006, pp. 105–10. There is a good article on the subject at http://en.wikipedia.org.

38 B. Glasner, *The Gospel of Food*, HarperCollins e-books (2007), loc. 118.

39 B. Luscombe, 'Do We Need $75,000 a Year to Be Happy?, *Time* (6 September 2010).

40 See A. Hardy, *The Epidemic Streets* (Oxford, 1991).

41 British Museum, 'Cradle to Grave by Pharmacopoeia', at www.britishmuseum.org.

42 *Yediot Aharonot* [Hebrew], 3 January 2013, at www.ynet.co.il; 'For Members of the U.S. Military, A Ban on Smoking Could Really Burn', *Stars and Stripes*, 25 June 2014, at www.stripes.com.

43 Anon, 'The History of Ecstasy', n.d., at www.drugs.iemallway.com; Conal Urquhart, 'Can MDMA Help to Cure Depression?', *The Guardian* (15 September 2012).

44 S. S. Wang, 'Value of Medical Checkups Doubted', *Wall Street Journal* (17 October 2012).

45 See, for a discussion of the persuasion techniques in use, E. M. Slater and J. E. Ward, 'How Risks of Breast Cancer and Benefits of Screening are Communicated to Women: Analysis of 58 Pamphlets', *British Medical Journal*, CCCXVII (1998).

46 See, for a short but very good overview of the subject, 'Workplace Wellness', at http://en.wikipedia.org.

47 Anon, 'Meet the Success Here: Denmark Institutes Fat Tax', 21 October 2011, at http://meetthesuccesshere.blogspot.co.il.

48 Sandra Haurant, 'French Government Banning Vegetarianism in School Canteens', *The Guardian* (26 October 2011).

49 U. Poschardt, 'Gesundheit is die Pflicht jede Burger', *Die Welt* (3 January 2013); 'Children's Day Celebrated with Fervor', *Chandigar Tribune* (6 October 2011).

50 See, for a short survey, 'Religious Views of Suicide', at http://en.wikipedia.org.

51 See, for a short introduction to the subject, S. P. James and D. E. Cooper, 'Buddhism and the Environment', *Contemporary Buddhism*, VIII/2 (2007), pp. 93–6.

52 Aristotle, *Politics* (I, 8).

53 See A. Bramwell, 'Blut und Boden', in *Deutsche Erinnerungsorte*, ed. E. Francois and H. Schulze (Munich, 2003), pp. 380–91.

54 See W. H. Rollins, 'Whose Landscape? Technology, Fascism and Environmentalism on the National Socialist Autobahn', *Annals of the Association of American Geographers*, LXXXV/3 (1995), pp. 494–520.

55 See for the regulations in question Edeltraud Klueting, 'Die gesetzlichen Regelungen der nationalsozialistischen Reichsregierung für den Tierschutz, den Naturschutz und den Umweltschutz', in *Naturschutz und Nationalsozialismus*, ed. J. Radkau and Frank Uekoetter (Frankfurt, 2003), pp. 77–106.

56 See, for example, D. Story, *Should Christians Be Environmentalists?* (Grand Rapids, MI, 2012); and M. Mies and V. Shiva, *Ecofeminism* (Halifax, NS, 1993).

57 See, for example, R. Ashworth, 'Gay Environmentalism', 22 February 2005, www.theslowlane.org.

58 The list 'Environmental and Animal Activists Injured or Killed' is available at www.sourcewatch.org.

59 See, for a useful short summary of their development, 'Green Party', at http://en.wikipedia.org.

60 A. Leopold, *A Sandy County Almanac* [1949] (New York, 2001), p. 262.

61 See David Biello, 'Is Birth Control the Answer to Environmental Ills?', *Scientific American* (23 September 2009).

62 The Impact Team, 'The Weather Conspiracy: The Coming of the New Ice Age' (New York, 1977).

63 D. Archibald, 'The CIA Documents the Global Cooling Research of the 1970s', NUWT, 25 May 2012, http://wattsupwiththat.com.

64 For these and other ideas see Jim Meyer, 'Geoengineering: A Mad Scientist's Guide to Fixing the Planet', n.d., http://grist.org.

65 See most recently, Anon, 'Dire Outlook Despite Global Warming "Pause"', 19 May 2013, http://phys.org; A. Watts, 'Russian Scientists Say Period of Global Cooling Ahead Owing to Changes in the Sun', 29 April 2013, at http://wattsupwiththat.com; Peter Ferrara, 'Sorry Global Warming Alarmists, the Earth Is Cooling', *Forbes* (31 May 2012).

66 See R. E. Goodin, 'Selling Environmental Indulgences', *Kyklos*, XLVII (1994), pp. 573–96.

67 Valerie Volcovici, 'U.S. Carbon Tax Could Halve Deficit in 10 Years', *Reuters*, 26 September 2012, http://uk.reuters.com.

68 See on this entire issue K. Knezevich, 'Hunting and Environmentalists: Conflict or Misperceptions', *Human Dimensions of Wildlife*, XIV/1 (2009), pp. 12–20.

69 Bryan Farrell, 'Green Camo: Seeing through the Military's New Environmentalism', War Resisters' League (2009), at www.warresisters.org.

70 See, above all, R. Bailey, *Ecoscam* (New York, 1994).

71 Diana Sander, 'Kann die Angst vor Elektrosmog den Menschen krank machen?', *Journal Expert.de*, 9 May 2013, at www.journalexpert.de.

VII. **The Man-machine**

1 Epicurus, 'Letter to Menoeceus', www.epicurus.net/en/menoeceus.html.

2 According to Lactantius, *Institutes* (III, 17).

3 Lucretius, *On the Nature of Things* (II, 251–60).

4 Ibid. (III, 54–5).

5 See on this W. R. Johnson, *Lucretius and the Modern World* (Bristol, 2000), pp. 3–4.

6 See on this fascinating story, S. Greenblatt, *The Swerve: How the Modern World Began* (New York, 2012), pp. 14–50.

7 On Calvin's views of Lucretius see H. N. Parker, ed., *Olympia Morala: The Complete Views of an Italian Heretic* (Chicago, IL, 2003), p. 39.

8 Thomas Creech's translation printed by London, Westminster, Booksellers of London, 1700.

9 Thomas Hobbes, *The Elements of Law* [1650] (New York, 1969), ch. 63.

10 Thomas Hobbes, *Leviathan* [1652] (London, 1961), p. 85.

11 Ibid., p. 99.

12 Paul-Henri d'Holbach, *Good Sense* [1772], p. 81, at e-Books, http://good-sense.t.ebooks2ebooks.com/81.html.

13 See J. A. Israel, *Radical Enlightenment* (Oxford, 2001), p. 710.

14 Denis Diderot, *Le Rêve de d'Alembert* [1769] (Paris, 1921), pp. 42, 70, 89, 95, 103 and 129.

15 See M. Wilson, *Diderot* (Oxford, 1972), p. 562.

16 See S. Gaukroger, *The Collapse of Mechanism and the Rise of Sensibility* (Oxford, 2010), pp. 394–420.

17 English translation in Gaukroger, *The Collapse of Mechanism*, p. 390.

18 Alfred Tennyson, *In Memoriam* [1833], 27.5 and 27.8.

19 See, for the history of this claim, L. Holford-Stevens, 'Horror Vacui in Lucrtian Biography', *Leeds International Classical Studies*, I/I (2002), p. 5.

20 See above all K. Lorenz, *On Aggression* (London, 1963), pp. 75–80.

21 B. F. Skinner, *Science and Human Behavior* (New York, 1953), pp. 350–58.

22 B. F. Skinner, *On Behaviorism* (New York, 1974), p. 17.

23 B. F. Skinner, *Beyond Freedom and Dignity* (New York, 1971), p. 215.

24 See B. F. Skinner, 'Two "Synthetic Social Relations"', *Journal of the Experimental Analysis of Behavior*, V/4 (1962), pp. 531–3.

25 Skinner, *On Behaviorism*, p. 150.

26 Skinner, *Science and Human Behavior*, p. 187.

27 Callistratus' *Descriptions* is available at www.theoi.com. The quotation is from chapter 8.

28 Ibid., chapter 9.

29 See J. W. Meri, *Medieval Islamic Civilization: An Encyclopaedia* (London, 2005), p. 711; C. B. Fowler, 'The Museum of Music: A History of

Mechanical Instruments', *Music Educators Journal*, LIV/2 (1967), pp. 45–9; M. E. Rosheim, *Robot Revolution: The Development of Anthrobotics* (1994), p. 36; and J. B. Needham, *Science and Civilization in China* (Cambridge, 1971), IV/2, pp. 133 and 508.

30 Needham, *Science and Civilization in China*, II, p. 53.

31 J. M. Levitt, *The Turk: Chess Automaton* (Jefferson, NC, 2000), pp. 39–43.

32 On this strange story, see T. Standage, *The Turk: The Life and Times of the Famous Eighteenth-century Chess-playing Machine* (New York, 2002).

33 See M. Hillier, *Automata and Mechanical Toys* (London, 1976), pp. 20 and 46.

34 C. R. Hills, *Power from Wind* (Cambridge, 1996), pp. 95–102.

35 Good descriptions of Aebo and Qrio are available at Wikipedia.

36 T. Maliq, 'Japanese Cargo Sends a Tiny Talking Robot to Space Station', NBC News, 4 August 2013, www.nbcnews.com.

37 A. Belford, 'That's Not a Droid, That's My Girlfriend', *Global Mail* (21 February 2013).

38 See Naho Kitano, 'Roboethics: A Comparative Analysis of Social Acceptance of Robots between the West and Japan' (2006), www.roboethics.org.

39 See, for some examples, 'Mechanical Marvels of the Nineteenth Century', at www.bigredhair.com/robots.

40 Jules Verne, *La maison à vapeur* (Paris, 1880).

41 The text is available at http://preprints/readingroo.ms/RUR/rur.pdf.

42 Isaac Asimov, 'Runaround', available at www.rci.rutgers.edu.

43 Ibid.

44 See, for example, a document named 'South Korean Robot Ethics Charter, 2012', at http://akikoko12um1.wordpress.com.

45 See, above all, P. Singer, *Wired for War: The Robotics Revolution and Conflict in the 21st Century*, Kindle Edition (2006).

46 G. C. Wilson, 'Navy Missile Downs Iranian Airliner', *Washington Post* (4 July 1988).

47 N. Schachtman, 'Robot Cannon Kills 9, Wounds 16', *Wired* (18 October 2007), at www.wired.com.

48 See Asimov's homepage at http://asimo.honda.com.

49 Singer, *Wired for War*, locs. 7780–97.

50 See D. Troop, 'Robots at War: Scholars Debate the Ethical Issues', *The Chronicle of Higher Education* (10 September 2012).

51 J. Pitrat, *Artificial Beings: The Conscience of a Conscious Machine* (London, 2013).

52 Homer, *The Odyssey* (I, 9–22).

53 M. Rose and J. M. Abi-Rasched, *Neuro: The New Brain Sciences and the Management of the Mind*, Kindle Edition (2013), locs. 321–2.

54 See on him C. Symonds, 'Thomas Willis, FRS (1621–1675)', *Notes and Records of the Royal Society of London*, XV (1960), pp. 91–7.

55 For a short account of this case, see M. MacMillan, 'Phineas Gage: Unravelling the Myth', *The Psychologist*, XXI/9 (2008), pp. 828–31.

56 Interview with Professor Idan Segev, a brain scientist at the Hebrew University of Jerusalem, 4 August 2013.

57 See, for an explanation of the technology aimed at lay persons, *Computed Tomography: History and Technology*, www.medica.siemens. com.

58 Thanks to Professor Avinoam Reches, of Hadassa Hospital, Jerusalem, neurologist and chairperson of the Ethics Commission of the Israel Medical Association, for drawing my attention to the existence of these devices.

59 I. Sample, 'Female Orgasm Captured in Series of Brain Scans', *The Guardian* (14 November 2011).

60 See J. Lewy, 'Drug Policy as an Ideological Challenge: Germany and the United States in the 19th and 20th Centuries', dissertation submitted to the Hebrew University, Jerusalem (2011), pp. 178–241.

61 See E. Shorter, *A History of Psychiatry* (New York, 1997), pp. 218–24, 406–7, 209–19, 225–9; also, more recently, Thomas Szasz, *Coercion as Cure: A Critical History of Psychiatry* (New Brunswick, NJ, 2009), pp. 125–6, 51–72, 129–40.

62 Daisy Yuhas, 'Throughout History: Defining Schizophrenia Remains a Challenge', *Scientific American Mind* (14 February 2013).

63 See J. Kingsland, 'The Rise and Fall of the Wonder Drugs', *New Scientist*, CLXXXII/2454 (2004), pp. 36–7.

64 Rose and Abi-Rasched, *Neuro*, locs. 213 and 295.

65 The most recent summary of the debate may be found in P. Belluck and B. Carey, '"Psychiatry's Guide Is Out of Touch with Science", Experts Say', *New York Times* (6 May 2013).

66 See A. Clark, 'Where Brain, Body and World Collide', *Daedalus*, CXXVII/2 (1998), pp. 257–80.

67　Hobbes, *Leviathan*, p. 85. The emphasis is Hobbes's own.

68　For example, Patricia Churchland, *Braintrust: What Neuroscience Tells Us about Morality*, Kindle edition (2011), esp. locs 544, 569 and 629.

69　Ryan Jaslow, 'CDC Finds Mental Health Woes in One in Five U.S. Kids', CBS News, 18 May 2013, at www.cbsnews.com; M. Konely, 'I in 5 Americans Suffers from Mental Illness', *Medical Unit*, 19 January 2012, at http://abcnews.go.com; K. Kelland, 'Nearly 40 Percent of Europeans Suffer Mental Illness', *Reuters*, 4 September 2011, at www.reuters.com.

70　See J. Moll et al., 'The Neural Basis of Human Moral Cognition', *Perspectives*, VI (2005), pp. 799–809.

71　See on them M. Iacobini, 'Imitation, Empathy and Mirror Neurons', *Annual Review of Psychology*, LX (2009), pp. 653–70.

72　See N. Cawthorn, *Serial Killers and Mass Murderers* (Berkeley, CA, 2007), p. 83.

73　'Report to the Governor, Medical Aspects, Charles J. Whitman Catastrophe', quoted in Wikipedia.

74　Churchland, *Braintrust*, locs 666 and 681.

75　Professor Siri Graff Lekness, 'Can We Blame the Brain?', *Science Nordic* (6 July 2012), at http://sciencenordic.com.

76　See M. Szalavitz, 'My Brain Made Me Do It: Psychopaths and Free Will', *Time* (17 August 2012).

77　See, for the XYY Syndrome and its standing in law, S. Horan, 'The XYY Supermale and the Criminal Justice System: A Square Peg in a Round Hole', *Loyola of Los Angeles Law Review*, XXV (1992), pp. 1342–76.

78　See, for a good short typology of the states of mind in question, Y. Ustinova, *Caves and the Ancient Greek Mind* (Oxford, 2009).

79　Greek law: Aristotle, *Politics* (1274b 19–23); Roman law: A Watson, *Studies in Roman Private Law* (London, 2003), pp. 24–51; Russian Law: 'Of Russian Origin', Russiapedia, at http://russiapedia.rt.com; medieval and early modern law: M. Zeegers, 'Diminished Responsibility: A Logical, Workable and Essential Concept', *International Journal of Law and Psychiatry*, IV/3–4 (1984), pp. 435 and 436.

80　*California Penal Code*, S. 22.

81　Hobbes, *Leviathan*, pp. 61–8.

82　P. Haggard, 'Decision Time for Free Will', *Neuron*, LXIX (2011), pp. 404–6.

83 Email from Professor Reches, 4 June 2013, and interview with him, *Mevasseret Zion* (29 July 2013).

84 *The Human Brain Project: A Report to the European Commission* (Lausanne, 2012).

Conclusion

1 See on him M. Hosenball and R. Cowan, 'Edward Snowden, NSA Whistleblower, Says He Acted out of Conscience to Protect "Basic Liberties"', *Huffington Post*, 10 June 2013, at www.huffingtonpost.com.

2 I. Kershaw, *The End: Germany, 1944–45* (London, 2011), especially pp. 207–46.

3 Quoted in G. Janouch et al., eds, *Conversations with Kafka* (New York, 1971), p. 120.

4 Friedrich Nietzsche, *Thus Spoke Zarathustra* [1884–5] (Harmondsworth, 1969), p. 74.

5 On the way Hitler understood the relationship between State and *Volk*, see Adolf Hitler, *Mein Kampf* [1924] (Mumbai, 1988), pp. 324–68.

6 See M. van Creveld, *The Rise and Decline of the State* (Cambridge, 1999), pp. 408–14.

7 Tertullian, *A Treatise on the Soul*, ch. 30. Thanks, again, to Jonathan for bringing this passage to my attention.

8 P. Malanima, 'Energy Consumption and Energy Crisis in the Roman World' (Rome, 2011), www.paolomalanima.it.

9 For example, Patricia Churchland, *Braintrust: What Neuroscience Tells Us about Morality*, Kindle edition (2011), loc. 3114.

10 M. Costandi, 'Scientists Read Dream', *Nature*, 19 October 2012, at www.nature.com.

11 See, for example, Celia Gorman, 'The Mind-reading Machine', *Spectrum* (9 July 2012).

12 N. Lennard, 'Judge Orders End to FBI Data Demands', *Salon*, 18 March 2013, at www.salon.com; *Augsburger Allgemeine*, 'BND will offenbar Internetueberwachung ausbauen', 16 June 2013, at www.augsburger-allgemeine.de.

Acknowledgements

The list of people whom I consulted while writing the present book is unusually short. That, however, merely means that I owe a lot to each of them. First I would like to thank my longtime friend and companion on my intellectual journeys, Dr Col. (ret.) Moshe Ben David, who read the manuscript from beginning to end and offered many useful suggestions. It is to him that this work is dedicated. Next come Dr Eado Bachelet, of Bar Ilan University, Ramat Gan, who tried to enlighten me concerning his work on nanorobotics; Prof. Idan Segev, of the Hebrew University, Jerusalem, who did the same in respect to neural networks; and Prof. Avinoam Reches, neurologist at Hadassah Hospital, Jerusalem, who kindly told me about some of the possibilities and limitations of his work. I also want to mention my stepson, Jonathan Lewy. With each passing year he is taking over more of my chores; where I would be without him I do not know.

Finally there is my son Uri van Creveld. Unusually, Uri is both a psychotherapist and a computer expert. I am told that, compared with him, most other such experts are what plumbers are to a highly qualified engineer. But for the many conversations I have had with him over the years, this book would hardly have taken the shape it has.

Index